6th Workshop on Cognitive Aspects of Computational Language Learning (CogACLL 2015)

Held at EMNLP 2015

Lisbon, Portugal
18 September 2015

ISBN: 978-1-5108-1193-5

Printed from e-media with permission by:

Curran Associates, Inc.
57 Morehouse Lane
Red Hook, NY 12571

Some format issues inherent in the e-media version may also appear in this print version.

Printed by Curran Associates, Inc. (2015)

For permission requests, please contact the Association for Computational Linguistics at the address below.

Association for Computational Linguistics
209 N. Eighth Street
Stroudsburg, Pennsylvania 18360

Phone: 1-570-476-8006
Fax: 1-570-476-0860

acl@aclweb.org

Additional copies of this publication are available from:

Curran Associates, Inc.
57 Morehouse Lane
Red Hook, NY 12571 USA
Phone: 845-758-0400
Fax: 845-758-2634
Email: curran@proceedings.com
Web: www.proceedings.com

EMNLP 2015

Conference on Empirical Methods in Natural Language Processing

Proceedings of the Sixth Workshop on Cognitive Aspects of Computational Language Learning (CogACLL-2015)

18 September 2015
Lisbon, Portugal

Preface

The Workshop on Cognitive Aspects of Computational Language Learning (CogACLL) took place on September 18, 2015 in Lisbon, Portugal, in conjunction with the EMNLP 2015. The workshop was endorsed by ACL Special Interest Group on Natural Language Learning (SIGNLL). This is the sixth edition of related workshops first held with ACL 2007, EACL 2009, 2012 and 2014 and as a standalone event in 2013.

The workshop is targeted at anyone interested in the relevance of computational techniques for understanding first, second and bilingual language acquisition and change or loss in normal and pathological conditions.

The human ability to acquire and process language has long attracted interest and generated much debate due to the apparent ease with which such a complex and dynamic system is learnt and used on the face of ambiguity, noise and uncertainty. This subject raises many questions ranging from the nature vs. nurture debate of how much needs to be innate and how much needs to be learned for acquisition to be successful, to the mechanisms involved in this process (general vs specific) and their representations in the human brain. There are also developmental issues related to the different stages consistently found during acquisition (e.g. one word vs. two words) and possible organizations of this knowledge. These have been discussed in the context of first and second language acquisition and bilingualism, with cross linguistic studies shedding light on the influence of the language and the environment.

The past decades have seen a massive expansion in the application of statistical and machine learning methods to natural language processing (NLP). This work has yielded impressive results in numerous speech and language processing tasks, including e.g. speech recognition, morphological analysis, parsing, lexical acquisition, semantic interpretation, and dialogue management. The good results have generally been viewed as engineering achievements. Recently researchers have begun to investigate the relevance of computational learning methods for research on human language acquisition and change. The use of computational modeling is a relatively recent trend boosted by advances in machine learning techniques, and the availability of resources like corpora of child and child-directed sentences, and data from psycholinguistic tasks by normal and pathological groups. Many of the existing computational models attempt to study language tasks under cognitively plausible criteria (such as memory and processing limitations that humans face), and to explain the developmental stages observed in the acquisition and evolution of the language abilities. In doing so, computational modeling provides insight into the plausible mechanisms involved in human language processes, and inspires the development of better language models and techniques. These investigations are very important since if computational techniques can be used to improve our understanding of human language acquisition and change, these will not only benefit cognitive sciences in general but will reflect back to NLP and place us in a better position to develop useful language models.

We invited submissions on relevant topics, including:

- Computational learning theory and analysis of language learning and organization
- Computational models of first, second and bilingual language acquisition

- Computational models of language changes in clinical conditions
- Computational models and analysis of factors that influence language acquisition and use in different age groups and cultures
- Computational models of various aspects of language and their interaction effect in acquisition, processing and change
- Computational models of the evolution of language
- Data resources and tools for investigating computational models of human language processes
- Empirical and theoretical comparisons of the learning environment and its impact on language processes
- Cognitively oriented Bayesian models of language processes
- Computational methods for acquiring various linguistic information (related to e.g. speech, morphology, lexicon, syntax, semantics, and discourse) and their relevance to research on human language acquisition
- Investigations and comparisons of supervised, unsupervised and weakly-supervised methods for learning (e.g. machine learning, statistical, symbolic, biologically-inspired, active learning, various hybrid models) from a cognitive perspective.

Acknowledgements

We would like to thank the members of the Program Committee for the timely reviews and the authors for their valuable contributions. Aline Villavicencio is partly funded by projects CNPq 551964/2011-1, 312184/2012-3 and 482520/2012-4 and Samsung/UFRGS 4287, Alessandro Lenci by project CombiNet (PRIN 2010-11 20105B3HE8) funded by the Italian Ministry of Education, University and Research (MIUR).

Robert Berwick
Anna Korhonen
Alessandro Lenci
Thierry Poibeau
Aline Villavicencio

Organizers:

Robert Berwick (Massachusetts Institute of Technology, USA)
Anna Korhonen (University of Cambridge, UK)
Alessandro Lenci (University of Pisa, Italy)
Thierry Poibeau (LATTICE-CNRS, France)
Aline Villavicencio (Federal University of Rio Grande do Sul, Brazil)

Program Committee:

Afra Alishahi, Tilburg University (Netherlands)
Colin J Bannard, University of Texas at Austin (USA)
Philippe Blache, LPL-CNRS (France)
Susana Bautista Blasco, Federal University of Rio Grande do Sul (Brazil)
Antal van den Bosch, Radboud University Nijmegen (Netherlands)
Ted Briscoe, University of Cambridge (UK)
Grzegorz Chrupała, Tilburg University (Netherlands)
Robin Clark, University of Pennsylvania (USA)
Matthew W. Crocker, Saarland University (Germany)
Walter Daelemans, University of Antwerp (Belgium)
Dan Dediu, Max Planck Institute for Psycholinguistics (The Netherlands)
Barry Devereux, University of Cambridge (UK)
Ted Gibson, Massachusetts Institute of Technology (USA)
Sharon Goldwater, University of Edinburgh (UK)
Marco Idiart, Federal University of Rio Grande do Sul (Brazil)
Mark Johnson, Macquarie University (Australia)
Aravind Joshi, University of Pennsylvania (USA)
Gianluca Lebani, University of Pisa (Italy)
Igor Malioutov, Massachusetts Institute of Technology (USA)
Marie-Catherine de Marneffe, The Ohio State University (USA)
Brian Murphy, Queen's University Belfast (UK)
Tim O'Donnel, Massachusetts Institute of Technology (USA)
Muntsa Padró, Nuance (Canada)
Lisa Pearl, University of California - Irvine (USA)
Massimo Poesio, University of Trento (Italy)
Ari Rappoport, The Hebrew University of Jerusalem (Israel)
Sabine Schulte im Walde, University of Stuttgart (Germany)
Ekaterina Shutova, University of California, Berkeley (USA)
Maity Siqueira, Federal University of Rio Grande do Sul (Brazil)
Mark Steedman, University of Edinburgh (UK)
Remi van Trijp, Sony Computer Science Laboratory Paris (France)
Charles Yang, University of Pennsylvania (USA)

Menno van Zaanen, Tilburg University (Netherlands)
Alessandra Zarcone, Saarland University (Germany)
Leonardo Zilio, Federal University of Rio Grande do Sul (Brazil)

Table of Contents

Using reading behavior to predict grammatical functions
Maria Barrett and Anders Søgaard 1

Reading metrics for estimating task efficiency with MT output
Sigrid Klerke, Sheila Castilho, Maria Barrett and Anders Søgaard 6

Evaluating Models of Computation and Storage in Human Sentence Processing
Thang Luong, Timothy O'Donnell and Noah Goodman 14

An agent-based model of a historical word order change
Jelke Bloem, Arjen Versloot and Fred Weerman 22

Towards a Model of Prediction-based Syntactic Category Acquisition: First Steps with Word Embeddings
Robert Grimm, Giovanni Cassani, Walter Daelemans and Steven Gillis 28

Which distributional cues help the most? Unsupervised contexts selection for lexical category acquisition
Giovanni Cassani, Robert Grimm, Walter Daelemans and Steven Gillis 33

Language Emergence in a Population of Artificial Agents Equipped with the Autotelic Principle
Miquel Cornudella and Thierry Poibeau 40

A Computational Study of Cross-situational Lexical Learning of Brazilian Portuguese
Pablo Faria 45

Units in segmentation: a computational investigation
Çağrı Çöltekin 55

Estimating Grammeme Redundancy by Measuring Their Importance for Syntactic Parser Performance
Aleksandrs Berdicevskis 65

Improving Coordination on Novel Meaning through Context and Semantic Structure
Thomas Brochhagen 74

Perceptual, conceptual, and frequency effects on error patterns in English color term acquisition
Barend Beekhuizen and Suzanne Stevenson 83

Motif discovery in infant- and adult-directed speech
Bogdan Ludusan, Amanda Seidl, Emmanuel Dupoux and Alex Cristia 93

Modeling dative alternations of individual children
Antal van den Bosch and Joan Bresnan 103

Workshop Program

Friday, September 18, 2015

09:00–09:10 Opening and Introduction

09:10–10:30 Session 1: Language Processing

09:10–09:30 *Using reading behavior to predict grammatical functions*
Maria Barrett and Anders Søgaard

09:30–10:00 *Reading metrics for estimating task efficiency with MT output*
Sigrid Klerke, Sheila Castilho, Maria Barrett and Anders Søgaard

10:00–10:30 *Evaluating Models of Computation and Storage in Human Sentence Processing*
Thang Luong, Timothy O'Donnell and Noah Goodman

10:30–11:00 ***Coffee Break***

11:00–11:50 Invited Talk by Afra Alishahi

11:50–12:10 Session 2: Language Change

11:50–12:10 *An agent-based model of a historical word order change*
Jelke Bloem, Arjen Versloot and Fred Weerman

12:10–13:00 Session 3: Poster Session

12:10–13:00 *Towards a Model of Prediction-based Syntactic Category Acquisition: First Steps with Word Embeddings*
Robert Grimm, Giovanni Cassani, Walter Daelemans and Steven Gillis

12:10–12:30 *Which distributional cues help the most? Unsupervised contexts selection for lexical category acquisition*
Giovanni Cassani, Robert Grimm, Walter Daelemans and Steven Gillis

12:10–13:00 *Language Emergence in a Population of Artificial Agents Equipped with the Autotelic Principle*
Miquel Cornudella and Thierry Poibeau

12:10–13:00 *A Computational Study of Cross-situational Lexical Learning of Brazilian Portuguese*
Pablo Faria

12:10–13:00 *Units in segmentation: a computational investigation*
Çağrı Çöltekin

12:10–13:00 *Estimating Grammeme Redundancy by Measuring Their Importance for Syntactic Parser Performance*
Aleksandrs Berdicevskis

13:00–14:10 *Lunch*

14:10–15:00 Invited Talk by Antal van den Bosch

Friday, September 18, 2015 (continued)

15:00–15:30 Session 4: Language Processing II

15:00–15:30 *Improving Coordination on Novel Meaning through Context and Semantic Structure*
Thomas Brochhagen

15:30–16:00 *Coffee Break*

16:00–17:30 Session 5: Language Acquisition

16:00–16:30 *Perceptual, conceptual, and frequency effects on error patterns in English color term acquisition*
Barend Beekhuizen and Suzanne Stevenson

16:30–17:00 *Motif discovery in infant- and adult-directed speech*
Bogdan Ludusan, Amanda Seidl, Emmanuel Dupoux and Alex Cristia

17:00–17:30 *Modeling dative alternations of individual children*
Antal van den Bosch and Joan Bresnan

17:30–17:35 Closing Session

Using reading behavior to predict grammatical functions

Maria Barrett and Anders Søgaard
University of Copenhagen
Njalsgade 140
DK-2300 Copenhagen S
{barrett,soegaard}@hum.ku.dk

Abstract

This paper investigates to what extent grammatical functions of a word can be predicted from gaze features obtained using eye-tracking. A recent study showed that reading behavior can be used to predict coarse-grained part of speech, but we go beyond this, and show that gaze features can also be used to make more fine-grained distinctions between grammatical functions, e.g., subjects and objects. In addition, we show that gaze features can be used to improve a discriminative transition-based dependency parser.

1 Introduction

Readers fixate more and longer on open syntactic categories (verbs, nouns, adjectives) than on closed class items like prepositions and conjunctions (Rayner and Duffy, 1988; Nilsson and Nivre, 2009). Recently, Barrett and Søgaard (2015) presented evidence that gaze features can be used to discriminate between most pairs of parts of speech (POS). Their study uses all the coarse-grained POS labels proposed by Petrov et al. (2011). This paper investigates to what extent gaze data can also be used to predict grammatical functions such as subjects and objects. We first show that a simple logistic regression classifier trained on a very small seed of data using gaze features discriminates between some pairs of grammatical functions. We show that the same kind of classifier distinguishes well between the four main grammatical functions of nouns, POBJ, DOBJ, NN and NSUBJ. In §3, we also show how gaze features can be used to improve dependency parsing. Many gaze features correlate with word length and word

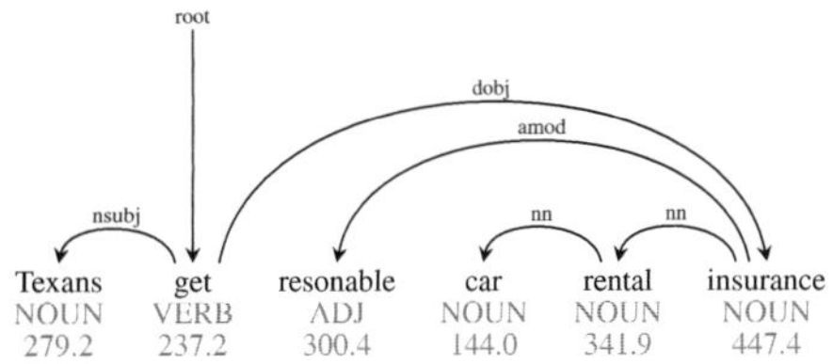

Figure 1: A dependency structure with average fixation duration per word

frequency (Rayner, 1998) and these could be as good as gaze features, while being easier to obtain. We use frequencies from the unlabelled portions of the English Web Treebank and word length as baseline in all types of experiments and find that gaze features to be better predictors for the noun experiment as well as for improving parsers.

This work is of psycholinguistic interest, but we show that gaze features may have practical relevance, by demonstrating that they can be used to improve a dependency parser. Eye-tracking data becomes more readily available with the emergence of eye trackers in mainstream consumer products (San Agustin et al., 2010). With the development of robust eye-tracking in laptops, it is easy to imagine digital text providers storing gaze data, which could then be used as partial annotation of their publications.

Contributions We demonstrate that we can discriminate between some grammatical functions using gaze features and which features are fit for the task. We show a practical use for data reflecting human cognitive processing. Finally, we use gaze features to improve a transition-based dependency parser, comparing also to dependency parsers augmented with word embeddings.

Proceedings of the Sixth Workshop on Cognitive Aspects of Computational Language Learning, pages 1–5,
Lisbon, Portugal, 18 September 2015.

2 Eye tracking data

The data comes from (Barrett and Søgaard, 2015) and is publicly available[1]. In this experiment 10 native English speakers read 250 syntactically annotated sentences in English (min. 3 tokens, max. 120 characters). The sentences were randomly sampled from one of five different, manually annotated corpora from different domains: Wall Street Journal articles (WSJ), Wall Street Journal headlines (HDL), emails (MAI), weblogs (WBL), and Twitter (TWI)[2]. See Figure 1 for an example.

Features It is not yet established which eye movement reading features are fit for the task of distinguishing grammatical functions of the words. To explore this, we extracted a broad selection of word- and sentence-based features. The features are inspired by Salojärvi et al. (2003) who used a similar exploratory approach. For a full list of features, see Appendix.

2.1 Learning experiments

In our binary experiments, we use L2-regularized logistic regression classifiers with the default parameter setting in SciKit Learn[3] and a publicly available transition-based dependency parser[4] trained using structured perceptron (Collins, 2002; Zhang and Nivre, 2011).

Binary classification We trained logistic regression models to discriminate between pairs of the 11 most frequent dependency relations where the sample size is above 100: (AMOD, NN, AUX, PREP, NSUBJ, ADVMOD, DEP, DET, DOBJ, POBJ, ROOT) only using gaze features. E.g., we selected all words annotated as PREP or NSUBJ and trained a logistic regression model to discriminate between the two in a five-fold cross validation setup. Our baseline uses the following features: word length, position in sentence and word frequency.

Some dependency relations are almost uniquely associated with one POS, e.g. determiners where

RANK	FEATURE NAME	% OF VOTES
0	Next word fixation probability	13.46
1	Fixation probability	11.14
2	n Fixations	9.66
3	Probability to get 2nd fixation	8.90
4	Previous word fixation probability	7.17
5	n Regressions from	5.65
6	First fixation duration on every word	5.45
7	Mean fixation duration per word	5.17
8	Previous fixation duration	4.93
9	Re-read probability	4.65
10	Probability to get 1st fixation	4.53
11	n Long regressions from word	3.77
12	Share of fixated words per sent	3.04
13	n Re-fixations	1.88
14	n Regressions to word	1.76

Table 1: Most predictive features for binary classification of 11 most frequent dependency relations using five-fold cross validation.

84.8% of words with the dependency relation DET are labeled determiners. This means that in some cases, the grammatical function of a word follows from its part of speech. In another binary experiment, we therefore focus on nouns to show that eye movements *do* make more fine-grained distinctions between different grammatical functions. Nouns are mostly four-way ambiguous: 74.6% of the 946 nouns in the dataset have one of four dependency relations to its head. Nouns with POBJ relations is 18.9% of all nouns, NSUBJ is 17.0%, NN is 27.0% and DOBJ is 14.9%. The remaining 25.4% of the nouns are discarded from the noun experiment since they have 28 different relations to their head.

Parsing In all experiments we trained our parsing models on four domains and evaluated on the fifth to avoid over-fitting to the characteristics of a specific domain. All parameters were tuned on the WSJ dataset. We did 30 passes over the data and used the feature model in Zhang and Nivre (2011) – concatenated with gaze vectors for the first token on the buffer, the first token in the stack, and the left sibling of the first token in the stack. We extend the feature representation of each parser configuration by 3×26 features. Our gaze vectors were normalized using the technique in Turian et al. (2010) ($\sigma \cdot E/SD(E)$) using a scaling factor of $\sigma = 0.001$. Gaze features such as fixation duration are known to correlate with word frequency and word length. To investigate whether word length and frequency are stronger features than gaze, we perform an experiment, +FREQ+LEN, where our baseline and system also use frequencies and word length as features.

[1]https://bitbucket.org/lowlands/release/src

[2]Wall Street Journal sentences are from OntoNotes 4.0 release of the English Penn Treebank. catalog.ldc.upenn.edu/LDC2011T03. Mail and weblog sentences come from the English Web Treebank. catalog.ldc.upenn.edu/LDC2012T13. Twitter sentences are from the work of (Foster et al., 2011)

[3]http://scikit-learn.org/stable/modules/generated/sklearn.linear_model.LogisticRegression.html

[4]https://github.com/andersjo/hanstholm

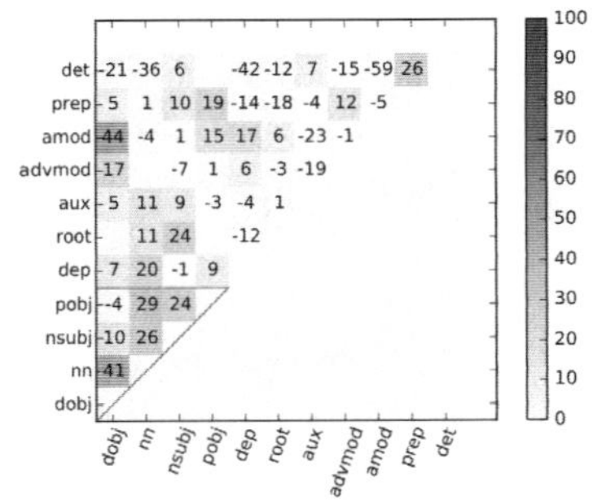

Figure 2: Error reduction over the baseline for binary classifications of 11 most frequent dependency relations. 5-fold cross validation. Dependency relations associated with nouns in triangle.

3 Results

Predictive features To investigate which gaze features were more predictive of grammatical function, we used stability selection (Meinshausen and Bühlmann, 2010) with logistic regression classification on binary dependency relation classifications on the most frequent dependency relations.

For each pair of dependencies, we perform a five-fold cross validation and record the informative features from each run. Table 1 shows the 15 most used features in ranked order with their proportion of all votes. The features predictive of grammatical functions are similar to the features that were found to be predictive of POS (Barrett and Søgaard, 2015), however, the probability that a word gets first and second fixation were not important features for POS classification, whereas they are contributing to dependency classification. This could suggest that words with certain grammatical functions are consistently more likely or less likely to get first and second fixation, but could also be due to a frequent syntactic order in the sample.

Binary discrimination Error reduction over the baseline can be seen in Figure 2. The mean accuracy using logistic regression on all binary classification problems between grammatical functions is 0.722. The frequency-position-word length baseline is 0.706. In other words, using gaze features leads to a 5.6% error reduction over the baseline. The worst performance (where our baseline outperforms using gaze features) is seen where one relation is associated with closed class words

RANK	FEATURE NAME	% OF VOTES
0	Next word fixation probability	20.66
1	Probability to get 2nd fixation	19.83
2	nRegressions from word	14.05
3	Previous word fixation probability	8.68
4	Probability to get 1st fixation	7.44

Table 2: Most predictive features for the binary classification of four most frequent dependency relations for nouns using five-fold cross validation.

(DET, PREP, AUX), and where discrimination is easier.

Noun experiment Error reductions for pairwise classification of nouns are between -4% and 41%. See Figure 2. The average accuracy for binary noun experiments is 0.721. Baseline accuracy is 0.647. For POBJ and DOBJ the baseline was better than using gaze, but for the other pairs, gaze was better. When doing stability selection for nouns with only the four most frequent grammatical functions, the most important features can be seen from Figure 2. The most informative feature is the fixation probability of the next word. Kernel density of this feature can be seen in Figure 3a, and it shows two types of behavior: POBJ and DOBJ, where the next word is less frequently fixated, and NN and NSUBJ, where the next word is more frequently fixated. Whether the next word is fixated or not, can be influenced by the word length, as well as the fixation probability of the current word: If the word is very short, the next word can be processed from a fixation of the current word, and if the current word is not fixated, the eyes need to land somewhere in order for the visual span to cover a satisfactory part of the text. Word length and fixation probabilities for the nouns are reported in Figure 3c and Figure 3b to show that the dependency labels have similar densities.

Dependency parsing We also evaluate our gaze features directly in a supervised dependency parser. Our baseline performance is relatively low because of the small training set, but comparable to performance often seen with low-resource languages. Evaluation metrics are labeled attachment scores (LAS) and unlabeled attachment scores (UAS), i.e. the number of words that get assigned the correct syntactic head w/o the correct dependency label.

Gaze features lead to consistent improvements across all five domains. The average error reduction in LAS is 5.0%, while the average error reduc-

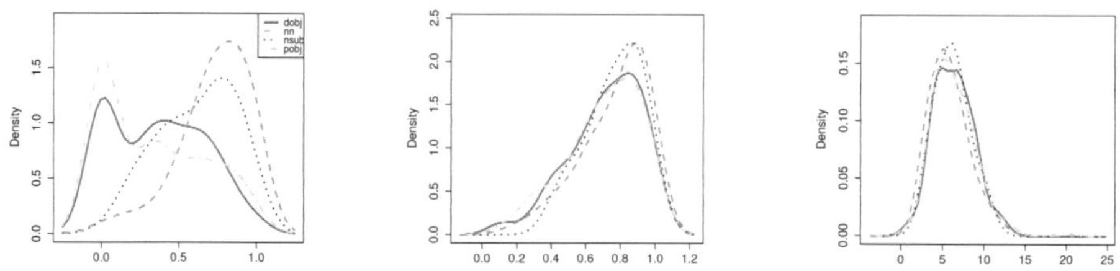

(a) Next word fixation probability (b) Fixation probability (c) Word length

Figure 3: Kernel density plots across four grammatical functions of nouns.

	LAS				+FREQ+LEN		UAS				+FREQ+LEN	
	BL	+SENNA	+EIGENW	+GAZE	BL	+GAZE	BL	+SENNA	+EIGENW	+GAZE	BL	+GAZE
HDL	0.539	0.539	0.526	**0.541**	0.535	**0.542**	0.583	**0.600**	0.564	0.589	0.582	**0.587**
MAI	0.667	0.651	0.668	*__0.684__	0.678	*__0.711__	0.715	0.699	0.715	*__0.747__	0.732	*__0.759__
TWI	0.532	0.569	**0.563**	*0.561	0.554	*__0.569__	0.576	**0.626**	0.615	*0.602	0.607	*__0.621__
WBL	0.604	0.629	0.592	*__0.638__	0.631	*__0.655__	0.668	0.670	0.666	*__0.711__	0.709	*__0.719__
WSJ	0.635	0.635	0.622	*__0.650__	0.629	**0.634**	0.672	0.681	0.674	*__0.695__	0.671	**0.677**
Average	0.595	0.605	0.594	*__0.615__	0.605	*__0.622__	0.643	0.655	0.647	*__0.669__	0.660	*__0.672__

Table 3: Dependency parsing results on all five test sets using 200 sentences (four domains) for training and 50 sentences (one domain) for evaluation. Best results are bold-faced, and significant ($p < 0.01$) improvements are asterisked.

tion in UAS is 7.3%. For the +FREQ+LEN experiment, +GAZE also lead to improvements for all domains, with error reductions of 3.3% for LAS and 4.7% for UAS.

For comparison we also ran our parser with SENNA embeddings[5] and EIGENWORDS embeddings.[6] The gaze vectors proved overall more informative.

4 Related work

In addition to Barrett and Søgaard (2015), our work relates to Matthies and Søgaard (2013), who study the robustness of a fixation prediction model across readers, not domains, but our work also relates in spirit to research on using weak supervision in NLP, e.g., work on using HTML markup to improve dependency parsers (Spitkovsky, 2013) or using click-through data to improve POS taggers (Ganchev et al., 2012).

There have been few studies correlating reading behavior and general dependency syntax in the literature. Demberg and Keller (2008), having parsed the Dundee corpus using MINIPAR, show that dependency integration cost, roughly the distance between a word and its head, is predictive of reading times for nouns. Our finding could be a side-effect of this, since NSUBJ, NN and DOBJ/POBJ typically have very different dependency integration costs, while DOBJ and POBJ have about the same. Their study thus seems to support our finding that gaze features can be used to discriminate between the grammatical functions of nouns. Most other work of this kind focus on specific phenomena, e.g., Traxler et al. (2002), who show that subjects find it harder to process object relative clauses than subject relative clauses. This paper is related to such work, but our interest is a broader model of syntactic influences on reading patterns.

5 Conclusions

We have shown that gaze features can be used to discriminate between a subset of grammatical functions, even across domains, using only a small dataset and explored which features are more useful. Furthermore, we have shown that gaze features can be used to improve a state-of-the-art dependency parsing model, even when trained on small seeds of data, which suggests that parsers can benefit from data from human processing.

[5]http://ronan.collobert.com/senna/

[6]http://www.cis.upenn.edu/~ungar/eigenwords/

Appendix: Gaze features

First fixation duration on every word, fixation probability, mean fixation duration per sentence, mean fixation duration per word, next fixation duration, next word fixation probability, probability to get 1st fixation, probability to get 2nd fixation, previous fixation duration, previous word fixation probability, re-read probability, reading time per sentence normalized by word count, share of fixated words per sentence, time percentage spent on this word out of total sentence reading time, total fixation duration per word, total regression from word duration, total duration of regressions to word, n fixations on word, n fixations per sent normalized by token count, n long regressions from word, n long regressions per sentence normalized by token count, n long regressions to word, n re-fixations on word, n re-fixations per sentence normalized by token count, n regressions from word, n regressions per sentence normalized by token count, n regressions to word.

References

Maria Barrett and Anders Søgaard. 2015. Reading behavior predicts syntactic categories. In *CoNLL 2015*, pages 345–249.

Michael Collins. 2002. Discriminative training methods for Hidden Markov Models. In *EMNLP*.

Vera Demberg and Frank Keller. 2008. Data from eye-tracking corpora as evidence for theories of syntactic processing complexity. *Cognition*, 109:193–210.

Jennifer Foster, Ozlem Cetinoglu, Joachim Wagner, Josef Le Roux, Joakim Nivre, Deirde Hogan, and Josef van Genabith. 2011. From news to comments: Resources and benchmarks for parsing the language of Web 2.0. In *IJCNLP*.

Kuzman Ganchev, Keith Hall, Ryan McDonald, and Slav Petrov. 2012. Using search-logs to improve query tagging. In *ACL*.

Franz Matthies and Anders Søgaard. 2013. With blinkers on: Robust prediction of eye movements across readers. In *EMNLP*, Seattle, Washington, USA.

Nicolai Meinshausen and Peter Bühlmann. 2010. Stability selection. *Journal of the Royal Statistical Society: Series B (Statistical Methodology)*, 72(4):417–473.

Matthias Nilsson and Joakim Nivre. 2009. Learning where to look: Modeling eye movements in reading. In *CoNLL*.

Slav Petrov, Dipanjan Das, and Ryan McDonald. 2011. A universal part-of-speech tagset. *arXiv preprint arXiv:1104.2086*.

Keith Rayner and Susan A. Duffy. 1988. On-line comprehension processes and eye movements in reading. In *Reading research: Advances in theory and practice*, pages 13–66, New York. Academic Press.

Keith Rayner. 1998. Eye movements in reading and information processing: 20 years of research. *Psychological bulletin*, 124(3):372.

Jarkko Salojärvi, Ilpo Kojo, Jaana Simola, and Samuel Kaski. 2003. Can relevance be inferred from eye movements in information retrieval. In *Proceedings of WSOM*, volume 3, pages 261–266.

Javier San Agustin, Henrik Skovsgaard, Emilie Mollenbach, Maria Barret, Martin Tall, Dan Witzner Hansen, and John Paulin Hansen. 2010. Evaluation of a low-cost open-source gaze tracker. In *Proceedings of the 2010 Symposium on Eye-Tracking Research & Applications*, pages 77–80. ACM.

Valentin Ilyich Spitkovsky. 2013. *Grammar Induction and Parsing with Dependency-and-Boundary Models*. Ph.D. thesis, STANFORD UNIVERSITY.

Matthew Traxler, Robin Morris, and Rachel Seely. 2002. Processing subject and object relative clauses: Evidence from eye movements. *Journal of Memory and Language*, 47:69–90.

Joseph Turian, Lev Ratinov, and Yoshua Bengio. 2010. Word representations: a simple and general method for semi-supervised learning. In *ACL*.

Yue Zhang and Joakim Nivre. 2011. Transition-based dependency parsing with rich non-local features. In *Proceedings of the 49th Annual Meeting of the Association for Computational Linguistics: Human Language Technologies: short papers-Volume 2*, pages 188–193. Association for Computational Linguistics.

Reading metrics for estimating task efficiency with MT output

Sigrid Klerke[†] **Sheila Castilho**[*] **Maria Barrett**[†] **Anders Søgaard**[†]
[†]CST, University of Copenhagen, Denmark
{skl, barrett, soegaard}@hum.ku.dk
[*]CNGL/SALIS, Dublin City University, Ireland
castils3@mail.dcu.ie

Abstract

We show that metrics derived from recording gaze while reading, are better proxies for machine translation quality than automated metrics. With reliable eye-tracking technologies becoming available for home computers and mobile devices, such metrics are readily available even in the absence of representative held-out human translations. In other words, reading-derived MT metrics offer a way of getting cheap, online feedback for MT system adaptation.

1 Introduction

What's a good translation? One way of thinking about this question is in terms of what the translations can be used for. In the words of Doyon et al. (1999), "a poor translation may suffice to determine the general topic of a text, but may not permit accurate identification of participants or the specific event." Text-based tasks can thus be ordered according to their tolerance of translation errors, as determined by actual task outcomes, and task outcome can in turn be used to measure the quality of translation (Doyon et al., 1999).

Machine translation (MT) evaluation metrics must be both adequate and practical. Human task performance, say participants' ability to extract information from translations, is perhaps the most adequate measure of translation quality. Participants' direct judgements of translation quality may be heavily biased by perceived grammaticality and subjective factors, whereas task performance directly measures the usefulness of a translation. Of course different tasks rely on different aspects of texts, but some texts are written with a single purpose in mind.

In this paper, we focus on logic puzzles. The obvious task in logic puzzles is whether readers can solve the puzzles when given a more or less erroneous translation of the puzzle. We assume task performance on logic puzzles is an adequate measure of translation quality *for logic puzzles*.

Task-performance is not always a practical measure, however. Human judgments, whether from direct judgments or from answering text-related questions, takes time and requires recruiting and paying individuals. In this paper, we propose various metrics derived from natural reading behavior as proxies of task-performance. Reading has several advantages over other human judgments: It is fast, is relatively unbiased, and, most importantly, something that most of us do effortlessly all the time. Hence, with the development of robust eye tracking methods for home computers and mobile devices, this can potentially provide us with large-scale, on-line evaluation of MT output.

This paper shows that reading-derived metrics are better proxies of task-performance than the standard automatic metric BLEU. Note also that on-line evaluation with BLEU is biased by what held-out human translations you have available, whereas reading-derived metrics can be used for tuning systems to new domains and new text types.

In our experiments, we include simplifications of logic puzzles and machine translations thereof. Our experiments show, as a side result, that a promising approach to optimizing machine translation for task performance is using text simplification for pre-processing the source texts. The intuition is that translation noise is more likely to make processing harder in more complex texts.

Proceedings of the Sixth Workshop on Cognitive Aspects of Computational Language Learning, pages 6–13,
Lisbon, Portugal, 18 September 2015.

1.1 Contributions

- We present an experimental eye-tracking study of 20 participants reading simplifications and human/machine translations of 80 logic puzzles.[1]
- This is, to the best of our knowledge, the first study to correlate reading-derived metrics, human judgments and BLEU with task performance for evaluating MT. We show that human judgments do not correlate with task performance. We also show that reading-derived metrics correlate significantly with task performance ($-.36 < r < -.35$), while BLEU does not.
- Finally, our results suggest that practical MT can benefit much from incorporating sentence compression or text simplification as a pre-processing step.

2 Summary of the experiment

In our experiments, we presented participants with 80 different logic puzzles and asked them to solve and judge the puzzles while their eye movements were recorded. Each puzzle was edited into five different versions: the original version in English (L2), a human simplification thereof (S(·)), a human translation into Danish (L1) and a machine translation of the original (M(·)), as well as a machine translation of the simplification (M(S(·))). Consequently, we used 400 different stimuli in our experiments. The participants were 20 native speakers of Danish with proficiency in English.

We record fixation count, reading speed and regression proportion (amount of fixations landing on previously read text) from the gaze data. Increased attention in the form of reading time and re-reading of previously read text are well-established indicators of increased cognitive processing load, and they correlate with typical readability indicators like word frequency, length and some complex syntactic structures (Rayner et al., 2013; Rayner, 1998; Holmqvist et al., 2011). We study how these measures correlate with MT quality, as reflected by human judgments and participants' task performance.

We thereby assume that the chance of quickly solving a task decreases when more resources are required for understanding the task. By keeping the task constant, we can assess the relative impact of the linguistic quality of the task formulation. We hypothesise that our five text versions (L1, L2, M(·), S(·), M(S(·))), can be ranked in terms of processing ease, with greater processing ease allowing for more efficient task solving.

The experiments are designed to test the following hypothesized partial ordering of the text versions (summarized in Table 1): text simplification (S(·)) eases reading processing relative to second language reading processing (L2) while professional human translations into L1 eases processing more (**H1**). In addition, machine translated text (M(·)) is expected to ease the processing load, but less so than machine translation of sim-

[1]The data will be made available from `https://github.com/coastalcph`

Math
A DVD player with a list price of $100 is marked down 30%. If John gets an employee discount of 20% off the sale price, how much does John pay for the DVD player?
1: 86.00
2: 77.60
3: 56.00
4: 50.00

Conclude
Erin is twelve years old. For three years, she has been asking her parents for a dog. Her parents have told her that they believe a dog would not be happy in an apartment, but they have given her permission to have a bird. Erin has not yet decided what kind of bird she would like to have.
Choose the statement that logically follows
1: Erin's parents like birds better than they like dogs.
2: Erin does not like birds.
3: Erin and her parents live in an apartment.
4: Erin and her parents would like to move.

Evaluate
Blueberries cost more than strawberries.
Blueberries cost less than raspberries.
Raspberries cost more than both strawberries and blueberries.
If the first two statements are true, the third statement is:
1: TRUE
2: FALSE
3: Impossible to determine

Infer
Of all the chores Michael had around the house, it was his least favorite. Folding the laundry was fine, doing the dishes, that was all right. But he could not stand hauling the large bags over to the giant silver canisters. He hated the smell and the possibility of rats. It was disgusting.
This paragraph best supports the statement that:
1: Michael hates folding the laundry.
2: Michael hates doing the dishes.
3: Michael hates taking out the garbage.
4: Michael hates cleaning his room.

Figure 1: Logic puzzles of four categories. The stimuli contain 20 of each puzzle category.

H1:	L1	$\prec$ S(·) $\prec$	L2
H2:	L1	$\prec$ M(S(·)) $\prec$ M(·) $\prec$	L2

Table 1: Expected relative difficulty of processing. L1 and L2 are human edited texts in the participants' native and non-native language, respectively, S(·) are manually simplified texts, M(·) are machine translated texts and M(S(·)) are machine translations of manually simplified texts.

plified text (M(S(·))), although both of these machine translated versions are still expected to be more demanding than the professionally translated original text (L1). Table 1 provides an overview of the hypotheses and the expected relative difficulty of processing each text version.

2.1 Summary of the findings

Our experimental findings are summarized as follows: The data supports the base assumption that L1 is easier than L2. We only find *partial* support for H1; While S(·) tends to be easier to comprehend than L2, also leading to improved task performance, S(·) is ranked as easier to process than L1 as often as the opposite, hypothesised ranking. This indicates that our proficient L2 readers may be benefitting as much from simplification as from translation in reasoning tasks. We also only find *partial* support for H2: The relative ordering of the human translations, L1, and the two machine translated versions, M(S(·)) and M(·), is supported and we find that the simplification improves MT a lot with respect to reading processing. However, participants tended to perform better with the original L2 logic puzzles compared to the machine translated versions. In other words, MT hurts while both manual simplification and translation help even proficient L2 readers. In sum, simplification seems necessary if L2-to-L1 MT is to ease comprehension, and not make understanding harder for readers with a certain L2 command level.

Importantly, we proceed to study the correlation of our eye-tracking measures, human judgments and BLEU (Papineni et al., 2002) with task performance. There has been considerable work on how various automatic metrics correlate with human judgments, as well as on inter-annotator consistency among humans judging the quality of translations (Callison-Burch et al., 2008). Various metrics have been proposed over the years, but BLEU (Papineni et al., 2002) remains the *de facto* state-of-the-art evaluation metric. Our findings, related to evaluation, are, as already mentioned, that (a) human judgments surprisingly do not correlate with task performance, and that (b) the reading-derived metrics TIME and FIXATIONS correlate strongly with task performance, while BLEU does not. This, in our view, questions the validity of human judgments and the BLEU metric and shows that reading-derived MT metrics may provide a better feedback in system development and adaptation.

3 Detailed description of the experiment

3.1 Stimuli

In this section, we describe the texts we have used for stimuli, as well as the experimental design and our participants.

We selected a set of 80 logic puzzles written in English, all with multiple-choice answers.[2] The most important selection criterium was that participants have to reason about the text and cannot simply recognize a few entities directly to guess the answer. The puzzles were of four different categories, all designed to train logic reasoning and math skills in an educational context. We chose 20 of each of the four puzzle categories to ensure a wide variety of reasoning requirements. Figure 1 shows an example question from each category.

The English (L2) questions and multiple choice answer options were translated into Danish (L1) by professional translators. The *question text* was manually simplified by the lead author (S(·)). Both of the English versions were machine-translated into Danish (M(·), M(S(·))).[3] This results in the five versions of the question texts, which were used for analysis. The multiple-choice answer options were not simplified or machine translated. Thus the participants saw either the original English answers or the human-translated Danish answers, matching the language of the question text. The average number of words and long words in each of the five versions are reported in Table 2.

Simplification is not a well-defined task and is often biased intentionally to fit a target audience or task. To allow for comparison with parallel simplification corpora, we classified the applied simplification operations into the following set of seven abstract simplification operations

[2]From LearningExpress (2005).

[3]Google Translate, accessed on 29/09/2014 23.33 CET.

Variant	# Long words mean	std	# Words mean	std
L2	9.56	6.67	38.33	19.29
s(·)	8.78	5.90	35.78	17.43
L1	10.22	6.97	38.87	21.28
M(s(·))	9.70	6.75	35.19	19.07
M(·)	10.35	6.74	36.53	19.04

Table 2: Mean and standard deviation of number of words and number of words with more than seven letters per question for all five versions.

Simplification	%
Lexical substitution	27.4
Paraphrase	24.2
Deletion	23.1
Information reordering	11.3
Anaphora substitution	7.5
Discourse marker insertion	4.3
Sentence splitting	2.2

Table 3: Simplification operations (SOps). The total number of applied SOps was 186, the average number of SOps applied per question was 2.0 (std 1.3).

and present their relative proportion in Table 3: Sentence splitting. information deletion and information reordering, discourse marker insertion (e.g., *and*, *but*), anaphora substitution (e.g., *Zoe's garden* vs. *the garden*), other lexical substitutions (e.g., *dogwoods* vs. *dogwood trees*) and paraphrasing (e.g., *all dogwoods* vs. *all kinds of dogwood trees*). On average 2.0 simplification operations was performed per question, while a total of 28.7% of the questions were left unchanged during simplification. All simplified questions still required the reader to understand and reason about the text. The simplifications were performed with the multiple answer texts in mind; leaving any information referenced in the answers intact in the question, even when deleting it would have simplified the question text.

3.2 Experimental design

The experiment followed a Latin-square design where each participant completed 40 trials, judging and solving 40 different puzzles, eight of each of the five versions.

A trial consisted of three tasks (see Figure 2): a comprehension task, a solving task and a comparison task. Each trial was preceded by a 1.5 second display of a fixation cross. The remainder of the trial was self-paced. During the entire trial - i.e., for the duration of the three tasks - the question text was presented on the top part of the screen. In the comprehension task, the participant was asked to rate the comprehensibility of the question text on a 7-point Likert scale that was presented at the bottom part of the screen. This score is called COMPREHENSION, henceforth. This is our rough equivalent of human judgments of translation quality. For the solving task, the multiple-choice answer options was presented in the middle part of the screen below the question text and the participant indicated an answer or "don't know" option in the bottom part of the screen. The measure EFFICIENCY, which was also introduced in Doherty and O'Brien (2014), is the number of correct answers given for a version, C_v over the time spent reading and solving the puzzles of that version, S_v: $E = \frac{C_v}{S_v}$. This score is our benchmarking metric below.

In the last task, COMPARISON, a different version of the same question text was presented below the first question text, always in the same language. Participants were asked to assess which version provided a better basis for solving the task using a 7-point Likert scale with a neutral midpoint. The three leftmost options favored the text at the top of the screen, while the three rightmost choices favored the text at the lower half of the screen.

Each participant completed three demo trials with the experimenter present. Participants were kept naïve with regards to the machine translation aspect of the study. They were instructed to solve the puzzles as quickly and accurately as possible and to judge COMPREHENSION and COMPARISON quickly. Each session included a 5-10 minute break with refreshments halfway through. At the end of the experiment a brief questionnaire was completed verbally. All participants completed the entire session in 70–90 minutes.[4]

3.2.1 Apparatus

The stimuli were presented in black letters in the typeface Verdana with a letter size of 20 pixels (ca. .4° visual angle) on a light gray background with 100 pixels margins. The eye tracker was a Tobii

[4]Participants received a voucher for 10 cups of tea/coffee upon completion.

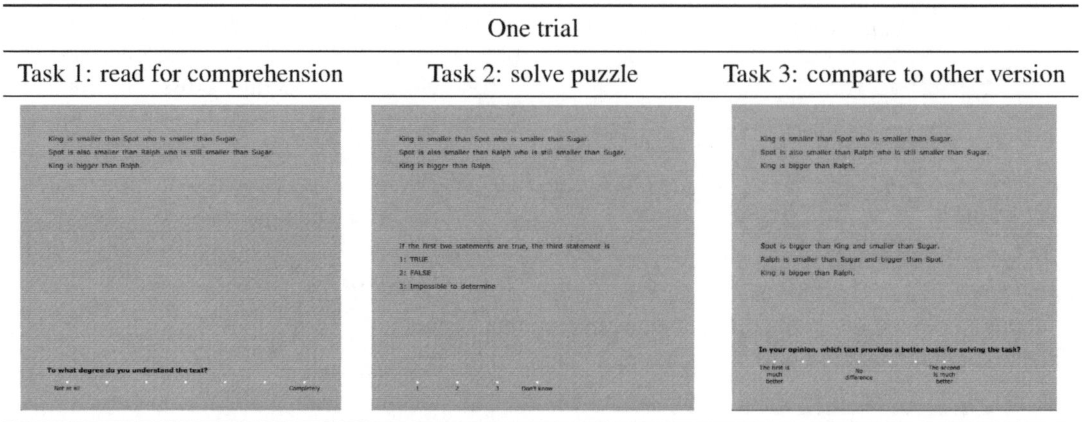

Figure 2: Illustration of one trial. Each trial consists of three individual tasks. The top third of the screen displays the target text and is fixed for the duration of the entire trial.

X120, recording both eyes with 120hz sampling rate. We used Tobii Studio standard settings for fixation detection. The stimuli was presented on a 19" display with a resolution of 1920 x 1080 pixels and a viewing distance of ca 65 cm. Here we focus on the initial reading task and report total reading time per word (TIME), number of fixations per word (FIXATIONS) and proportion of regressions (REGRESSIONS). The calculations of the eyetracking measures are detailed in Section 4.3.

3.2.2 Participants

We recruited participants until we obtained a total of 20 recordings of acceptable quality. In this process we discarded two participants due to sampling loss. Another two participants were dismissed due to unsuccessful calibration. All participants completed a pre-test questionnaire identifying themselves as native Danish speakers with at least a limited working proficiency of English. None of the participants had been diagnosed with dyslexia, and all had normal or corrected to normal vision. The 20 participants (4 males) were between 20 and 34 years old (mean 25.8) and minimum education level was ongoing bachelor's studies.

4 Results

The mean values for all metrics and the derived rankings of the five versions are presented in Table 4. Significance is computed using Student's paired t-test, comparing each version to the version with the largest measured value. Table 5 presents correlations with task performance (EFFICIENCY) for each measure. We describe the correlations, and their proposed interpretation, in Section 4.4.

4.1 Subjective measures

We elicited subjective evaluations of text comprehension and pairwise comparisons of versions' usefulness for solving the puzzles. Note that participants evaluate MT output significantly lower than human-edited versions.

We treated the pairwise COMPARISON scores as votes, counting the preference of one version as equally many positive and negative votes on the preferred version and the dis-preferred version, respectively. With this setup, we maintain zero as a neutral evaluation. COMPARISON was only made within the same language, so the scores should not be interpreted across languages. Note, however, how COMPARISON results show a clear ranking of versions within each language.

4.2 Task performance measures

The task performance is reported as the EFFICIENCY, i.e., correct answers per minute spent reading and solving puzzles. We observe that the absolute performance ranges from 48% to 52% correct answers. This is well above chance level (27%), and does not differ significantly between the five versions, reflecting that the between-puzzles difference in difficulty level, as expected, is much larger than the between-versions difference.

EFFICIENCY, however, reveals a clearer ranking. Participants were less efficient solving logic

VERSION	L1	M(S(·))	μ M(·)	S(·)	L2	RANKINGS
COMPREHENSION	5.58	**4.51	**4.50	5.61	5.46	S(·) $\prec$ L1 $\prec$ L2 $\prec$ M(S(·)) $\prec$ M(·)
COMPARISON	1.62	**−.54	**−1.07	.43	**−.43	L1 $\prec$ M(S(·)) $\prec$ M(·) | S(·) $\prec$ L2
EFFICIENCY	.94	.90	**0.80	1.0	.87	S(·) $\prec$ L1 $\prec$ M(S(·)) $\prec$ L2 $\prec$ M(·)
TIME	.54	.62	.65	.55	.54	L1 $\prec$ L2 $\prec$ S(·) $\prec$ M(S(·)) $\prec$ M(·)
REGRESSIONS	15.59	16.49	16.78	13.76	14.40	S(·) $\prec$ L2 $\prec$ L1 $\prec$ M(S(·)) $\prec$ M(·)
REGRESSIONS	17.77	18.46	19.15	15.55	16.55	S(·) $\prec$ L2 $\prec$ L1 $\prec$ M(S(·)) $\prec$ M(·)

Table 4: Mean values for the five text versions. COMPREHENSION and COMPARISON are Likert scale scores respectively ranging from 0 to 7 and from −3 to 3, EFFICIENCY is correct answers relative to reading speed, TIME is seconds per word, FIXATIONS is number of fixations per word and REGRESSIONS is proportion of re-fixations (**: Student's paired t-test relative to largest mean value $p < 0.001$)

puzzles when presented with machine translations of the original puzzles. The machine translations of the simplified puzzles actually seemingly *eased* task performance, compared to using the English originals, but differences are not statistically significant. The simplified English puzzles led to the best task performance.

4.3 Eye-tracking measures

The reading times in seconds per word (TIME) are averages over reading times while fixating at the question text located on the upper part of the screen during the first sub-task of each trial (judging comprehension). This measure is comparable to normalized total reading time in related work. Participants spent most time on the machine translations, whether of the original texts or the simplified versions.

The measure FIXATIONS similarly was recorded on the question part of the text during the initial comprehension task, normalized by text length, and averaged over participants and versions. Again we observe a tendency towards more fixations on machine translated text, and fewest on the human translations into Danish.

Finally, we calculated REGRESSIONS during initial reading as the proportion of fixations from *the furthest word read* to a preceding point in the text. Regressions may indicate confusion and on average account for 10-15% of fixations during reading (Rayner, 1998). Again we see more regressions with machine translated text, and fewest with simplified English puzzles.

4.4 Correlations between measures

We observe the following correlations between our measures. All correlations with EFFICIENCY are shown in Table 5. First of all, we found no

	Data used	r	$p \leq .001$
COMPREHENSION	all	.25	-
	M(S(·))	.36	-
	M(·)	-.27	-
COMPARISON	all	.13	-
	M(S(·))	.06	-
	M(·)	.26	-
TIME	all	-.35	✓
	M(S(·))	-.19	-
	M(·)	-.54	-
FIXATIONS	all	-.36	✓
	M(S(·))	-.26	-
	M(·)	-.57	-
REGRESSIONS	all	-.17	-
	M(S(·))	.01	-
	M(·)	-.33	-
BLEU	M(S(·))	-.13	-
	M(·)	-.17	-

Table 5: Correlations with EFFICIENCY (Pearson's r). BLEU only available on translated text. Correlation reported on these subsets for comparability.

correlations between subjective measures and eye-tracking measures nor between subjective measures and task performance. The two subjective measures, however, show a strong correlation (Spearman's $r = .50$ $p < .001$). EFFICIENCY shows significant negative correlation with both of the eye-tracking measures TIME (Pearson's $r = -.35$ $p < .001$ and FIXATIONS (Pearson's $r = -.36$ $p < .001$), but not REGRESSIONS . Within the group of eye-tracking measures TIME and FIXATION exhibit a high correlation ($r = 0.94$ $p < .001$). REGRESSIONS is significantly negatively correlated with both of these (Pearson's $r = -.38$ $p < .001$ and Pearson's $r = -.43$ $p < .001$, respectively).

We obtain BLEU scores (Papineni et al., 2002)

by using the human-translated Danish text (L1) as reference for both of the MT outputs, M(·) and M(S(·)). The overall BLEU score for M(·) version is .691, which is generally considered very good, and .670 for M(S(·)). The difference is not surprising, since M(S(·)) inputs a different (simpler) text to the MT system. On the other hand, given that our participants tended to be more efficiently comprehending and solving the logic puzzles using M(S(·)), this already indicates that BLEU is not a good metric for talking about the usefulness of translations of instructional texts such as logic puzzles.

Our most important finding is that BLEU does not correlate with EFFICIENCY, while two of our reading-derived metrics do. In other words, the normalised reading time and fixation counts are better measures of task performance, and thereby of translation quality, than the state-of-the-art metric, BLEU in this context. This is an important finding since reading-derived metrics are potentially also more useful as they do not depend on the availability of professional translators.

5 Discussion

Several of our hypotheses were in part falsified. L2 is solved more efficiently by our participants than M(·), not the other way around. Also, M(S(·)) is judged as harder to comprehend than S(·) and consistently ranked so by all metrics. These observations suggest that MT is not assisting our participants despite the fact that L2 ranks lower than L1 in four out of five comparisons. Our participants are university students and did not report to have skipped any questions due to the English text suggesting generally very good L2 skills.

If we assume that EFFICIENCY – as a measure of task performance – is a good measure of translation quality (or usefulness), we see that the best indicator of translation quality that only takes the initial reading into account are FIXATIONS and TIME. This indicates that FIXATIONS and TIME may be better MT benchmarking metrics than BLEU.

6 Related work

Eye tracking has been used for MT evaluation in both post-editing and instruction tasks (Castilho et al., 2014; Doherty and O'Brien, 2014).

Doherty et al. (2010) also used eye-tracking measures for evaluating MT output and found fixation count and gaze time to correlate negatively with binary quality judgments for translation segments, whereas average fixation duration and pupil dilation were not found to vary reliably with the experimental conditions. A notable shortcoming of that study is that the translated segments in each category were different, making it impossible to rule out that the observed variation in both text quality and cognitive load was caused in part by an underlying variation in content complexity.

This shortcoming was alleviated in a recent reanalysis of previous experiments (Doherty and O'Brien, 2014; Doherty et al., 2012) which compares the usability of raw machine translation output in different languages and the original, well-formed English input. In order to test usability, a plausible task has to be set up. In this study the authors used an instructional text on how to complete a sequence of steps using a software service, previously unknown to the participants. MT output was obtained for four different languages and three to four native speakers worked with each output. Participants' subjective assessment of the usability of the instructions, their performance in terms of efficiency and the cognitive load they encountered as measured from eye movements were compared across languages. The results of this study supports the previous finding that fixation count and total task time depends on whether the reader worked with the original or MT output, at least when the quality of the MT output is low. In addition, goal completion and efficiency (total task time relative to goal completion) as well as the number of shifts (between instructions and task performance area) were shown to co-vary with the text quality.

Castilho et al. (2014) employed a similar design to compare the usability of lightly post-edited MT output to raw MT output and found that also light post-editing was accompanied by fewer fixations and lower total fixation time (proportional to total task time) as well as fewer attentional shifts and increased efficiency.

In contrast, Stymne et al. (2012) found no significant differences in total fixation counts and overall gaze time (proportional to total task time), when directly comparing output of different MT systems with expected quality differences. However, they showed that both of these two eye-tracking measures were increased for the parts of the text containing errors in comparison with error-free passages. In addition, they found gaze time to vary with specific error types in machine translated text.

From an application perspective, Specia (2011) suggested the time-to-edit measure as an objective and accessible measure of translation quality. In their study it outperformed subjective quality assessments as annotations for a model for translation candidate ranking. Their tool was aimed at optimizing the productivity in post-editing tasks.

Eye tracking can be seen as a similarly objective metric for fluency estimation (Stymne et al., 2012). The fact that eye tracking does not rely on translators makes annotation even more accessible.

Both Doherty and O'Brien (2014) and Castilho et al. (2014) found subjective comprehensibility, satisfaction and likelihood to recommend a product to be especially sensitive to whether the instructional text for the product was raw MT output. This suggests that the lower reliability of subjective evaluations as annotations could be due to a bias against MT-specific errors. Only Stymne et al. (2012) report the correlations between eye movement measures and subjective assessments and found only moderate correlations.

This work is to the best of our knowledge the first to study the correlation of reading-derived MT metrics and task performance. Since we believe task performance to be a more adequate measure of translation quality – especially when the texts are designed with a specific task in mind – we therefore believe this to be a more adequate study of the usefulness of reading-derived MT metrics than previous work.

7 Conclusion

We presented an eye-tracking study of participants reading original, simplified, and human/machine translated logic puzzles. Our analysis shows that the reading-derived metrics TIME and FIXATIONS obtained from eye-tracking recordings can be used to assess translation quality. In fact, such metrics seem to be much better proxies of task performance, i.e., the practical usefulness of translations, than the state-of-the-art quality metric, BLEU.

References

Chris Callison-Burch, Cameron Fordyce, Philipp Koehn, Christof Monz, and Josh Schroeder. 2008. Further meta-evaluation of machine translation. In *Proceedings of the Third Workshop on Statistical Machine Translation*, pages 70–106. Association for Computational Linguistics.

Sheila Castilho, Sharon O'Brien, Fabio Alves, and Morgan O'Brien. 2014. Does post-editing increase usability? a study with Brazilian Portuguese as target language. In *EAMT*.

Stephen Doherty and Sharon O'Brien. 2014. Assessing the usability of raw machine translated output: A user-centered study using eye tracking. *International Journal of Human-Computer Interaction*, 30(1):40–51.

Stephen Doherty, Sharon O'Brien, and Michael Carl. 2010. Eye tracking as an mt evaluation technique. *Machine translation*, 24(1):1–13.

Stephen Doherty, Dorothy Kenny, and Andrew Way. 2012. A user-based usability assessment of raw machine translated technical instructions. In *AMTA*.

Jennifer Doyon, Kathryn B Taylor, and John S White. 1999. Task-based evaluation for machine translation. In *Proceedings of Machine Translation Summit VII*, volume 99.

Kenneth Holmqvist, Marcus Nyström, Richard Andersson, Richard Dewhurst, Halszka Jarodzka, and Joost Van de Weijer. 2011. *Eye tracking: A comprehensive guide to methods and measures*. Oxford University Press.

LearningExpress. 2005. *501 Challenging Logic and Reasoning Problems*. 501 Series. LearningExpress.

Kishore Papineni, Salim Roukus, Todd Ward, and Wei-Jing Zhu. 2002. BLEU: a method for automatic evaluation of machine translation. In *ACL*.

Keith Rayner, Alexander Pollatsek, and D Reisberg. 2013. Basic processes in reading. *The Oxford Handbook of Cognitive Psychology*, pages 442–461.

Keith Rayner. 1998. Eye movements in reading and information processing: 20 years of research. *Psychological bulletin*, 124(3):372.

Lucia Specia. 2011. Exploiting objective annotations for measuring translation post-editing effort. In *Proceedings of the 15th Conference of the European Association for Machine Translation*, pages 73–80.

Sara Stymne, Henrik Danielsson, Sofia Bremin, Hongzhan Hu, Johanna Karlsson, Anna Prytz Lillkull, and Martin Wester. 2012. Eye tracking as a tool for machine translation error analysis. In *LREC*, pages 1121–1126.

Evaluating Models of Computation and Storage in Human Sentence Processing

Minh-Thang Luong*
Stanford University
lmthang@stanford.edu

Timothy J. O'Donnell*
MIT
timod@mit.edu

Noah D. Goodman
Stanford University
ngoodman@stanford.edu

Abstract

We examine the ability of several models of computation and storage to explain reading time data. Specifically, we demonstrate on both the Dundee and the MIT reading time corpora, that fragment grammars, a model that optimizes the tradeoff between computation and storage, is able to better explain people's reaction times than two baseline models which exclusively favor either storage or computation. Additionally, we make a contribution by extending an existing incremental parser to handle more general grammars and scale well to larger rule and data sets.[1]

1 Introduction

A basic question for theories of language representation, processing, and acquisition is how the linguistic system balances storage and reuse of lexical units with productive computation. At first glance, the question appears simple: words are stored; phrases and sentences are computed. However, a closer look quickly invalidates this picture. Some canonically computed structures, such as phrases, must be stored, as witnesses by verbal idioms like *leave no stone unturned*[2] (Nunberg et al., 1994). There is also compositionality at the sub-word level: affixes like *ness* in *pine-scentedness*, are almost always composed productively, whereas other affixes, e.g., *th* in *warmth*, are nearly always stored together with stems (O'Donnell, 2015). Facts such as these have led to a consensus in the field that storage and computation are properties that cut across different kinds of linguistic units and levels of linguistic structure (Di Sciullo and Williams, 1987)—giving rise to *hetergeneous lexicon*[3] theories, in the terminology of Jackendoff (2002b).

Naturally, the question of what is computed and what is stored has been the focus of intense empirical and theoretical research across the language sciences. On the empirical side, it has been the subject of many detailed linguistic analyses (e.g., Jackendoff (2002a)) and specific phenomena such as composition versus retrieval in word or idiom processing have been examined in many studies in experimental psycholinguistics (Hay, 2003; O'Donnell, 2015). On the theoretical side, there have been many proposals in linguistics regarding the structure and content of the heterogeneous lexicon (e.g., Fillmore et al. (1988), Jackendoff (2002b)). More recently, there have been a number of proposal from computational linguistics and natural language processing for how a learner might infer the correct pattern of computation and storage in their language (De Marcken, 1996; Bod et al., 2003; Cohn et al., 2010; Post and Gildea, 2013; O'Donnell, 2015).

However, there remains a gap between detailed, phenomenon-specific studies and broad architectural proposals and learning models. Recently, however, a number of methodologies have emerged which promise to bridge this gap. These methods make use of broad coverage probabilistic models which can encode representational and inferential assumptions, but which can also be applied to make detailed predictions on large psycholinguistic datasets encompassing a wide vari-

* indicates equal contribution.

[1] Our code and data are available at http://stanford.edu/~lmthang/earleyx/.

[2] Meaning: *prevent any rock from remaining rightside up.*

[3] A hetergeneous lexicon contains not only words but also affixes, stems, and phrasal units such as idioms.

Proceedings of the Sixth Workshop on Cognitive Aspects of Computational Language Learning, pages 14–21, Lisbon, Portugal, 18 September 2015.

ety of linguistic phenomena. In the realm of syntax, one recent approach has been to use probabilistic models of sentence structures, paired with incremental parsing algorithms, to produce precise quantitative predictions for variables such as reading times (Roark et al., 2009) or eye fixation times (Demberg and Keller, 2008; Mitchell et al., 2010; Frank and Bod, 2011; Fossum and Levy, 2012; van Schijndel and Schuler, 2013). To date, no models of storage and computation in syntax have been applied to predict measures of human reading difficulty.

In this work, we employ several of the models of computation and storage studied by O'Donnell (2015), to examine human sentence processing. We demonstrate that the fragment grammars model (O'Donnell et al., 2009; O'Donnell et al., 2011)—a model that treats the question of what to store and what to compute productively as a probabilistic inference—better explains human reading difficulty than two "limiting-case" baselines, MAP adaptor grammars (maximal storage) and Dirichlet-multinomial PCFG (maximal computation), in two datasets: the Dundee eye-tracking corpus (Kennedy and Pynte, 2005) and the MIT reading time dataset (Bachrach et al., 2009).

2 Goals and Scope of the Paper

Before moving on, we remark on the goals and scope of the current study. The emergence methods connecting wide-coverage probabilistic grammars and psycholinguistic data offer great potential to test theoretical models quantitatively, at scale, and on a variety of detailed phenomena. However, studies using these methods also involve many moving parts, often making their results difficult to interpret.

To connect probabilistic models of syntactic computation and storage to reading time or eye fixation data, practioners need to:

1. Preprocess train and test data sets by tokenizing words, limiting sentence lengths, and handling unknown words.

2. Decide on a suitable grammatical formalism: determine a hypothesis space of stored items and specify a probability model over that space.

3. Choose and implement a probabilistic model to extract grammars from the training set.

4. Pick a test set annotated with reading difficulty information, e.g., eye fixation or reading times.

5. Choose a specific incremental parsing algorithm to generate word-by-word parsing predictions.

6. Determine the theoretical quantity that will be used as a predictor, e.g., *surprisal* or *entropy reduction*.

7. Choose a suitable linking model to regress theoretical predictions against human data, controlling for participant-specific factors and nuisance variables.

Given this wide array of design decisions, it is often difficult to compare results across studies or to determine which theoretical assumptions are crucial to the performance of models. For the field to make progress, studies must be replicable and each of the above factors (and potentially others) must be varied systematically in order to isolate their specific consequences. We contribute towards this process in three ways.

First, we report results for three models which differ only in terms of how they address the problem of what to store and what to compute (see Section 3). Otherwise, modeling and analysis assumptions are exactly matched. Moreover, the models represent three "limiting cases" in the space of storage and computation — store all maximal structures, store only minimal structures, and treat the problem as a probabilistic inference. Although none of the models represents a state-of-the-art model of syntactic structure, this study should provide important baselines against which to compare in future proposals.

Second, to make this study possible, we extend an existing incremental parser to address two technical challenges by: (a) handling more general input grammars and (b) scaling better to extremely large rule sets. This parser can be used with any model that can be projected to or approximated by a probabilistic context-free grammar. We make this parser available to the community for future research.

Third, and finally, unlike previous studies which only report results on a single dataset, we demonstrate consistent findings over two popular datasets, the Dundee eye-tracking corpus and the MIT reading times corpus. We make available our predicted values for all examined data points together with our analysis scripts. This should facilitate the replication of these specific results and direct numerical comparison with later proposals.

3 Approaches to Computation and Storage

In this paper we study the ability of three models to predict reading difficulty as measured by either eye-fixation or reading times — the *full-parsing* model, implemented by Dirichlet-multinomial probabilistic context-free grammars (DMPCFG) (Kurihara and Sato, 2006; Johnson et al., 2007), the *full-listing* mode, implemented by maximum a posteriori adaptor grammars (MAG) (Johnson et al., 2006), and the *inference-based* model, implemented by fragment grammars (FG) (O'Donnell, 2015).

All three models start with the same underlying *base system*—a context-free grammar (CFG) specifying the space of possible syntactic derivations—and the same training data—a corpus of syntactic trees. However, the models differ in what they store and what they compute. The full-parsing model can be understood as a fully-compositional baseline equivalent to a Bayesian version of the underlying CFG. The full-listing model, by contrast, stores all full derivations (i.e., all derivations down to terminal symbols) and subderivations in the input corpus. These stored (sub)trees can be thought of as extending the CFG base component with rules that directly rewrite nonterminal symbols to sequence of terminals in a single derivational step.

Finally, the inference-based model treats the problem of what tree fragments to store, and which parts of derivations to compute as an inference in a Bayesian framework, learning to store and and reuse those subtrees which best explain the data while taking into account two prior biases for simplicity. The first bias prefers to explain the data in terms of a smaller lexicon of stored tree fragments. The second bias prefers to account for each input sentence with smaller numbers of derivational steps (i.e., fragments). Note that these two biases compete and thus give rise to a tradeoff. Storing smaller, more abstract fragments allows the model to represent the input with a more compact lexicon, at the cost of using a greater number of rules, on average, in individual derivations. Storing larger, more concrete fragments allows the model to derive individual sentences using a smaller number of steps, at the cost of expanding the size of the stored lexicon. The inference-based model can be thought of as extending the base CFG with rules, inferred from the data, that expand larger portions of derivation-tree structure in single steps, but can also include nonterminals on their right-hand side (unlike the full-listing model).

As we mentioned above, none of these models take into account various kinds of structure—such as headedness or other category-refinements—that are known to be necessary to achieve state-of-the-art syntactic parsing results (Petrov et al., 2006; Petrov and Klein, 2007). However, the results reported below should be useful for situating and interpreting the performance of future models which do integrate such structure. In particular, these results will enable ablation studies which carefully vary different representational devices.

4 Human Reading Time Prediction

To understand the effect of different approaches to computation and storage in explaining human reaction times, we employ the surprisal theory proposed by Hale (2001) and Levy (2008). These studies introduced *surprisal* as a predictor of the difficulty in incremental comprehension of words in a sentence. Because all of the models described in the last section can be used to compute surprisal values, they can be used to provide predictions for processing complexity and hence, gain insights about the use of stored units in the human sentence processing. The surprisal values for these different models are dervied by means of a probabilistic, incremental Earley parser (Stolcke, 1995; Earley, 1968), which we describe below.

4.1 Surprisal Theory

The surprisal theory of incremental language processing characterizes the lexical predictability of a word w_t in terms of a surprisal value, the negative log of the conditional probability of a word given its preceding context, $-\log P(w_t|w_1 \ldots w_{t-1})$. Higher surprisal values mean smaller conditional probabilities, that is, words that are less predictable are more surprising to the language user and thus harder to process. Surprisal theory was first introduced in Hale (2001) and studied more extensively by Levy (2008). It has also been shown to have a strong correlation with reading time duration in both eye-tracking and self-paced reading studies (Boston et al., 2008; Demberg and Keller, 2008; Roark et al., 2009; Frank, 2009; Wu et al., 2010; Mitchell et al., 2010).

4.2 The Incremental Parser

The computation of surprisal values requires access to an incremental parser which can compute the *prefix probabilities* associated with a string s under some grammar—the total probability over all derivation using the grammar which generate strings prefixed by s (Stolcke, 1995). The prefix probability is an important concept in computational linguistics because it enables probabilistic predictions of possible next words (Jelinek and Lafferty, 1991) via the conditional probabilities $P(w_t|w_1 \ldots w_{t-1}) = \frac{P(w_1 \ldots w_t)}{P(w_1 \ldots w_{t-1})}$. It also allows estimation of incremental costs in a stack decoder (Bahl et al., 1983). Luong et al. (2013) used prefix probabilities as scaling factors to avoid numerical underflow problems when parsing very long strings.

We extend the implementation by Levy (2008) of the probabilistic Earley parser described in Stolcke (1995) which computes exact prefix probabilities. Our extension allows the parser (a) to handle arbitrary CFG rewrite rules and (b) to scale well to large grammars.[4]

The implementation of Levy (2008) only extracts grammars implicit in treebank inputs and restricts all pre-terminal rules to single-terminal rewrites. To approximate the incremental predictions of the models in this paper, we require the ability to process rules that include sequences of multiple terminal and non-terminal symbols on their right-hand side. Thus, we extend the implementation to allow efficient processing of such structures (property a).

With regards to property (b), we note that parsing against the full-listing model (MAG) is prohibitively slow because the approximating grammars for the model contain PCFG rules which exhaustively list the mappings from every nonterminal in the input corpus to its terminal substring, leading to thousands of rules. For example, for the Brown corpus section of the Penn Treebank (Marcus et al., 1993), we extracted 778K rules for the MAG model, while the number of rules in the DMPCFG and the inference-based (FG) grammars are 75K and 146K respectively. Parsing the MAG is also memory intensive due to multi-terminal rules that rewrite to long sequences of terminals, because, for example, an S node must rewrite to an entire sentence. Such rules result in an exploding number of states during parsing as the Earley dot symbol moves from left to right.

To tackle this issue, we utilize a *trie* data structure to efficiently store multi-terminal rules and quickly identify (a) which rules rewrite to a particular string and (b) which rules have a particular prefix.[5] These extensions allow our implementation to incorporate multi-terminal rules in the prediction step of the Earley algorithm, and to efficiently incorporate which of the many rules can contribute to the prefix probability in the Earley scanning step.

We believe that our implementation should be useful to future studies of reading difficulty, allowing efficient computation of prefix probabilities for any model which can be projected to (or approximated by) a PCFG—even if that approximation is very large. publicly available at `http://url`.

5 Experiments

5.1 Data

Our three models models are trained on the Wall Street Journal (WSJ) portion of the Penn Treebank (Marcus et al., 1994). In particular, because we have access to gold standard trees from this corpus, it is possible to compute the exact maximum a posteriori full-parsing (DMPCFG) and full-listing (MAG) models, and output PCFGs corresponding to these models.[6]

We evaluate our models on two different corpora: (a) the *Dundee corpus* (Kennedy and Pynte, 2005) with eye-tracking data on naturally occurring English news text and (b) the *MIT corpus* (Bachrach et al., 2009) with self-paced reading data on hand-constructed narrative text. The for-

[4]Other recent studies of human reading data have made use of the parser of Roark (2001). However, this parser incoporates many specific design decisions and optimizations—"baking in" aspects of both the incremental parsing algorithm and a model of syntactic structure. As such, since it does not accept arbitrary PCFGs, it is unsuitable for this present study.

[5]Specifically, terminal symbols are used as keys in our trie and at each trie node, e.g., corresponding to the key sequence a b c, we store two lists of nonterminals: (a) the *complete* list – where each non-terminal X corresponds to a multi-terminal rule $X \rightarrow a\ b\ c$, and (b) the *prefix* list – where each non-terminal X corresponds to a multi-terminal rule $X \rightarrow a\ b\ c \ldots d$. We also accumulated probabilities for each non-terminal in these two lists as we traverse the trie.

[6]Note that for DMPCFG, this PCFG is exact, whereas for MAG, it represents a truncated approximation.

mer has been a popular choice in many sentence processing studies (Demberg and Keller, 2008; Mitchell et al., 2010; Frank and Bod, 2011; Fossum and Levy, 2012; van Schijndel and Schuler, 2013). The latter corpus, with syntactically complex sentences constructed to appear relatively natural, is smaller in size and has been used in work such as Roark et al. (2009) and Wu et al. (2010). We include both corpora to demonstrate the reliability of our results.

Detailed statistics of these corpora are given in Table 1. The last column indicates the number of data points (i.e., word-specific fixation or reading times) used in our analyses below. This dataset was constructed by excluding data points with zero reading times and removing rare words (with frequencies less than 5 in the WSJ training data). We also exclude long sentences (of greater than 40 words) for parsing efficiency reasons.

	sent	**word**	**subj**	**orig**	**filtered**
Dundee	2,370	58,613	10	586,131	228,807
MIT	199	3,540	23	81,420	69,702

Table 1: **Summary statistics of reading time corpora** – shown are the number of sentences, words, subjects, data points before (*orig*) and after filtering (*filtered*).

5.2 Metrics

Following (Frank and Bod, 2011; Fossum and Levy, 2012), we present two analyses of the surprisal predictions of our models: (a) a *likelihood* evaluation and (b) a *psychological* measure of the ability of each model to predict reading difficulty.

For the former, we simply average the negative surprisal values, i.e., $\log p(w_n|w_1 \dots w_{n-1})$, of all words in the test set, computing the average log likelihood of the data under each model.[7] This can be understood as simply a measure of goodness of fit of each model on each test data set.

For the latter, we perform a linear mixed-effects analysis (Baayen et al., 2008) to evaluate how well the model explains reading times in the test data. The `lme4` package (Bates et al., 2011) is used to fit our linear mixed-effects models. Following (Fossum and Levy, 2012), eye fixation and reading times are log-transformed to produce more normally distributed data.[8] We include the following common predictors as fixed effects for each word/participant pair: (i) position of the word in the sentence, (ii) the number of characters in the word, (iii) whether the previous word was fixated, (iv) whether the next word was fixated, and (v) the log of the word unigram probability.[9]

All fixed effects were centered to reduce collinearity. We include by-word and by-subject intercepts as random effects. The *base* model results reported below include only these fixed and random factors. To test the ability of our three theoretical models of computation and storage to explain the reading time data, we include surprisal predictions from each model as an additional fixed effect. To test the signficance of these results, we perform nested model comparisons with χ^2 tests.

5.3 Results

For the *likelihood* evaluation, the values in Table 2 demonstrate that the FG model provides the best fit to the data. The results also indicate a ranking over the three models, FG $\succ$ DMPCFG $\succ$ MAG.

	Dundee	**MIT**
DMPCFG	-6.82	-6.80
MAG	-6.91	-6.95
FG	-6.35	-6.35

Table 2: **Likelihood Evaluation** – the average negative suprirsal values given by each model (DMPCFG, MAG, FG) on all words in each corpus (Dundee, MIT).

For the *psychological* evaluation, we present results of our nested model comparisons under two settings: (a) *additive* in which we independently add each of the surprisal measures to the *base* model and (b) *subtractive*, in which we take the *full* model consisting of all the surprisal measures and independently remove one surprisal measure each time.

Results of the additive setting are shown in Table 3, demonstrating the same trend as observed in the likelihood evaluation. In particular, the FG model yields the best improvement in terms of model fit as captured by the $\chi^2(1)$ statistics, indicating that it is more explanatory of reaction times when added to the *base* model as compared to the DMPCFG and the MAG predictions. The ranking

[7]Exponentiating this value gives the perplexity score.

[8]For the Dundee corpus, we use the first-pass reading time.

[9]The unigram probability was estimated from the WSJ training data, the written text portion of the BNC corpus, and the Brown corpus. We make use of the SRILM toolkit (Stolcke, 2002) for such estimation.

is also consistent with the likelihood results: FG $\succ$ DMPCFG $\succ$ MAG.

Models	Dundee		MIT	
	$\chi^2(1)$	p	$\chi^2(1)$	p
base+DMPCFG	70.9	< 2.2E-16	38.5	5.59E-10
base+MAG	10.9	9.63E-04	0.1	7.52E-01
base+FG	118.3	< 2.2E-16	62.5	2.63E-15

Table 3: **Psychological accuracy, additive tests** – $\chi^2(1)$ and p values achieved by performing nested model analysis between the models *base+X* and the *base* model.

For the subtractive setting, results in Table 4 highlight the fact that several models significantly ($p < 0.01$) explains variance in fixation times above and beyond the other surprisal-based predictors. The FG measure proves to be the most influential predictor (with $\chi^2(1) = 62.5$ for the Dundee corpus and 42.9 for the MIT corpus). Additionally, we observe that DMPCFG does not significantly explain more variance over the other predictors. This, we believe, is partly due to the presence of the FG model, which captures much of the same structure as the DMPCFG model.

Models	Dundee		MIT	
	$\chi^2(1)$	p	$\chi^2(1)$	p
full-DMPCFG	4.0	4.65E-02	3.5	6.18E-02
full-MAG	14.3	1.58E-04	23.6	1.21E-06
full-FG	62.5	2.66E-15	42.9	5.88E-11

Table 4: **Psychological accuracy, subtractive test** – $\chi^2(1)$ and p values achieved by performing nested model analysis between the models *full-X* and the *full* model.

Additionally, we examine the coefficients of the surprisal predictions of each model. We extracted coefficients for individual surprisal measures independently from each of the models *base+X*. As shown in the columns *Indep* in Table 5, all coefficients are positive, implying, sensibly, that the more surprising a word, the longer time it takes to process that word.

Moreover, when all surprisal measures appear together in the same *full* model (columns *Joint*), we observe a consistent trend that the coefficients for DMPCFG and FG are positive, whereas that of the MAG is negative.

Models	Dundee		MIT	
	Indep.	Joint	Indep.	Joint
DMPCFG	5.94E-03	1.95E-03	8.08E-03	3.24E-03
MAG	1.00E-03	-1.41E-03	1.54E-04	-2.82E-03
FG	5.13E-03	5.49E-03	5.88E-03	6.97E-03

Table 5: **Mixed-effects coefficients** – the *Indep.* columns refer to the coefficients learned by the mixed-effects models *base+X* (one surprisal measure per model), whereas the *Joint* columns refer to coefficients of all surprisal measures within the *full* model.

5.4 Discussion

Our results above indicate that the inference-based model provides the best account of our test data, both in terms of the likelihood it assigns to the test corpora and in terms of its ability to explain human fixation times. With respect to the full-parsing model this result is unsurprising. It is widely known that the conditional independence assumptions of PCFGs make them poor models of syntactic strcutre, and thus—presumably—of human sentence processing. Other recent work has shown that reasonable (though not state-of-the-art) parsing results can be achieved using models which relax the conditional independence assumptions of PCFGs by employing inventories of stored tree-fragments (i.e., *tree-substitution grammars*) similar to the fragment grammars model (De Marcken, 1996; Bod et al., 2003; Cohn et al., 2010; Post and Gildea, 2013; O'Donnell, 2015).

The comparison with the full-listing model is more interesting. Not only does the full-listing model produce the worst performance of the three models in both corpora and for both evaluations, it actually produces negative correlations with reading times. We believe this result is indicative of a simple fact: while it has become clear that there is lexical storage of many syntactic constructions, and—in fact—the degree of storage may be considerably more than previously believed (Tremblay and Baayen, 2010; Bannard and Matthews, 2008)—syntax is still a domain which is mostly compositional. The full-listing model overfits, leading to nonsensical reading time predictions. In fact, this is likely a logical necessity—the vast combinatorial power implicit in natural language syntax means that even for a system with tremendous memory capacity, only a small fraction of potential structures can be stored.

6 Conclusion

In this paper, we have studied the ability of several models of computation and storage to explain human sentence processing, demonstrating that a model which treates the problem as a case-by-case probabilistic inference provides the best fit to reading time datasets, when compared to two "limiting case" models which always compute or always store. However, as we emphasized in the introduction we see our contribution as primarily methodological. None of the models studied here represent state-of-the-art proposals for syntactic structure. Instead, we see these results together with the tools that we make available to the community, as providing a springboard for later research that will isolate exactly which factors, alone or in concert, best explain human sentence processing.

Acknowledgment

We gratefully acknowledge the help of Asaf Bachrach for making the MIT reading time dataset available to us. We thank the annonymous reviewers for their valuable comments and feedbacks.

References

R. Harald Baayen, Doug J. Davidson, and Douglas M. Bates. 2008. Mixed-effects modeling with crossed random effects for subjects and items. *Journal of Memory and Language*, 59(4):390–412.

Asaf Bachrach, Brian Roark, Alex Marantz, Susan Whitfield-Gabrieli, Carlos Cardenas, , and John D.E. Gabrieli. 2009. Incremental prediction in naturalistic language processing: An fmri study.

Lalit R. Bahl, Frederick Jelinek, and Robert L. Mercer. 1983. A maximum likelihood approach to continuous speech recognition. *IEEE Transactions on Pattern Analysis and Machine Intelligence*, PAMI-5(2):179 –190.

Colin Bannard and Danielle Matthews. 2008. Stored word sequences in language learning: The effect of familiarity on children's repetition of four-word combinations. *Psychological Science*, 19(3):241–248.

Douglas Bates, Martin Maechler, and Ben Bolker, 2011. *lme4: Linear mixed-effects models using S4 classes*. R package version 0.999375-42.

Rens Bod, Remko Scha, and Khalil Sima'an, editors. 2003. *Data-Oriented Parsing*. CSLI, Stanford, CA.

Marisa F. Boston, John T. Hale, Reinhold Kliegl, Umesh Patil, and Shravan Vasishth. 2008. Parsing costs as predictors of reading difficulty: An evaluation using the potsdam sentence corpus. *Journal of Eye Movement Research*, 2(1):1–12.

Trevor Cohn, Phil Blunsom, and Sharon Goldwater. 2010. Inducing tree-substitution grammars. *Journal of Machine Learning Research*, 11:3053–3096.

Carl De Marcken. 1996. *Unsupervised Language Acquisition*. Ph.D. thesis, Massachusetts Institute of Technology.

Vera Demberg and Frank Keller. 2008. Data from eye-tracking corpora as evidence for theories of syntactic processing complexity. *Cognition*, 109(2):193–210.

Anna Maria Di Sciullo and Edwin Williams. 1987. *On the Definition of Word*. MIT Press, Cambridge, MA.

Jay Earley. 1968. *An Efficient Context-Free Parsing Algorithm*. Ph.D. thesis, Carnegie Mellon University.

Charles J. Fillmore, Paul Kay, and Mary Catherine O'Connor. 1988. Regularity and idiomaticity in grammatical constructions: The case of let alone. *Language*, 64(3):501–538, September.

Victoria Fossum and Roger Levy. 2012. Sequential vs. hierarchical syntactic models of human incremental sentence processing. In *CMCL*.

Stefan L Frank and Rens Bod. 2011. Insensitivity of the human sentence-processing system to hierarchical structure. *Psychological Science*, 22(6):829–34.

Stefan L. Frank. 2009. Surprisal-based comparison between a symbolic and a connectionist model of sentence processing. In *CogSci*.

John Hale. 2001. A probabilistic Earley parser as a psycholinguistic model. In *NAACL*.

Jennifer Hay. 2003. *Causes and Consequences of Word Structure*. Routledge, New York, NY.

Ray Jackendoff. 2002a. *Foundations of Language*. Oxford University Press, New York.

Ray Jackendoff. 2002b. What's in the lexicon? In S. Nooteboom, F. Weerman, and F. Wijnen, editors, *Storage and Computation in the Language Faculty*. Kluwer Academic Press, Dordrecht.

Frederick Jelinek and John D. Lafferty. 1991. Computation of the probability of initial substring generation by stochastic context-free grammars. *Computational Linguistics*, 17(3):315–323.

Mark Johnson, Thomas L. Griffiths, and Sharon Goldwater. 2006. Adaptor grammars: A framework for specifying compositional nonparametric bayesian models. In *NIPS*.

Mark Johnson, Thomas Griffiths, and Sharon Goldwater. 2007. Bayesian inference for PCFGs via Markov chain Monte Carlo. In *NAACL*.

Alan Kennedy and Joel Pynte. 2005. Parafoveal-on-foveal effects in normal reading. *Vision Research*, 45(2):153–168.

Kenichi Kurihara and Taisuke Sato. 2006. Variational bayesian grammar induction for natural language. In *ICGI*.

Roger Levy. 2008. Expectation-based syntactic comprehension. *Cognition*, 106(2):1126–1177.

Minh-Thang Luong, Michael C. Frank, and Mark Johnson. 2013. Parsing entire discourses as very long strings: Capturing topic continuity in grounded language learning. *TACL*, 1(3):315–323.

Mitchell P. Marcus, Mary Ann Marcinkiewicz, and Beatrice Santorini. 1993. Building a large annotated corpus of English: the Penn treebank. *Computational Linguistics*, 19(2):313–330.

Mitchell Marcus, Grace Kim, Mary Ann Marcinkiewicz, Robert MacIntyre, Ann Bies, Mark Ferguson, Karen Katz, and Britta Schasberger. 1994. The Penn treebank: Annotating predicate argument structure. In *HLT*.

Jeff Mitchell, Mirella Lapata, Vera Demberg, and Frank Keller. 2010. Syntactic and semantic factors in processing difficulty: an integrated measure. In *ACL*.

Geoffrey Nunberg, Ivan A. Sag, and Thomas Wasow. 1994. Idioms. *Language*, 70(3):491–538.

Timothy J. O'Donnell, Noah D. Goodman, and Joshua B. Tenenbaum. 2009. Fragment grammars: Exploring computation and reuse in language. Technical Report MIT-CSAIL-TR-2009-013, MIT Computer Science and Artificial Intelligence Laboratory Technical Report Series, Cambridge, MA.

Timothy J. O'Donnell, Jesse Snedeker, Joshua B. Tenenbaum, and Noah D. Goodman. 2011. Productivity and reuse in language. In *CogSci*.

Timothy J. O'Donnell. 2015. *Productivity and Reuse in Language: A Theory of Linguistic Computation and Storage*. The MIT Press, Cambridge, Massachusetts.

Slav Petrov and Dan Klein. 2007. Improved inference for unlexicalized parsing. In *HLT-NAACL*.

Slav Petrov, Leon Barrett, Romain Thibaux, and Dan Klein. 2006. Learning accurate, compact, and interpretable tree annotation. In *COLING-ACL*.

Matt Post and Daniel Gildea. 2013. Bayesian tree substitution grammars as a usage-based approach. *Language and Speech*, 56(3):291–308.

Brian Roark, Asaf Bachrach, Carlos Cardenas, and Christophe Pallier. 2009. Deriving lexical and syntactic expectation-based measures for psycholinguistic modeling via incremental top-down parsing. In *EMNLP*.

Brian Roark. 2001. Probabilistic top-down parsing and language modeling. *Computational Linguistics*, 27:249–276.

Andreas Stolcke. 1995. An efficient probabilistic context-free parsing algorithm that computes prefix probabilities. *Computational Linguistics*, 21(2):165–201.

Andreas Stolcke. 2002. Srilm-an extensible language modeling toolkit. In *ICSLP*.

Antoine Tremblay and R. Harald Baayen. 2010. Holistic processing of regular four-word sequences: A behavioral and ERP study of the effects of structure, frequency, and probability on immediate free recall. In *Perspectives on Formulaic Language: Acquisition and Communication*, pages 151–173. Continuum.

Marten van Schijndel and William Schuler. 2013. An analysis of frequency- and memory-based processing costs. In *NAACL-HLT*.

Stephen Wu, Asaf Bachrach, Carlos Cardenas, and William Schuler. 2010. Complexity metrics in an incremental right-corner parser. In *ACL*.

An agent-based model of a historical word order change

Jelke Bloem **Arjen Versloot** **Fred Weerman**

Amsterdam Center for Language and Communication
University of Amsterdam
1012 VB Amsterdam, Netherlands
{j.bloem, a.p.versloot, f.p.weerman}@uva.nl

Abstract

We aim to demonstrate that agent-based models can be a useful tool for historical linguists, by modeling the historical development of verbal cluster word order in Germanic languages. Our results show that the current order in German may have developed due to increased use of subordinate clauses, while the English order is predicted to be influenced by the grammaticalization of the verb *to have*. The methodology we use makes few assumptions, making it broadly applicable to other phenomena of language change.

1 Introduction

Agent-based modeling is a method for simulating the behaviour of individual agents (i.e. a speaker of a language) in a larger community of agents (i.e. all speakers of the language). While agent-based models have been successfully used as tools in the field of evolutionary linguistics to study how linguistic structures may have emerged, they have not yet spread to the field of historical linguistics, which is more interested in describing and modeling change in existing natural languages. Both fields are concerned with changing language models, although the starting assumptions and context are different. In historical linguistics there is data available about structures in earlier and more modern states of the language, while in evolutionary linguistics the structures have to emerge from the implemented mechanisms. Nevertheless, the mechanisms described, such as grammaticalization, are often similar and lend themselves to study using similar methodology.

In the field of evolutionary linguistics, agent-based models are used to model language as a complex dynamic system, whose structure depends on the interactions of its speakers. An early overview of such work is provided by Steels (1997), who emphasizes the possibilities of modeling various aspects of language in this way. Among this work is a study by Briscoe (1997) on the default word order of languages, though it assumes a framework of universal grammar in which learning consists of setting parameters. Subsequent work included the application of this method to specific domains of linguistics, such as the emergence of vowel systems (De Boer, 2000) and the development of agent-based models specific to language, such as the iterated learning model of Kirby and Hurford (2002). Language change was often only discussed in terms of the emergence of new structures, and lacked comparisons to historical data (de Boer and Zuidema, 2009), or used artificial languages, as noted by Choudhury et al. (2007), whose own work is an exception. A few other studies that relate to historical linguistics can be found. Daland et al. (2007) and Van Trijp (2012) model some apparent idiosyncrasies in inflectional paradigms of natural languages, Daland et al. (2007) doing so with a model that includes social structure, and Van Trijp (2012) using the Fluid Construction Grammar framework. A further example is Landsbergen et al. (2010)'s study that models some mechanisms of language change from the perspective of cultural evolution. Overall, agent-based language studies informed by historical data are not widespread, and often involve many assumptions or dependence on a framework. A recent exception to this is a study by Pijpops and Beuls (2015) on Dutch regular and irregular verbs.

Our emphasis in this work is on creating an agent-based model that makes minimal assumptions, in order for the presented methodology to be useful for any theory of language that allows for functionalism in language change. Our case study, the historical development of verbal cluster order in Germanic languages, involves a word order variation in which multiple constructions are grammat-

Proceedings of the Sixth Workshop on Cognitive Aspects of Computational Language Learning, pages 22–27,
Lisbon, Portugal, 18 September 2015.

ical. This kind of phenomenon has not been investigated with an agent-based model before. Besides syntactic analyses (Evers, 1975), recent work on verb clusters has also discussed non-syntactic factors influencing word order, using frequency-based methods (De Sutter, 2005; Arfs, 2007; Bloem et al., 2014) and historical data (Coussé, 2008). We follow up on this line of work with our agent-based model, in which a functional bias induces language change. Using this model, we will show how the current orders of verb clusters in modern West-Germanic languages might have developed and diverged from the proto-Germanic cluster orders.

In the next section, we briefly outline the phenomenon of verbal cluster order variation. We then describe the methodology of the simulation and its initial state, followed by the results and a discussion of those results

2 Verbal clusters

Many verbal cluster word orders are attested in different Germanic languages (Wurmbrand, 2006). We will illustrate this with a Dutch example, a language where the ordering of these verbs is relatively free. In two-verb clusters, the finite verb can be positioned before or after the infinitive:

(1) Ik denk dat ik het **heb begrepen**.
I think that I it have understood
'I think that I have understood it'

(2) Ik denk dat ik het **begrepen heb**.
I think that I it understood have
'I think that I have understood it'

In the literature, construction 1 is called the 1-2 order (ascending order or red order), and construction 2 is called the 2-1 order (descending order or green order). Both orders are grammatical in Dutch, and express the same meaning, though there are differences in usage. German and Frisian only allow order (2) for two-verb clusters, while English and Scandinavian languages only allow order (1) [1]. Despite these differences, all of these languages evolved from Proto-West-Germanic.

This raises the question of why some of the West Germanic languages ended up with verbal clusters in 2-1 order, and others with the 1-2 order. To study this, we need to select some factors that may have influenced the change, and the best place to look for this is the Dutch language, in which both orders are possible. Language variation often indicates language change, with the variation being a state of transition from one structure to another, in which both structures can be used. Factors that correlate with different word order preferences in modern Dutch may therefore be involved in the change as well.

[1]English and Scandinavian verb groups are generally not called verb clusters in the literature because they can be interrupted by nonverbal material, but for the purposes of this study the distinction is not important.

% 1-2	mod+inf	have+PP	cop+PP
main	97%	50%	10%
sub	80%	50%	5%

Table 1: Reconstructed proto-Germanic probabilities for the 1-2 order.

The order variation in Dutch has been claimed to be an instance of language change in progress. In the 15th century, the 2-1 order was used almost exclusively. After this, the 1-2 order starts appearing in texts, and becomes increasingly frequent, moving towards the current state of the language (Coussé, 2008). This was not the first time the 1-2 order had been attested though, it also appears in some of the oldest Dutch texts.

3 Methodology

Our simulation consists of a group of agents that can function as speakers and recipients of verbal cluster utterances. Each agent has its own instance of a probabilistic language model that stores and produces such utterances. We will first describe the language model and the linguistic features of verbal clusters that it stores, and then we will explain what happens when the simulation is ran and the agents interact.

To find linguistic features that may be associated more with one order than with the other, we rely on synchronic corpus studies of Dutch, the language in which both orders are possible. Associations have been found with a variety of factors, including contextual factors such as regional differences between speakers (Coussé et al., 2008). When creating a language model for an agent, we are only interested in factors that may cause a particular speaker (or agent) to choose a particular word order. A recent study found that verbal cluster order variation correlates with both constructional factors (the use of a particular linguistic form) and processing factors (such as sentence length) (Bloem et al., 2014). We will examine only the constructional factors, because those are likely to be stored in the lexicon with their own associated word order preferences. The most important of these are the main clause / subordinate clause distinction (there are more 2-1 orders in main clauses), and the type of auxiliary verb (there are more 2-1 orders when a copula verb is used in a cluster). These two factors not only have different order preferences in modern Dutch, but have also undergone historical changes that may have triggered our word order change: subordinate clauses have become more prevalent, and one type of auxiliary verb, *to have*, grammaticalized during the time period we are interested in.

We will assume that the two factors, clause type and auxiliary type, are stored as features, each with their own word order preferences. This way of storing features is based on the bidirectional model in Versloot (2008), though our models learn by interacting rather than iterating.

Table 1 shows all of the possible combinations of feature values a verbal cluster can have in our model. Our model assumes two clause types (main and subordinate) and three different types of auxiliary verbs, reflecting the historical sources of verb clusters:

1. Clause type feature
   (a) Main clause context
   (b) Subordinate clause context
2. Auxiliary type feature
   (a) modal + infinitive: the origin of verb clusters in Germanic
   (b) 'to have' + participial main verb (PP): arose only later in history to extend the possibilities of expressing temporal and aspectual features
   (c) copula + PP: originally a passive, predicative, construction — not purely verbal, rather adjectival.

A cluster can have either of two word orders: the 1-2 and the 2-1 order.

The simulation consists of a language agents, each starting out with n exemplars of verbal clusters, stored in the agent's language model. An agent's language model contains the type of information shown in Table 1: for each possible combination of feature values, exemplars are stored. In addition to their features they have the property of being either in the 2-1 or 1-2 order (from which a percentage can be calculated, as in the table). The agents' language models do not contain any other structures. We did not use an existing framework in order to have as few parameters as possible. The simulation was implemented in the Python programming language.

When the model is run, each run consists of $a * n * i$ interactions. In an interaction i, a random agent is picked as the speaker and another random agent as the recipient. The speaker agent generates a verbal cluster based on its language model, and the recipient agent stores it as an exemplar. When a speaker agent generates a verbal cluster, it picks the features of a random exemplar from its language model, and then assigns word order based on the word order probabilities of both of its features individually. A 1-2 (ascending) realization of a modal subordinate clause cluster may be produced according to the following:

$$P(asc|x) = P(asc|x_{sub}) + P(asc|x_{modinf}) \quad (1)$$

where x is a set of feature values. $P(asc|x_{sub})$ is the probability of a subordinate clause being in 1-2 order, and $P(asc|x_{modinf})$ for the modal+infinitive construction type. These probabilities are calculated from the stored frequency of the features in 1-2 contexts:

$$P(asc|x_{sub}) = \frac{F(sub, asc)}{F(sub)} \quad (2)$$

So, the probability of a modal subordinate clause cluster being expressed in the 1-2 order depends on how many exemplars the agent has stored in which a subordinate clause cluster was in the 1-2 order (relative to 2-1), as well as exemplars in which a modal cluster was in the 1-2 order (relative to 2-1). Example (3) is an example of a modal subordinate clause cluster in 1-2 order, though our language model is more abstract and does not use actual words, only the features.

(3) Ik denk dat ik het **wil** **horen**
    I think that I it want hear
    'I think that I want to hear it'

After producing this exemplar, the agent normally deletes it from its own storage, because we do not want the relative frequencies of the various feature values (i.e. the number of copular verbs) to vary randomly. We are only interested in the word order. Furthermore, this avoids an endless growth of the agents' language models. Only when a growth factor applies, this deletion does not happen. The simulation includes two growth factors g_have and g_sub to simulate two relevant historical changes: the grammaticalization of 'to have' as an auxiliary verb, and an increase in the use of subordinate clauses. When these growth factors are set to 1, after every a interactions, an exemplar with the relevant feature is kept where it otherwise would have been deleted from the language model. A growth factor of 2 doubles the rate. g_have applies while there are fewer *have*-clusters than clusters of either of the other types, and g_sub while there are fewer subordinate clause clusters than main clause clusters.

When an agent is the recipient of a verbal cluster exemplar, it simply stores it in its language model, including the word order. So, when example (3) is perceived, the 1-2 order production probability of subordinate clause clusters and that of modal clusters will go up (separately) in the language model of the recipient agent. A critical learning bias is simulated here: the tendency to decompose an utterance into features and storing information about the features, rather than storing it as a whole. This is the only assumption we make about the language faculty in this model, and it is a functional one. It simulates the fact that people do not perfectly copy a language from each other.

We initialize each experiment with 30 agents ($a = 30$), and $i = 5000$ to simulate a long time course in which simulations will almost always stabilize in the end. With fewer agents, some agents lose all of their exemplars during the simulation. Each agent starts with a language model of 73 exemplars ($n = 73$) that follows frequency patterns as reconstructed for 6th century Germanic, based on a comparison of verb cluster frequencies in Old English, Old High German and Old Frisian texts. These figures are also summarized in table 1. For any unattested combination of features and word order a single exemplar is included to simulate noise.

4 Results

Figures (a) and (b) show example results of the agent-based model simulation, with different parameter settings. The graphs show the results of 50 different simulation runs overlaid, each run being a possible language. The X-axis represents time (in number of interactions) and the Y-axis represents the proportion of 1-2 orders, a value between 0 and 1. The proportions are calculated over all of the agents in the simulation. When the simulation is ran for long enough, it will always stabilize into a situation where a language either has only 1-2 or only 2-1 orders, though some feature combinations stabilize faster than others. Due to space constraints, we only show results for subordinate clause clusters (with any auxiliary type), but the general patterns are similar for all of the features, though some change sooner than others. We can observe that the model correctly predicts both languages with dominant 1-2 orders such as English, and dominant 2-1 orders as in German.

However, a model that predicts everything is not very interesting. We would like to know when a language in the model becomes English-like or German-like. We can do this by changing the growth factors: the rise of subordinate clauses (g_sub) and of *to have* (g_have). Figure (a) shows simulations in which *to have* grammaticalizes faster, while in Figure (b), subordinate clauses catch on more quickly. A clear difference can be observed — Figure (a) shows more languages gaining English-like 1-2 orders (35% 1-2, 56% 2-1 and the rest had not stabilized yet), while Figure (b) shows more German-like 2-1 orders (92% 2-1, 7% 1-2). Different speeds of grammaticalization of *to have* and growth of subordinate clauses result in different dominant word orders.

5 Discussion

With this study, we hope to have shown that an agent-based model with just a single learning bias can be used to gain insight into processes of change in natural languages, and generate new hypotheses. Specifically, the model makes two predictions: that *to have* grammaticalized faster in English, and that subordinate clauses gained use more quickly in German. These predictions can be tested using historical corpora of these languages in future work.

In the model, the 2-1 order is supported by subordinate clauses. Due to verb-second (V2) movement in these languages, the finite verb (the 1) precedes the other verb in main clauses (the 2). This 1-2 order differentiates main clauses from subordinate clauses, motivating the preservation of a 2-1 order in the subordinate clauses. Increased use of subordinate clauses may then have supported the 2-1 order as the default order. However, if *to have* grammaticalizes earlier, the 1-2 order is sup-

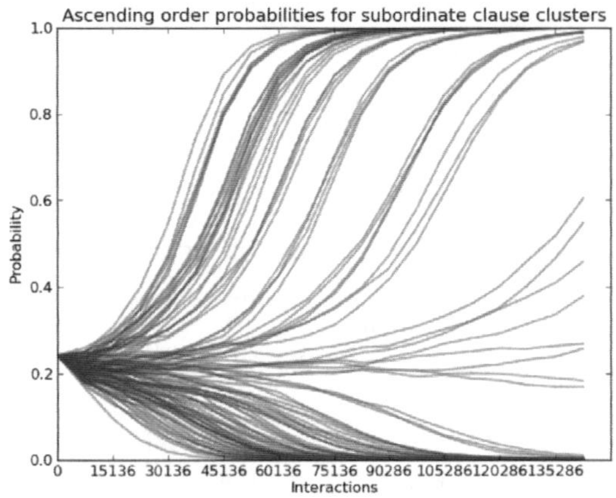

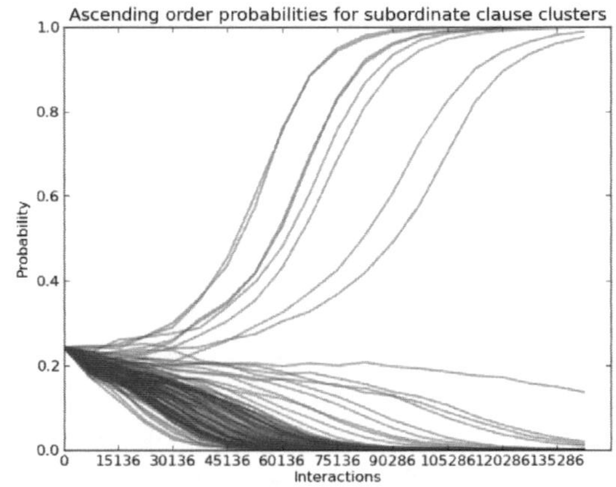

(a) 50 runs with faster growth of have+pp constructions ($g\_have = 2$, $g\_sub = 1$)

(b) 50 runs with faster growth of subordinate clauses ($g\_have = 1$, $g\_sub = 2$)

ported. This new grammatical verb becomes associated with the most prevalent word order at the time, and pushes the language further in the direction of that word order. In the beginning this is the 1-2 order, more associated with main clauses in proto-West-Germanic due to V2 movement, but later on the 2-1 order is more prevalent, due to its association with subordinate clauses.

Our model cannot yet account for the current state of the Dutch language, which first moved towards mainly 2-1 orders like German, and then shifted towards 1-2 orders again (Coussé, 2008), a change that is still in progress. There is evidence that the 1-2 order has become the default order (Meyer and Weerman, submitted), and this second change was likely caused by a factor outside the scope of our model, such as language contact.

Nevertheless, we believe that agent-based modelling can be a useful tool for historical linguists, particularly those working with frequency-based explanations. The present work and the study of Pijpops and Beuls (2015) show that testing of different mechanisms and parameters in a simulation, informed by historical data, can provide additional evidence for theories on what may or may not have been possible in a case of language change, given the assumptions built into the model. We believe it is particularly interesting to test how few assumptions are necessary to explain the observed historical data, which previous work has not focused on.

We would like to emphasize that this method is applicable to other cases of language change in which the use of structures changed over time. Any processes of historical change that can be captured in terms of frequencies and features may be used as factors to be investigated, and the fact that the model makes few assumptions also means that no particular social or cultural phenomena need to have happened for the model to be applicable. However, these simplifications also limit the extend of what can be modeled. In future work, contact phenomena could be simulated by including non-learning agents, or influxes of agents with different language models. Subsequent work on other cases of historical change may need to include such additional assumptions, if they are known to have been historically relevant.

References

Mona Arfs. *Rood of groen? De interne woordvolgorde in tweeledige werkwoordelijke eindgroepen met een voltooid deelwoord en een hulpwerkwoord in bijzinnen.* Göteborg University, 2007.

Jelke Bloem, Arjen Versloot, and Fred Weerman. Applying automatically parsed corpora to the study of language variation. In *Proceedings of COLING 2014, the 25th International Conference on Computational Linguistics: Technical Papers*, pages 1974–1984, Dublin, Ireland, August 2014. Dublin City University and Association for Computational Linguistics. URL http://www.aclweb.org/anthology/C14-1186.

Ted Briscoe. Co-evolution of language and of the language acquisition device. In *Proceedings of the eighth conference on European chapter of the Association for Computational Linguistics*, pages 418–427. Association for Computational Linguistics, 1997.

Monojit Choudhury, Vaibhav Jalan, Sudeshna Sarkar, and Anupam Basu. Evolution, optimization, and language change: The case of bengali verb inflections. In *Proceedings of Ninth Meeting of the ACL Special Interest Group in Computational Morphology and Phonology*, pages 65–74. Association for Computational Linguistics, 2007.

Evie Coussé. *Motivaties voor volgordevariatie. Een diachrone studie van werkwoordvolgorde in het Nederlands.* Universiteit Gent, 2008.

Evie Coussé, Mona Arfs, and Gert De Sutter. Variabele werkwoordsvolgorde in de Nederlandse werkwoordelijke eindgroep. Een taalgebruiksgebaseerd perspectief op de synchronie en diachronie van de zgn. rode en groene woordvolgorde. *Taal aan den lijve. Het gebruik van corpora in taalkundig onderzoek en taalonderwijs*, pages 29–47, 2008.

Robert Daland, Andrea D Sims, and Janet Pierrehumbert. Much ado about nothing: A social network model of russian paradigmatic gaps. In *ANNUAL MEETING-ASSOCIATION FOR COMPUTATIONAL LINGUISTICS*, volume 45, page 936. Citeseer, 2007.

Bart De Boer. Self-organization in vowel systems. *Journal of phonetics*, 28(4):441–465, 2000.

Bart de Boer and Willem Zuidema. Models of language evolution: Does the math add up. *ILLC Preprint Series PP-2009-49, University of Amsterdam*, 2009.

Gert De Sutter. *Rood, groen, corpus! Een taalgebruiksgebaseerde analyse van woordvolgordevariatie in tweeledige werkwoordelijke eindgroepen.* University of Leuven: PhD thesis, 2005.

Arnold Evers. *The transformational cycle in Dutch and German*, volume 75. Indiana University Linguistics Club Bloomington, 1975.

Simon Kirby and James R Hurford. The emergence of linguistic structure: An overview of the iterated learning model. In *Simulating the evolution of language*, pages 121–147. Springer, 2002.

Frank Landsbergen, Robert Lachlan, Carel ten Cate, and Arie Verhagen. A cultural evolutionary model of patterns in semantic change. *Linguistics*, 48(2):363–390, 2010.

Caitlin Meyer and Fred Weerman. Cracking the cluster: The acquisition of verb raising in Dutch. *Manuscript in preparation*, submitted.

Dirk Pijpops and Katrien Beuls. Strong "island of resilience" in the weak flood. Dutch strategies for past tense formation implemented in an agent-based model. Presented at Computational Linguistics in the Netherlands (CLIN) 25, Antwerp, 2015.

Luc Steels. The synthetic modeling of language origins. *Evolution of communication*, 1(1):1–34, 1997.

Remi Van Trijp. Self-assessing agents for explaining language change: A case study in german. In *ECAI*, pages 798–803, 2012.

Arjen Pieter Versloot. Mechanisms of language change: vowel reduction in 15th century West Frisian. 2008.

Susi Wurmbrand. Verb clusters, verb raising, and restructuring. *The Blackwell companion to syntax*, pages 229–343, 2006.

Towards a Model of Prediction-based Syntactic Category Acquisition: First Steps with Word Embeddings

Robert Grimm **Giovanni Cassani** **Walter Daelemans** **Steven Gillis**
University of Antwerp, CLiPS
{name.surname}@uantwerpen.be

Abstract

We present a prototype model, based on a combination of count-based distributional semantics and prediction-based neural word embeddings, which learns about syntactic categories as a function of (1) writing contextual, phonological, and lexical-stress-related information to memory and (2) predicting upcoming context words based on memorized information. The system is a first step towards utilizing recently popular methods from Natural Language Processing for exploring the role of prediction in childrens' acquisition of syntactic categories.[1]

1 Introduction

Evidence is mounting that during language processing, the brain is predicting upcoming elements at different levels of granularity (Huettig, 2015). This could serve at least two purposes: (1) to facilitate understanding in dialogue and (2) to acquire abstract syntactic structure.

With respect to (1), Pickering and Garrod (2007) review evidence suggesting that people predict upcoming elements in their interlocutors' speech streams using the production system. This is thought to facilitate understanding in dialogue. One reason to postulate (2) is that length of memory span for syntactically well-formed sequences is positively correlated with an individual's ability to predict upcoming words (Conway, 2010; see Huettig, 2015, for further arguments).

We thus have evidence that people predict linguistic elements, and there is reason to suspect that this could be linked to the acquisition of syntactic structure. Models of prediction in language processing should therefore aim to demonstrate the emergence of such structure as a function of learning to predict upcoming elements.

Perhaps the most explicit account of such a process can be found in the work of Chang et al. (2006), who use a recurrent neural network in combination with an event semantics, in order to generate sentences with unseen bindings between words and semantic roles – i.e., the types of novel sentential constructions that could be afforded by abstract syntactic structure.

It is noteworthy, given this line of work, that prediction is central to recently popular methods from Natural Language Processing (NLP) for obtaining distributional representations of words (Mikolov et al., 2013; Pennington et al., 2014). Vector representations (often called *word embeddings*) obtained using these methods cluster closely in terms of semantic and syntactic types – an achievement due to engineering efforts, without emphasis on psychological constraints. Thus, if these methods are to be used for modelling aspects of human language processing, they should be modified to reflect such constraints.

Here, we attempt to take a first step into this direction: we modify the skipgram model from the *word2vec* family of models (Mikolov et al., 2013) – which predicts both the left and right context of a word – to predict only the righ context. Word counts from the left context form the basis for prediction and are tuned to maximize the likelihood of correctly predicting words from the right context. Throughout, we measure the organization of word embeddings in terms of syntactic categories – and find that embeddings of the same category cluster more closely after each training stage.

In addition to word frequencies from the left context, we experiment with phonological information and features related to lexical stress as the basis of predicting words from the right context.

[1]The work reported here was implemented in the Theano framework (Bastien et al., 2012; Bergstra et al., 2010). The code is freely available at: https://github.com/RobGrimm/prediction_based (commit ID: 6d60222)

Proceedings of the Sixth Workshop on Cognitive Aspects of Computational Language Learning, pages 28–32,
Lisbon, Portugal, 18 September 2015.

2 Language Model

The model is trained in two consecutive stages: (1) for each word in the vocabulary, create a vector of frequency counts for words from its left context. Concatenate this with phonological and / or lexical stress features, and project the result into a joint dimensionality-reduced space. (2) Use the embeddings obtained in stage 1 to predict words from the right context, and modify the input embeddings via the backpropagation algorithm.

Stage 1 is meant to correspond to a memory component which tracks backward statistical regularities, while stage 2 is meant to correspond to a forward-looking predictive mechanism. On the NLP side, the model is a combination of count-based distributional semantics (stage 1) and prediction-based neural word embeddings (stage 2). While count-based and prediction-based approaches can produce similar results, provided the parameters are tweaked in a certain way, (Levy et al., 2015), it seems intuitively that adding counts is more like memorizing context, whereas an explicitly predictive component is more suited for modelling prediction in language processing.

To the best of our knowledge, there exists no other work which combines counting and predicting to derive word embeddings, nor work which attempts to relate this to language acquisition. The current model, being a result of preliminary explorations, is only loosely based on possible principles of cognitive processing; it may, nevertheless, have the potential to move currently successful methods from NLP closer to language acquisition research.

2.1 Memory Component: Auto Encoder

During the first stage, we use a denoising Auto Encoder to (a) reduce the dimensionality of the feature vectors and (b) project concatenated feature vectors (e.g. contextual and phonological) into a shared space. As a result, we see some first improvements of the vectors' clustering in terms of syntactic categories.

An Auto Encoder is a neural network that learns to transform a given input $x^{(i)}$ into an intermediate representation $h(x^{(i)}) = s(W \cdot x^{(i)} + b_v)$, so that a faithful reconstruction $y^{(i)} = s(W' \cdot h(x^{(i)}) + b_h)$ can be recovered from $h(x^{(i)})$ (Bengio, 2009), where s is a non-linear activation function. We set $s(z) = max(0, min(1, z))$ and $W' = W^T$, i.e. we use a truncated linear rectified activation function and work with tied weights.

The parameters of the network are the weight matrix W, the visible bias b_v and the hidden bias b_h. The Auto Encoder is trained via gradient descent to produce faithful reconstructions of a set of input vectors $\{x^{(1)}, ...x^{(n)}\}$ by minimizing the average, across training examples, of the reconstruction error $||x^{(i)} - y^{(i)}||^2$.

After training, the latent representation $h(x^{(i)})$ is often used for some other task. One strategy to force $h(x^{i)})$ to retain useful features is to train on a partially corrupted version $\tilde{x}^{(i)}$ of $x^{(i)}$. This is the idea behind the denoising Auto Encoder (dAE), where part of the input vector $\tilde{x}^{(i)}$ is set to 0.0 with probability v (the *corruption level*). The dAE is then trained to reconstruct the uncorrupted input.

2.2 Predictive Component: Softmax Model

In stage 2, the model learns to predict words from the embeddings obtained in stage 1. This is done by maximizing the probability $p(c|w;\theta)$ of context word c given target word w, for all pairs of target and context words $(w, c) \in D$. To obtain D, we first define an integer $t > 0$ as the context window. Considering each sentence S from the training corpus, for each target word $w_n \in S$ at position $n \leq length(S)$, we sample an integer t_n from the uniform distribution $\{1, ...t\}$. We then add the target-context word pairs $\{(w_n, w_{n+j}) : 0 < j \leq t_n, w_i \in S\}$ to D. Note that we only sample words from the right context, instead of from both left *and* right context. Aside from this difference, stage 2 is comparable to the *word2vec* skipgram model (Mikolov et al., 2013).

Here as there, the probability of a context word given its target word can be defined as:

$$p(c|w;\theta) = \frac{e^{v_c \cdot T_{w*}}}{\sum_{c' \in V} e^{v_{c'} \cdot T_{w*}}} \quad (1)$$

where the embedding T_{w*} of target word w is a row in the embeddings matrix T, v_c is a vector representation for context word c, and V is the vocabulary. (1) is computed by a neural network with a softmax output layer and weight matrix W, such that v_c is a row in W, and the parameters θ are W and T. The training objective is the minimization of the negative sum of log probabilities across all target word – context word pairs.

3 Data

3.1 Corpus and Vocabulary

Training data are based on a concatenation of 18 POS-tagged English corpora[2] from the CHILDES database (MacWhinney, 2000). We only consider utterances from the father and mother, i.e. utterances whose speaker was coded with either *FAT* or *MOT* (child-directed speech, or CDS). The concatenated North American and English corpora contain 1.555.311 and 1.575.548 words of CDS, respectively (3.130.859 words).

The vocabulary consists of the 2000 most frequent nouns, verbs, adjectives, and closed class words (words that are tagged as adverbs, communicators, conjunctions, determiners, infinitival *to*, numerals, particles, prepositions, pronouns, quantifiers, auxiliaries, wh-words, or modifiers), with homophones disambiguated by POS tags. In total, we end up with 1010 nouns, 522 closed class words, 302 verbs, and 166 adjectives.

3.2 Phonology and Lexical Stress

For each word from the vocabulary, we construct a phonological feature vector by first extracting its sequence of phonemes from the CELEX database (Baayen et al., 1995). Each phoneme is then placed on a trisyllabic consonant-vowel-grid, which is transformed into a 114-dimensional binary vector by concatenating the phonemes' vector-representations, as given by Li and MacWhinney (2002) (empty consonant-vowel slots are assigned a vector of zeros). Once done for every word, embeddings of similar-sounding words tend to be close to one another in the embeddings space. Finally, in order to learn more abstract phonological representations, the feature vectors are reduced to 30 dimensions, using a dAE trained for 200 epochs, with a learning rate of 0.1 and a corruption level of 0.1.

For each word, we also extract a lexical stress component from the CELEX database, which we transform into a binary vector of length three. Each index corresponds to one of three possible syllables, such that a one signifies the presence of primary stress and a zero indicates its absence.

[2] *UK corpora*: Belfast, Manchester. *US corpora*: Bates, Bliss, Bloom 1973, Bohannon, Brown, Demetras – Trevor, Demetras – Working, Feldman, Hall, Kuczaj, MacWhinney, New England, Suppes, Tardif, Valian, Van-Kleeck. See the CHILDES manuals for references: http://childes.psy.cmu.edu/manuals/

3.3 Training Set

Given the vocabulary V, we create the embeddings matrix T of size $|V| \times |V|$, where each row T_{w*} is a word embedding corresponding to a unique target word $w \in V$ and each column T_{*c} corresponds to a unique context word $c \in V$. A cell T_{wc} is then the frequency with which c occurs within a sentence-internal window of $t = 3$ words to the left of w, across all occurrences of w in CDS. Rows are normalized to unit interval.

The model is trained in three conditions, with the rows in T constituting the training set: (1) *context*: T remains unchanged; (2) *context + stress*: each row T_{w*} is concatenated with the lexical stress feature vector of w; (3) *context + phonology*: each row is concatenated with a phonological feature vector.

4 Training Procedure and Evaluation

While the task is to predict words, we are interested in a side effect of the learning process: the induction of representations whose organization in vector space reflects syntactic categories. To measure this, we train a 10-NN classifier on the embeddings after each training epoch, with embeddings labeled by syntactic category, and we stop training as soon as the micro F_1 score does not increase anymore.[3] To avoid premature termination of training due to fluctuations in F_1 scores during stage 1, we keep track of the epoch E at which we got the best score A. If scores stay smaller than or equal to A for 10 epochs, we terminate training and obtain the dimensionality-reduced embeddings for further training in stage 2 from the dAE's state at E. In stage 2, as there are no such fluctuations, it is safe to terminate as soon as there is no increase anymore. This procedure allows for as many training epochs as are necessary for achieving the best results – between 22 and 30 in the first and between 4 and 5 epochs in the second stage.

Performance is compared across stages as well as to a majority vote baseline (each data point is assigned the most common class) and a stratified sampling baseline (class labels are assigned in accordance with the class distribution). The expected pattern is that performance at each training stage is both above baseline and significantly bet-

[3] We track the micro instead of the macro F_1 measure because we think it is important for potential models of language acquisition to correctly categorize a majority of words, even at the expense of minority categories.

progress	category	context				context + stress				context + phonology			
		prec.	rec.	ma. F_1	mi. F_1	prec.	rec.	ma. F_1	mi. F_1	prec.	rec.	ma. F_1	mi. F_1
before stage 1	nouns	89	92	**0.746**	**0.819**	88	92	**0.751**	**0.821**	72	94	**0.566**	**0.734**
	verbs	66	92			70	90			67	77		
	adj.	68	48			68	48			58	4		
	clos. cl.	82	68			82	70			88	52		
after stage 1	nouns	91	93	**0.785**	**0.847**	89	92	**0.778**	**0.840**	81	94	**0.707**	**0.804**
	verbs	73	93			75	91			72	86		
	adj.	74	54			70	53			70	30		
	clos. cl.	84	73			83	73			89	66		
after stage 2	nouns	90	96	**0.810**	**0.865**	88	96	**0.799**	**0.858**	79	97	**0.725**	**0.812**
	verbs	81	87			81	86			82	83		
	adj.	76	60			75	54			75	32		
	clos. cl.	86	77			86	76			90	66		

Table 1: Precision and recall (in percent), together with micro and macro F_1 scores, based on a 10-NN classifier trained on the word embeddings at different stages during the training process.

ter than performance at the previous stage. Significance of differences is computed via approximate randomization testing (Noreen, 1989),[4] a statistical test suitable for comparing evaluation metrics such as F-scores (cf. Yeh, 2000).

Results are based on a dAE with 400 hidden units, trained with a learning rate of 0.01, and a corruption level of 0.1. The softmax model was trained with a learning rate of 0.008, with context words sampled from a sentence-internal window of $t = 3$ words to the right. Both models were optimized via true stochastic gradient descent.

5 Results and Discussion

Table 1 shows precision, recall and F_1 scores based on a 10-NN classifier trained on the word embeddings at three different points in time: (a) before training begins, with scores based on the input embeddings, (b) after stage 1, with embeddings projected into a lower-dimensional space, and (c) after stage 2, with embeddings modified as a result of predicting words from the right context.

F_1 scores at every stage are highly significantly different ($p \leq 0.001$) from both the majority vote baseline (macro F_1 = 0.168, micro F_1 = 0.505) and the stratified sampling baseline (macro F_1 = 0.247, micro F_1 = 0.354). Across conditions, F_1 scores after stage 1 are very significantly different ($p \leq 0.01$) from scores obtained before stage 1. Scores calculated after stage 2 are still significantly different ($p \leq 0.05$) from scores at the previous stage in the *context* and *context + stress* conditions, although there is no such significant difference in the *context + phonology* condition (but $p \approx 0.07$ for the difference between micro F_1 scores). There is no significant difference between the *context* and *context + stress* conditions at any stage, whereas the within-stage differences between F_1 scores in the *context* and *context + phonology* conditions are all highly significant.

We can make at least three observations. (1) The model performs as expected, in that there is a significant increase in performance after every stage – i.e., the induced word representations cluster more closely in terms of syntactic categories as training progresses. (2) The phonological component does not improve on the *context* condition, likely because phonological similarity often conflicts with syntactic similarity – most notably with homophones, but also with words such as the verb *tickle* and the noun *pickle*. (3) The lexical stress features do not seem to help, as there is no significant difference between the *context* and *context + stress* conditions.

6 Conclusions and Future Work

In general, the model demonstrates that it is possible to augment prediction-based word embeddings with a count based component, such that frequency counts serve as the basis of prediction and are further refined as a result of predicting right context. This can serve as a first step towards utilizing prediction-based methods in order to model childrens' acquisition of syntactic categories through a process of (1) tracking backward statistical regularities by writing to memory and

[4]We used an implementation by Vincent Van Asch, available at: http://www.clips.uantwerpen.be/scripts/art

(2) tracking forward regularities via prediction

Apart from that, the model can be used to compare the utility of different types of features. It makes explicit the distinction, identified by Huettig (2015), between *cue of prediction* (what is used as the basis of prediction) and *content of prediction* (what is predicted). Neither of the two possible *cues of prediction* we investigated turned out to be helpful for the induction of syntactic categories.

The initial experiments described in this paper emphasize different *cues of prediction*. In the future, we plan to also predict different kinds of features. Moreover, we plan to replace the psychologically implausible stage-like organization of the model with a more incremental architecture.

Acknowledgments

The present research was supported by a BOF/TOP grant (ID 29072) of the Research Council of the University of Antwerp.

References

Alexander Yeh. 2000. More accurate tests for the statistical significance of result differences. *Proceedings of the 18th conference on Computational Linguistics. Volume 2 (947–953).*

Brian MacWhinney. 2000. The CHILDES project: Tools for analyzing talk: Volume I: Transcription format and programs, volume II: The database. *Computational Linguistics*, 26(4):657–657.

Christopher M. Conway, Althea Baurnschmidt, Sean Huang, and David B. Pisoni. 2010. Implicit statistical learning in language processing: word predictability is the key. *Cognition*, 114(3):356–371.

Eric W. Noreen. 1989. *Computer Intensive Methods for Testing Hypotheses: An Introduction.* Wiley, Hoboken, New Jersey.

Falk Huettig (in press). 2015. Four central questions about prediction in language processing. *Brain Research*, doi:10.1016/j.brainres.2015.02.014.

Franklin Chang, Gary S. Dell, and Kathryn Bock. 2006. Becoming Syntactic. *Psychological Review*, 113(2):234–272.

Frédéric Bastien, Pascal Lamblin, Razvan Pascanu, James Bergstra, Ian Goodfellow, Arnaud Bergeron, Nicolas Bouchard, David Warde-Farley, Yoshua Bengio. 2012. Theano: new features and speed improvements. *NIPS 2012 deep learning workshop.*

Harald Baayen, Richard Piepenbrock, and Leon Gulikers. 1995. *The CELEX lexical database (CD-ROM release 2).* Linguistic Data Consortium, University of Pennsylvania, Philadelphia, PA.

Jeffrey Pennington, Richard Socher, and Christopher Manning. 2014. Glove: Global vectors for word representation. *Proceedings of the 2014 Conference on Empirical Methods in Natural Language Processing (EMNLP), pages 1532–1543,* Doha, Qatar, October. Association for Computational Linguistics.

James Bergstra, Olivier Breuleux, Frédéric Bastien, Pascal Lamblin, Razvan Pascanu, Guillaume Desjardins, Joseph Turian, David Warde-Farley, Yoshua Bengio 2010. Theano: A CPU and GPU Math Compiler in Python. *Proceedings of the Python for Scientific Computing Conference (SciPy) 2010.* Austin, Texas.

Martin J. Pickering and Simon Garrod. 2007. Do people use language production to make predictions during comprehension? *Trends in cognitive sciences*, 11(3):105–110.

Omer Levy, Yoav Goldberg, and Ido Dagan. 2015. Improving distributional similarity with lessons learned from word embeddings. *Transactions of the Association for Computational Linguistics*, 3.

Ping Li and Brian MacWhinney. 2002. PatPho: A phonological pattern generator for neural networks. *Behavior Research Methods, Instruments, & Computers*, 34(3):408–415.

Tomas Mikolov, Kai Chen, Greg Corrado, and Jeffrey Dean. 2013. Efficient estimation of word representations in vector space. *arXiv:1301.3781 [Computation and Language (cs.CL)]*

Yoshua Bengio. 2009. Learning Deep Architectures for AI. *Foundations and Trends in Machine Learning*, 2(1):1–127.

Which distributional cues help the most?
Unsupervised contexts selection for lexical category acquisition

Giovanni Cassani **Robert Grimm** **Walter Daelemans** **Steven Gillis**
University of Antwerp, CLiPS
{name.surname}@uantwerpen.be

Abstract

Starting from the distributional bootstrapping hypothesis, we propose an unsupervised model that selects the most useful distributional information according to its salience in the input, incorporating psycholinguistic evidence. With a supervised Parts-of-Speech tagging experiment, we provide preliminary results suggesting that the distributional contexts extracted by our model yield similar performances as compared to current approaches from the literature, with a gain in psychological plausibility. We also introduce a more principled way to evaluate the effectiveness of distributional contexts in helping learners to group words in syntactic categories.

1 Introduction and related work

The psycholinguistic research about language acquisition has long been concerned with how children crack the linguistic input to infer the underlying structures. In this respect, bootstrapping (Gillis and Ravid, 2009) has been an important concept, which generated a number of hypotheses. After semantic bootstrapping, introduced by Pinker (1984), other proposals were put forward, each strengthening one aspect as the starting level that informs the others (syntactic bootstrapping (Gleitman, 1990; Gleitman and Gillette, 1995), prosodic bootstrapping (Christophe et al., 2008), distributional bootstrapping (Maratsos and Chalkley, 1980; Mintz, 2003)). This debate is tightly interwoven with the more general controversy between a nativist (Chomsky, 1965) and an emergentist account (Bates and MacWhinney, 1987; MacWhinney, 1998; Tomasello, 2000): our work was set up to explore the possibility of learning useful linguistic information from the Primary Linguistic Data (PLD), only using general-purpose learning mechanisms. Thus, we look at language acquisition from an emergentist perspective, exploring the fruitfulness of the distributional bootstrapping hypothesis.

Starting with Cartwright and Brent (1997), a variety of models for Parts-of-Speech (PoS) induction has been proposed (Clark, 2000; Mintz et al., 2002; Mintz, 2003; Parisien et al., 2008; Leibbrandt, 2009; Chrupała and Alishahi, 2010; St. Clair et al., 2010), showing that PLD are rich enough in distributional cues to provide the child with enough information to group words according to their syntactic category. Among such models, two major approaches can be identified: i) a frame-based one which starts by selecting the relevant cues and then evaluate how these help categorization, and ii) a probabilistic approach that considers all possible contexts in a left and right window whose size is set in advance, and determines the best category for each word based on a probabilistic match between the context of each new word and the previously encountered contexts for all words. While the first approach has been more concerned with finding the right cues or the most useful type of context (Monaghan and Christiansen, 2004), usually by focusing on certain distributional patterns and assessing their effectiveness in inducing lexical categories, the second one has tackled the problem from a more global perspective, inducing categories – not necessarily syntactic – and evaluating them using other linguistic tasks (Frank et al., 2008).

The first approach has been more influential in the acquisition literature, and is the topic of active behavioral research with both adults (Reeder et al., 2013; Mintz et al., 2014) and infants (Zhang et al., 2015). The second approach has been more distinctive of the computational psycholinguistic literature, but has been largely neglected by the acquisition literature. In this short paper, we try

Proceedings of the Sixth Workshop on Cognitive Aspects of Computational Language Learning, pages 33–39,
Lisbon, Portugal, 18 September 2015.

to suggest that the approach and the methods used in the second stream of research can be applied to the first, not only to induce plausible categories, but also a set of cues, without focusing on a specific kind of distributional pattern which is set in advance using linguistic knowledge. In this respect, we will review some of the major problems of the frame-based approach before suggesting a first way of tackling them.

In his seminal paper, Mintz (2003) suggested that the 45 most frequent A_x_B frames, defined as two words flanking a variable slot, are a plausible and accurate type of information – see also Wang and Mintz (2007) for an incremental model. This hypothesis was further tested on French by Chemla et al. (2009) with good success; however, its cross-linguistic validity was challenged by Erkelens (2009) for Dutch and Stumper et al. (2011) for German[1]. More recently, the *frequent frames* hypothesis was challenged by St. Clair et al. (2010), who proposed to use *flexible frames*, i.e. left and right bi-grams defined through the 45 most frequent words in a corpus, that can be combined on the fly to provide tri-gram level information – but see Mintz et al. (2014).

The main problem we see in both frequent and flexible frames, is the arbitrariness in deciding which contexts are important (Leibbrandt, 2009). While frequency drives the decision, what makes A_x_B (or A_x + x_B) frames so special that the child commits to them to infer lexical categories?

Moreover, restricting to token frequency can lead to retain contexts that do not help categorization, since they only occur with one word (like the frequent frame *have_X_look*), which in turn causes the model to not scale well to unseen data. Where the goal is explicitly to deal with reduced computational capacities, such behavior is far from desirable since it stores information that does not help to group words in more abstract categories.

A further problem of frequent frames, at least with English, is a strong verb bias: such cues provide information about a greater number of verbs, while the PLD typically contain many more nouns than verbs. This bias is a by-product of the definition of frames as fully lexical contexts: the shortest sentence from which a frame can be derived consists of three words, where the medial slot is usually taken up by a verb.

[1]However, better results were obtained with frames defined at the morpheme level, rather than at the word level (Wang et al., 2011).

At the same time, flexible frames suffer from other problems. Behavioral evidence suggests that children and adults store longer sequences as units (Bannard and Matthews, 2008; Arnon and Clark, 2011)[2], and arbitrarily excluding them does not seem a good strategy. Moreover, they were evaluated using a feed-forward neural network that was trained and tested *on the same data* (St. Clair et al., 2010). Since the utility of a set of distributional contexts cannot be restricted to its accuracy, the extent to which it scales to new, unseen words also needs to be taken into account.

Some of these problems have been addressed by Leibbrandt (2009), although his models are not incremental and rely heavily on arbitrary thresholds to remove very infrequent elements: while some sort of threshold seems to be unavoidable in a fully unsupervised model, a multitude of thresholds make it arbitrary and difficult to evaluate.

We will now introduce our model and then discuss the experiment that was set up to assess its effectiveness. We finally highlight the limitations of this work, sketch some ways to improve on it and draw the conclusions.

2 Model

We propose a model as a solution to the problems we highlighted in the previous section: it is entirely data-driven (reducing arbitrariness in the choice of the relevant dimensions) and more consistent with psycholinguistic evidence.

Three different pieces of information concerning a distributional context can be useful to the task at hand: i) its token frequency, i.e. how many times it occurs in the input; ii) its type frequency, i.e. the number of different words it occurs with; iii) the strength to which a context is predicted by a word, averaging across all the words it occurs with. Since it is hard to think to frequency without a comparison threshold, we divide token and type frequencies of a context by the average token and type frequencies across all contexts stored in memory at each sentence in the input.

These pieces of information can be combined in the following way:

$$score = token\_F \cdot type\_f \cdot p \qquad (1)$$

where each context is represented by a score resulting from the product of three pieces of infor-

[2]Although, see Baayen et al (2011) for an account in which n-grams effects are explained in a different way.

mation, defined as follows:

$$token\_F = \frac{log_2(count(c_i))}{avg(log_2(count(c))} \quad (2)$$

$$type\_f = \frac{log_2(\|W_{ci}\|)}{avg(log_2(\|W_c\|))} \quad (3)$$

$$p = \frac{1}{\|W_{ci}\|} \sum_{j=1}^{\|W_{ci}\|} \frac{log_2(count(w_j, c_i))}{log_2(count(w_j))} \quad (4)$$

In these formulas, c_i represents a distributional cue, W_{ci} is the set of words the cue occurs with; w_j represents a word and $count(w_j, c_i)$ the number of times a cue occurs with a specific word.

Raw counts are transformed with a base-2 logarithm to account for the fact that, as frequency grows, the contribution of every new occurrence to the total frequency is less and less important (Keuleers et al., 2010). Moreover, since the goal of this model is to discover structure, we assume that an item is only considered when it occurs more than once (items whose log is 0 are not considered). The formula in (4) closely resemble an average conditional probability – which children are likely to use to infer structure in language (Saffran et al., 1996) –, but differs from it since counts are again log-transformed for consistency with (2) and (3).

Salience can be thought of as the importance that a context might play in grouping words into categories, and the score we propose serves the purpose of selecting the most salient contexts. In this work, any context whose score is > 1 is considered to be salient, since 1 is the theoretical upper boundary of the *p* term, that can be increased or decreased by the following terms.

The formula in (1) is plugged into an incremental model that computes averages for token and type frequencies at every sentence *s*, and updates scores for contexts encountered in *s*. Contexts are harvested in a 2-word left/right window, looking at 2 bi-grams (*A_x; x_B*) and 3 tri-grams (*A_B_x, A_x_B* and *x_A_B*). A window cannot exceed a sentence boundary. At sentence initial and final positions, two dummy words were inserted, since sentence boundary information has been shown to be a useful distributional cue (Freudenthal et al., 2006; Freudenthal et al., 2008).

3 Experiment

3.1 Data

The experiment was carried out on the Aran section of the Manchester corpus (Theakston et al., 2001) from the CHILDES database (MacWhinney, 2000). In order to evaluate our model on unseen data, we divided the corpus chronologically in two sections: the first is used to select the distributional cues, the second for the evaluation phase.

We only considered sentences uttered by the mother, obtaining a corpus of 35K sentences. Our section for context selection (*selection set* henceforth) contains roughly 20K sentences, the section for the evaluation phase 15K. The corpus was not lemmatized. We removed false starts, onomatopoeia and other words based on their MOR PoS tags [3].

3.2 Setup

Different models - where each term from (1) is knocked out separately to assess its importance - were run on the selection set using only bi-grams, only tri-grams or both as contexts. The salient contexts at the end of this process were used as features in a supervised PoS experiment over types (not tokens) to evaluate their usefulness. As one reviewer pointed out, this evaluation is problematic for a number of reasons (Frank et al., 2008): however, we decided to use such approach because it is easy to interpret and provide a first indication about the potential effectiveness of the selected cues, serving as a first proof of concept.

In the selection set, only surface forms are considered[4]. We used the TiMBL package for memory-based learning (Daelemans et al., 2009), selecting the IB1 algorithm (Aha et al., 1991), weighted overlap as a distance metric with no feature weighting, and 1 nearest neighbor. In order to perform the experiment, the second part of the corpus was divided into a training and a test set (10K and 5K sentences, respectively), and two vector spaces were constructed, containing information about ho many times a word occurred with each cue.

The salient contexts harvested on the selection set were used as columns and the words occur-

[3] This is the list of MOR tags that were removed: *neo, on, chi, wplay, meta, fam, sing, L2, none*. Words without a tag were also removed, like errors, marked by a *0* before the tag, as in *0aux*.

[4] *Dog* and *dogs* are two different types, the modal *can* and the noun *can* are not.

Model	# contexts	Useless	Missed words (%)	Hits	Acc.
frequent frames	45	3 (6.7%)	83.7	290	**.83**
flexible frames	90	**0**	16.6	1405	.66
		$p \cdot token\_F$			
2grams_bound	75	**0**	10.2	1559	.671
3grams_bound	348	13 (3.7%)	37.3	1073	.681
all_bound	490	11 (2.2%)	3.8	**1669**	.664
		$p \cdot type\_f$			
2grams_bound	21	**0**	19.5	1377	.674
3grams_bound	42	**0**	56.7	788	.756
all_bound	97	**0**	8.7	1611	.679
		$p \cdot token\_F \cdot type\_f$			
2grams_bound	211	**0**	2.6	1624	.641
3grams_bound	659	7 (1%)	25.5	1249	.653
all_bound	964	8 (0.8%)	**1.2**	1562	.609

Table 1: Evaluation of several sets of distributional cues, with baselines at the top and our models grouped according to the information included. Column 2 shows the number of salient contexts; column 3 shows how many of them could not be used for categorization. Column 4 provides the percentage of words from the training set (total = 3191) that could not be categorized by the contexts. Columns 5 and 6 raw number of hits (test set = 2600 words) and accuracy on supervised PoS tagging.

ring with at least one such context as rows. Words that never occurred with any of the salient contexts were not categorized. In the training and test sections, homographs were disambiguated when they were tagged differently: thus, the list of target words may well include *dog_noun*, *dogs_noun*, *can_verb* and *can_noun*.

Performances were evaluated on a tag-set consisting of 5 categories: nouns (including pronouns), verbs (including auxiliaries), adjectives, adverbs and function words, since we were mainly interested in content words, which make up the productive part of the lexicon. Performance is evaluated along 5 aspects: i) the number of salient contexts; ii) the percentage of salient contexts that could not be used in the training section, either because they were absent or because they only occurred with one word; iii) the proportion of words that were missed on the training set; iv) number of hits on the PoS-tagging experiment, and v) accuracy.

3.3 Results and discussion

Table 1 shows performances of all models on the five dimensions we introduced in (§3.2). Best scores on each dimensions are highlighted in bold. Intuitively, a model is good when it (i) selects a limited set of contexts, reducing the dimensionality of the vector space in which similar words are searched; (ii) minimizes the number of selected contexts that do not scale to new data; (iii) ensures high coverage on new data; (iv) allows to correctly categorize a high number of words; and (v) achieves a high accuracy, resulting in a reliable categorization.

While *frequent frames* achieve the highest accuracy, they also have the worst coverage and lowest number of hits. Plus, it is interesting that 3 contexts out of 45 are useless for categorization. When we turn to *flexible frames*, we see that they scale perfectly and achieve rather good accuracy, but do not ensure wide coverage and many hits.

A first global trend involves accuracy, which is inversely correlated with the number of selected contexts (Pearson r = -0.68), suggesting that distributional information is noisy and it is vital to focus on certain cues and discard the majority of them[5] to achieve reliable categorization. Finally, conflating bi-grams and tri-grams - which is closer to the psycholinguistic evidence we have - does not harm the model.

Turning to model-specific features[6], $p{\cdot}token\_F$ results in a rather large set of contexts, some of them being useless. Coverage is generally high, as the number of hits. When all three terms are in-

[5] A further analysis, not reported, was conducted by retaining all contexts and showed that both accuracy and number of hits were worse than most of the models evaluated here.

[6] The $token\_F \cdot type\_f$ models performed much worse than the others, thus results are not reported.

cluded, we still have large sets of contexts, few of which don't scale to new data. Coverage is high as the raw number of hits, but each model here is less accurate than its twin models. The reason for this behavior could be that *type_f* strongly correlates with *token_ F* (the first cannot exceed the latter), and when they are both considered their contribution is inflated, resulting in more contexts and noise.

The $p \cdot type\_f$ models result in the smallest set of contexts, with perfect scalability and high accuracy. The downsides pertain coverage, and number of hits. Overall, no model performs high across all dimensions. However, the model combining p and *type_ f* displays parsimony, scalability, coverage and accuracy, although it is not the best on any dimension (it is also similar to flexible frames, but with better coverage, hits and accuracy). As we noted earlier, $token\_F$ and $type\_f$ are strongly positively correlated: this result suggests that the latter can be more useful to categories induction, since high type frequency ensures that a cue is systematic. We also evaluated contexts' token frequencies because of the well-attested frequency effects in language acquisition (Bybee, 1995), but the results suggest its effect in category formation can be better accounted for by contexts' type frequency. Nevertheless, further evidence is needed to confirm this hypothesis.

4 Limitations and future work

As one reviewer pointed out, this approach should be extended to be fully incremental and categorize tokens instead of types and evaluated with external linguistic task (see §3.2). However, unlike the probabilistic approach to category induction (§1), the focus of this paper was on the cues rather that on the categories: our goal was to show that it is possible to explicitly select the most informative distributional cues that infants are likely to rely on using a principled metric that does not simply rely on token frequency and predetermined distributional patterns. At the same time, if the presented model is indeed relevant can be only determined by directly evaluating categories of tokens induced in an unsupervised way on several linguistic task and looking at the time-course of learning, which was not discussed here.

A further limitation of the current work is that it arbitrarily focuses on words, neglecting morphological information, which is crucial in languages such as German, Turkish, Finnish and alike. A full model for distributional bootstrapping should automatically decide which are the relevant cues to categories, with no a priori restrictions on which units to focus on – see Hammerström and Borin (2011) for a review on unsupervised learning of morphology. This work only suggests a first way of moving away from pre-defined distributional patterns, since it can be equally applied to morphemes but it needs a pre-segmented input. A possible solution would be that of combining segmentation and category formation, looking at which cues are given more importance by the model and how useful they are to grouping words. Again, this falls outside of the scope of this paper and will be addressed in the future.

Finally, our model can be degraded in a variety of ways to introduce more plausible cognitive constraints in the form of free parameters that can reproduce attention and memory limitations. Such degraded versions would constitute a further and more informative test for this model, but are left for future work.

5 Conclusions

While no strong conclusion can be drawn without more data from typologically different languages, we think the goal of the paper was matched: we showed that the limitations of current frame-based approaches to distributional bootstrapping can be tackled with a simple model that incorporates evidence from psycholinguistic experiments and takes the number of different words a cues occurs with into account to decide whether the cue is informative. Furthermore, we showed that a model should be evaluated on different levels, since it is hard to achieve globally good performances.

The work by Mintz (2003) was crucial in showing that the PLD were rich enough to support an emergentist account of language learning. However, we contend that it is better to evaluate a process and its output, rather than a pre-selected set of cues, since it will more likely shed light on how certain cues but not others become important. It appears clear that focusing on fewer contexts is better: the central issue in a frame-based account of distributional bootstrapping should be to devise a model that identifies which cues give the best information.

Acknowledgments

The presented research was supported by a BOF/TOP grant (ID 29072) of the Research Council of the University of Antwerp.

References

David W. Aha, Dennis Kibler, and Marc K. Albert. 1991. Instance-based learning algorithms. *Machine Learning*, 6:37-66.

Inbal Arnon and Eve V. Clark. 2011. Why *Brush your teeth* is better than *Teeth*. Children's word production is facilitated in familiar sentence-frames. *Language Learning and Development*, 7:107-129.

Harald R. Baayen, Petar Milin, Dusica F. Durdević, Peter Hendrix, and Marco Marelli. 2011. An amorphous model for morphological processing in visual comprehension based on naive discriminative learning. *Psychological Review*. 118(3):438.

Elizabeth Bates and Brian J. MacWhinney. 1987. Competition, variation, and language learning. in Brian MacWhinney (Ed.), *Mechanisms of Language Acquisition*. Hillsdale, NJ:Lawrence Erlbaum.

Joan L. Bybee. 1995. Regular morphology and the lexicon. *Language and Cognitive Processes*, 10:425-455.

Colin Bannard and Danielle Matthews. 2008. Stored word sequences in language learning. The effect of familiarity on children's repetition of four word combinations. *Psychological Science*, 3:241-248.

Timothy A. Cartwright and Michael R. Brent. 1997. Syntactic categorization in early language acquisition: Formalizing the role of distributional analysis. *Cognition*, 63:121-170.

Emmanuel Chemla, Toben H. Mintz, Savita Bernal, and Anne Christophe. 2009. Categorizing words using "frequent frames": What cross-linguistic analyses reveal about distributional acquisition strategies. *Developmental Science*, 12:396-406.

Noam Chomsky. 1965. *Aspects of the theory of syntax*. MIT Press.

Anne Christophe, Séverine Millotte, Savita Bernal, and Jeffrey Lidz. 2008. Bootstrapping lexical and syntactic acquisition. *Language and Speech*, 51:61-75.

Grzegorz Chrupała and Afra Alishahi. 2010. Online entropy-based model of lexical category acquisition. *Proceedings of the 14th Conference on Computational Natural Language Learning*, ACL:Stroudsburg, PA. 182:191

Alexander Clark. 2000. Inducing syntactic categories by context distribution clustering. *Proceedings of the 2nd workshop on Learning language in logic and the 4th conference on Computational Natural Language Learning, Vol 7. ACL:Stroudsburg.*

Walter Daelemans, Jakub Zavrel, Ko van der Sloot, and Antal van den Bosch. 2009. *TiMBL: Tilburg Memory Based Learner, version 6.3, Reference Guide.* ILK Technical Report 10-01

Marian A. Erkelens. 2009. Restrictions of frequent frames as cues to categories: the case of Dutch. *Supplement to the Proceedings of the 32nd Boston University Conference on Language Development (BU-CLD 32)*. Boston, MA.

Stella Frank, Sharon Goldwater, and Frank Keller. 2009. Evaluating models of syntactic category acquisition without using a gold standard. *Proceedings of the 31st Annual Conference of the Cognitive Science Society*.

Daniel Freudenthal, Julian M. Pine, and Fernand Gobet. 2006. Modeling the development of children's use of optional infinitives in Dutch and English using MOSAIC. *Cognitive Science*, 30:277-310.

Daniel Freudenthal, Julian M. Pine, and Fernand Gobet. 2008. On the utility of conjoint and compositional frames and utterance boundaries as predictors of word categories. *Proceedings of the 30th Annual Conference of the Cognitive Science Society*. Washington, DC.

Steven Gillis and Dorit Ravid. 2009. Language Acquisition. In Dominik Sandra, Jan-Ola Östman and Jef Verschueren (Ed.), *Cognition and pragmatics*. Amsterdam: Benjamin.

Lila R. Gleitman. 1990. The structural sources of verb meaning. *Language Acquisition*, 1:3-55.

Lila R. Gleitman and Jane Gillette. 1995. The role of syntax in verb-learning. In Paul Fletcher & Brian MacWhinney (Ed.), *The Handbook Of Child Language*. Oxford: Blackwell. 413-427.

Harald Hammarström and Kars Borin. 2011. Unsupervised learning of morphology. *Computational Linguistics*, 37(2):309-350.

Emmanuel Keuleers, Kevin Diependaele, and Marc Brysbaert. 2010. Practice effects in large-scale visual word recognition studies: A lexical decision study on 14,000 Dutch mono-and disyllabic words and nonwords. *Frontiers in Psychology*, 1:174.

Richard E. Leibbrandt. 2009. Part-of-speech Bootstrapping using Lexically-specific Frames (PhD). *Flinders University, School of Computer Science, Engineering and Mathematics*.

Brian J. MacWhinney 1998. Models of the emergence of language. *Annual Review of Psychology*, 49:199-227.

Brian J. MacWhinney. 2000. *The CHILDES Project: Tools for analyzing talk. Third Edition*. Mahwah, NJ:Lawrence Erlbaum Associates.

Michael P. Maratsos and Mary A. Chalkley. 1980. The Internal Language of Children Syntax. In K. Nelson (Ed.) *Children's language*, Hillsdale, NJ: Erlbaum. 2:127-213.

Toben H. Mintz, Elissa L. Newport, and Thomas G. Bever. 2002. The distributional structure of grammatical categories in speech to young children. *Cognitive Science*, 26:393-424.

Toben H. Mintz. 2003. Frequent frames as a cue for grammatical categories in Child-Directed Speech. *Cognition*, 90(1):91-117.

Toben H. Mintz, Felix Hao Wang, and Jia Li. 2014. Word categorization from distributional information: Frames confer more than the sum of their (bigram) parts. *Cognitive Psychology*, 75:1-27.

Padraic Monaghan and Morten H. Christiansen. 2004. What distributional information is useful and usable for language acquisition? *Proceedings of the 26th annual conference of the Cognitive Science Society.*

Christopher Parisien, Afsaneh Fazly, and Suzanne Stevenson. 2008. An incremental Bayesian model for learning syntactic categories. *Proceedings of the twelfth conference on Computational Natural Language Learning, ACL:Stroudsburg.*

Steven Pinker. 1984. *Language learnability and language development.* Cambridge, MA: Harvard University Press.

Patricia A. Reeder, Elissa L. Newport, and Richard N. Aslin. 2013. From shared contexts to syntactic categories: The role of distributional information in learning linguistic form-classes. *Cognitive Psychology*, 66:30-54.

Jenny R. Saffran, Elissa L. Newport, and Richard N. Aslin. 1996. Word segmentation: The role of distributional cues. *Journal of Memory and Language*, 35:606-621.

Michelle C. St. Clair, Padraic Monaghan, and Morten H. Christiansen. 2010. Learning grammatical categories from distributional cues: Flexible frames for language acquisition. *Cognition*, 116:341-360.

Barbara Stumper, Colin Bannard, Elena V. M. Lieven, and Michael Tomasello. 2011. "Frequent Frames" in German Child-Directed Speech: A limited cue to grammatical categories. *Cognitive Science*, 35:1190-1205.

Anne L. Theakston, Elena V. M. Lieven, Julian M. Pine, and Caroline F. Rowland. 2001. The role of performance limitations in the acquisition of "mixed" verb-argument structure at stage I. *Journal of Child Language*, 28:127-152.

Michael Tomasello. 2000. Do young children have adult like syntactic competence?. *Cognition*, 74:209-253.

Hao Wang and Toben H. Mintz. 2007. A dynamic learning model for categorizing words using frames. *Proceedings of the 32nd Annual Boston University Conference on Language Development (BUCLD 32).* Boston, MA.

Hao Wang, Barbara Höhle, F. Nihan Ketrez, Aylin C. Küntay, and Toben H. Mintz. 2011. Cross-linguistic distributional analyses with frequent frames: the cases of german and turkish.. *Proceedings of 35th Annual Boston University Conference on Language Development (BUCLD 35).* Boston, MA.

Zhao Zhang, Rushen Shi, and Aijun Li. 2015. Grammatical categorization in Mandarin-Chinese-learning infants. *Language Acquisition*, 22:104-115.

Language Emergence in a Population of Artificial Agents Equipped with the Autotelic Principle

Miquel Cornudella
Sony Computer Science Laboratory Paris
6 rue Amyot, 75005
Paris, France
cornudella@csl.sony.fr

Thierry Poibeau
Laboratoire LATTICE-CNRS
1 rue Maurice Arnoux, 92120
Montrouge, France
thierry.poibeau@ens.fr

Abstract

Experiments on the emergence of a shared language in a population of agents usually rely on the control of the complexity by the experimenter. In this article we show how agents provided with the autotelic principle, a system by which agents can regulate their own development, progressively develop an emerging language evolving from one word to multi-word utterances, increasing its discriminative power.

1 Introduction

The evolution of communication has been a topic in artificial life since early 90s (Werner, 1991; Ackley and Littman, 1994). Short after that, a group of Alife researchers started to focus on the origins and emergence of human language-like communication systems through experiments with populations of artificial agents (Smith et al., 2003; Steels, 2003; Wagner et al., 2003). This line of research has shed light on the emergence of spatial terms and categories (Spranger, 2013), case systems (van Trijp, 2012), quantifiers (Pauw and Hilferty, 2012) or syntax (Kirby, 1999; Steels and Casademont, 2015). However, the success of these experiments usually relies on the control of complexity by the experimenter.

In order to let the agents manage complexity themselves it is necessary to provide them with a mechanism to regulate complexity in an autonomous way. Research in AI and robotics has explored systems that allow embodied agents to develop themselves in open-ended environments by means of error reduction (Andry et al., 2001), reinforcement learning (Huang and Weng, 2002), prediction (Marshall et al., 2004) or curiosity (Oudeyer et al., 2007; Kaplan and Oudeyer, 2007). This mechanisms are highly inspired by psychological studies on the role of motivation (Hull, 1943; Skinner, 1953; White, 1959; Graham, 1996). Motivation can be defined as "to be moved to do something" (Ryan and Deci, 2000) and it is commonly divided in *extrinsic motivation*, when an activity is done to attain some separable outcome, and *intrinsic motivation*, when an activity is done for its inherent satisfactions.

This paper investigates the role of intrinsic motivation in language emergence. It presents an agent-based experiment where a population of artificial agents has to develop a language to refer to objects in a complex environment. In addition to mechanisms to invent and adopt words and syntactic patterns, agents are provided with an operational version of the Flow theory (Csikszentmihalyi, 1990) that enables them to self-regulate their development.

2 Flow Theory

The model of intrinsic motivation in a population of artificial agents used in this experiment is based on the Flow theory developed by the psychologist Csikszentmihalyi (1990). He studied what moves people to be deeply involved in a complex activity that does not present a direct reward. He called these activities *autotelic*, as the motivational driving force (*telos*) comes from the individual herself (*auto*).

Csikszentmihalyi states that in an autotelic activity there is a relation between *challenge*, how difficult a particular task is, and *skill*, the abilities a person requires to face that particular task. As a consequence of this relation, a person involved in an autotelic activity can experience three mental states: *boredom*, when the challenge is too low for the skills this person has, *flow*, when there is a balance between challenge and skills, and *anxiety*, when the challenge is too high for the available skills. The flow state produces an intense enjoyment in a person involved in an autotelic activ-

Proceedings of the Sixth Workshop on Cognitive Aspects of Computational Language Learning, pages 40–44,
Lisbon, Portugal, 18 September 2015.

ity. The flow state is not static but in continuous movement, since the balance between challenge and skills creates the ideal conditions to develop skills. As a consequence this person becomes self-motivated, as she tries to stay in the flow state to experience this strong form of enjoyment.

3 Autotelic Principle

The autotelic principle is an operational version of the flow theory that provides agents with a system to self-regulate their development (Steels, 2004). It was first designed for developmental robotics (Steels, 2005) but it has also been used to study language emergence (Steels and Wellens, 2007). This principle proposes the balancing between challenge and skills as the motivational driving force in agents. Agents are therefore provided with mechanisms to set their own challenges and evaluate their performance to determine their *emotional state*. Depending on their emotional state, agents autonomously decide to increase their challenge (*boredom*), decrease it (*anxiety*) or continue with the current challenge to keep developing their skills (*flow*).

Challenges are defined as a specific configuration of a set of parameters. For example, parameters can be the number of objects or the number of properties of an object that agents can refer to. Challenges are formally represented as $< p_{i,1}, ..., p_{i,n} >$ in a multi-dimensional parameter space P, where $p_{i,j}$ corresponds to the configuration of the parameter j in the challenge i. Steels found advantageous to initialize the system with the lowest challenge configuration and grow in a bottom-up manner. There are no studies on the effect of a higher challenge configuration initialization in agents, but it will probably result in a slower development of skills.

Agents can estimate their skills by measuring their *performance*. Performance is measured taking into account an overall estimation of the interaction (if they have succeed or failed) and specific performance measures for each component used. Components are subsystems of the agent that are responsible for specific tasks, such as selecting a topic, conceptualise it into a meaning predicate or formulate an utterance given a meaning predicate. For example, in a communicative challenge the conceptual component has a performance measure of how well the resulting conceptualisation discriminates the topic or the language component a measure that evaluates if it could formulate an utterance covering the conceptualisation.

Agents also keep track of how *confident* they are to succeed on the challenge they have posed to themselves. The confidence in a challenge is related to the skills agents require to deal with that challenge. In a challenge where agents have to come up with names for objects, the development of a lexicon increases its communicative success and the confidence in being able to cope with the challenge.

Agents are constantly alternating between the operational and the shake-up phases. The operational phase takes place when the challenge parameters are fixed. The agent explores this configuration and tries to develop its skills to reach a certain level of performance. The shake-up phase occurs when the performance and confidence measures are stable. Agents employ this measures to determine how the challenge parameters should be adjusted. If the performance and confidence measures are low, agents perceive that they are in an anxious state and decrease the challenge parameters. Alternatively, when both performance and confidence measures are high, agents enter a boredom state and increase the challenge parameters.

4 Experiment configuration

The aim of this experiment is to show how a population of artificial agents provided with the autotelic principle develop a shared language without any control on the complexity by the experimenter. Agents play a *language game*, which consist in situated communicative interactions between two agents of a population (Steels, 2012). These agents are randomly selected from a population of ten agents. One of them assumes the role of *speaker* and the other the role of *hearer*.

4.1 World

In the experiment, agents share a world, which consist of ten different scenes. Each scene is composed of two objects and a spacial relation between them, such as *close*, *far* or *left of*. Objects are characterised by three feature-value pairs: *prototype* (e.g.: chair, box, table), *color* (e.g.: green, blue, purple) and *shape* (e.g.: round, hexagonal, square). Objects and scenes are unique, but a particular feature-value can be shared by two or more objects. In an interaction speaker and hearer share the same context, which consist of a randomly selected scene from the world.

4.2 Language game

The specific language game that agents play is called *multi-word guessing game*. The speaker selects a topic form the context of the interaction, based on his current communicative challenge. It conceptualises this concept into a meaning predicate and uses its language component to formulate an utterance which is transmitted as text to the hearer. The hearer tries to comprehend the utterance and construct hypotheses about the topic. If the hearer has only one hypothesis, it points to the interpreted topic. If the hypothesis corresponds to the topic, the speaker gives positive feedback and the interaction ends. On the other hand, if the hypothesis does not correspond to it, the speaker gives negative feedback to the hearer and points to the intended topic. When the hearer has multiple hypotheses, it signs to the speaker that it could not identify the topic. The speaker then gives feedback by pointing to the intended topic. The interaction is a success only when the hearer has one hypothesis about the topic that corresponds with the topic selected by the speaker. In all other cases, the result of the interaction is a failure.

4.3 Challenges

Agents refer to one or two objects in the scene, and minimally express the *prototype* of the object(s). Apart from the prototype, agents can refer to one or more properties of objects or to the relation between them. The challenge configuration is therefore based on two parameters: the number of properties agents refer to and if the relation is expressed or not. Challenges have a *confidence* value between 0.0 and 1.0, initialised at 0.0. After each interaction, speaker and hearer update their confidence value with a score obtained computing the average between the result of the interaction (success or failure) and the performance evaluation of the components used by the agent. The update score has a low value (between 0.008 and -0.032) to provide agents enough time to develop the skills necessary to cope with the challenge.

The challenge level one (refer only to prototypes of objects) is set as the initial challenge. In the experiment agents can adjust the challenge configuration up to level four: refer to up to two objects expressing three of their properties or to relations between objects.

Challenge Level	Properties	Relation
1	0	0
2	1	0
3	2	0
4	3	0
	2	1

Table 1: Challenge levels.

4.4 Mechanisms

Agents are equipped with *conceptualisation* and *interpretation* mechanisms to map between the world model and meaning predicates that refer to it. For example, a blue table is conceptualised into *(blue(x), table(x))*. Agents start without any form-meaning mappings (also called *constructions*). This mappings will emerge during interactions by using three mechanisms: *diagnostics*, *repairs* and *alignment*.

Diagnostics are a set of processes by which agents can identify problems during formulation (when agents go from a meaning predicate to an utterance) and comprehension (when agents reconstruct the meaning predicate from an input utterance). In the experiment agents can identify *unknown meanings*, *unknown words*, *unsolved word orders* and *referent problems*.

Repairs are strategies used by agents to solve diagnosed problems. For example, an unknown meaning can be solved by the speaker with a repair that creates a new word for that meaning, or an unknown word can be solved by the hearer with a repair that uses the feedback of the speaker to identify which meaning corresponds to that word. Notice that the later is only possible when the hearer can unambiguously deduce the meaning of the unknown word. Unsolved word orders and referent problems appear when agents start to build multi-word utterances. This problem can be solved by creating grammatical constructions that introduce constraints on how properties and prototypes are ordered when formulating and comprehending multi-word utterances.

There is a competition of form-meaning mappings (both lexical and grammatical) during the emergence of a shared language. This competition occurs either when multiple forms refer to the same meaning or when one word can express several meanings. Each mapping has a score between 0.0 and 1.0 and is initialised at 0.5. Alignment is a mechanism that guides the choice of which constructions agents use based on the score of their constructions. The scores of the mappings used by the speaker and hearer are updated after each interaction. When a form-meaning mapping gets a score of 0.0 is deleted from the construction inventory of the agent. The alignment used in this experiment follows the dynamics of *lateral inhibition* (De Vylder and Tuyls, 2006).

When there is communicative success, both speaker and hearer align, which means that they increase the scores of the mappings used by 0.1 and decrease its competitors by 0.1. Note that the mapping competitors for the speaker are those constructions that express the same meaning, while mapping competitors for the hearer are those that contain the same form. When there is communicative failure, the alignment differs for speaker and hearer. If the speaker has formulated one word utterance, it decreases the score of the construction used by 0.1. The hearer aligns only when the intended topic by the speaker is among its hypotheses. It increases the score of the constructions used by 0.1 and decreases the score of its form competitors by 0.1. In all other cases agents are not able to identify what caused the communicative failure and do not align.

5 Experimental results

The results of ten experimental runs for a population of ten agents equipped with the autotelic principle are shown in Figure 1.

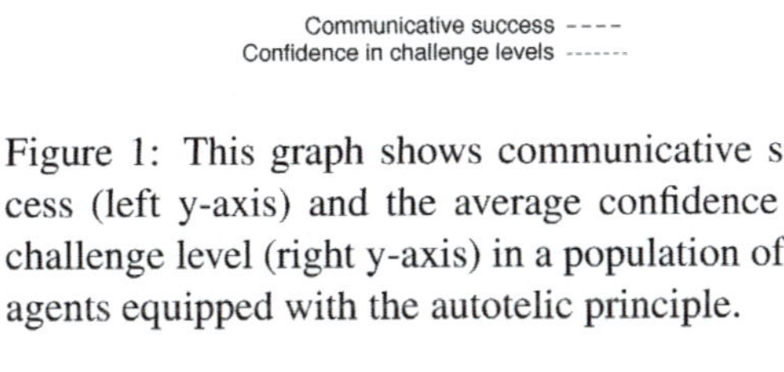

Figure 1: This graph shows communicative success (left y-axis) and the average confidence on challenge level (right y-axis) in a population of 10 agents equipped with the autotelic principle.

Agents start with an empty construction inventory and with the challenge of emerging a shared language for prototypes. They develop it rapidly, increasing their confidence on the first challenge up to its maximum value around interaction 2000. Note that the communication success starts to drop before the average confidence value in the population has come to its maximum. This is due to the fact that some agents have already reached the highest confidence score and therefore they have moved to the next challenge.

Communicative success and the speed at which agents gain confidence decreases at this point, as agents begin to refer also to the color and shape of objects. Agents have to agree now on form-meaning mappings to refer to color and shape and grammatical constructions to manage reference problems in multi-word utterances. Communicative success and confidence in challenge levels two and three grow steadily until they reach its maximum value around interaction 5500. The population has reached the maximum level of confidence for the first three challenge levels and start to address challenges of level four. The communicative success slightly diminishes at this point due to the fact that agents have to agree on how to refer to relations. By interaction 9000 all agents have reached the maximum confidence for each challenge.

There are differences on the percentage of communicate success that agents are able to reach for each challenge level. These differences are due to the fact that some topic descriptions are ambiguous. The discriminative power of an utterance increases when agents refer to more properties of objects or the relation between them. This accounts for the differences observed on Figure 1, where agents reach a higher percentage of communicative success once they have agreed on how to refer to properties and relations.

The results obtained show that a population of agents equipped with the autotelic principle manage to autonomously increase the complexity of a shared language through recurrent interactions. Agents succeed in progressively develop their communicative skills when trying to stay in a state of flow. As a result, agents reach a higher communicative success in their interactions, as they can successfully refer to more informative topic descriptions which are less ambiguous.

Acknowledgments

Miquel Cornudella is partially supported by a CIFRE grant (agreement no. 2013/0730). The authors wish to thank their colleagues for their feedback and support, particularly Remi van Trijp and Paul Van Eecke.

References

David H Ackley and Michael L Littman. 1994. Altruism in the evolution of communication. *Artificial life IV*, pages 40–48.

Pierre Andry, Philippe Gaussier, Sorin Moga, Jean-Paul Banquet, and Jacqueline Nadel. 2001. Learning and communication via imitation: An autonomous robot perspective. *Systems, Man and Cybernetics, Part A: Systems and Humans, IEEE Transactions on*, 31(5):431–442.

Mihaly Csikszentmihalyi. 1990. *Flow: The psychology of optimal experience*. Harper and Row, New York.

Bart De Vylder and Karl Tuyls. 2006. How to reach linguistic consensus: A proof of convergence for the naming game. *Journal of Theoretical Biology*, 242(4):818 – 831.

Sandra Graham. 1996. Theories and principles of motivation. *Handbook of educational psychology*, 4:63–84.

Xiao Huang and John Weng. 2002. Novelty and reinforcement learning in the value system of developmental robots. In *Lund University Cognitive Studies*, pages 47–55.

Clark Leonard Hull. 1943. *Principles of behavior: an introduction to behavior theory.* Appleton-Century.

Frédéric Kaplan and Pierre-Yves Oudeyer. 2007. The progress-drive hypothesis: an interpretation of early imitation. *Models and mechanims of imitation and social learning: Behavioural, social and communication dimensions*, pages 361–377.

Simon Kirby. 1999. Syntax out of learning: The cultural evolution of structured communication in a population of induction algorithms. In D. Floreano, J.D. Nicoud, and F. Mondada, editors, *Advances in Artificial Life: Proceedings of the 5th European Conference on Artificial Life*, pages 694–703, Berlin. Springer.

James B. Marshall, Douglas Blank, and Lisa Meeden. 2004. An emergent framework for self-motivation in developmental robotics. In *Proceedings of the 3rd international conference on development and learning, Salk Institute, San Diego*, volume 10.

Pierre-Yves Oudeyer, Frédéric Kaplan, and Verena Vanessa Hafner. 2007. Intrinsic motivation systems for autonomous mental development. *Evolutionary Computation, IEEE Transactions on*, 11(2):265–286.

Simon Pauw and Joseph Hilferty. 2012. The emergence of quantifiers. *Experiments in Cultural Language Evolution*, 3:277.

Richard M Ryan and Edward L Deci. 2000. Intrinsic and extrinsic motivations: Classic definitions and new directions. *Contemporary educational psychology*, 25(1):54–67.

Burrhus Frederic Skinner. 1953. *Science and human behavior*. Simon and Schuster.

Kenny Smith, Simon Kirby, and Henry Brighton. 2003. Iterated learning: A framework for the emergence of language. *Artificial Life*, 9(4):371–386.

Michael Spranger. 2013. Evolving grounded spatial language strategies. *KI-Künstliche Intelligenz*, 27(2):97–106.

Luc Steels and Emília Garcia Casademont. 2015. Ambiguity and the origins of syntax. *The Linguistic Review*, 32(1):37–60.

Luc Steels and Pieter Wellens. 2007. Scaffolding language emergence using the autotelic principle. In *Artificial Life, 2007. ALIFE'07. IEEE Symposium on*, pages 325–332. IEEE.

Luc Steels. 2003. Evolving grounded communication for robots. *Trends in cognitive sciences*, 7(7):308–312.

Luc Steels. 2004. The autotelic principle. In Fumiya Iida, Rolf Pfeifer, Luc Steels, and Yasuo Kuniyoshi, editors, *Embodied Artificial Intelligence*, volume 3139 of *Lecture Notes in Computer Science*, pages 231–242. Springer Berlin Heidelberg.

Luc Steels. 2005. The emergence and evolution of linguistic structure: from lexical to grammatical communication systems. *Connection Science*, 17(3-4):213–230, December.

Luc Steels. 2012. *Experiments in Cultural Language Evolution*. Advances in interaction studies. John Benjamins Publishing Company.

Remi van Trijp. 2012. Not as awful as it seems: Explaining german case through computational experiments in fluid construction grammar. In *Proceedings of the 13th Conference of the European Chapter of the Association for Computational Linguistics*, EACL '12, pages 829–839, Stroudsburg, PA, USA. Association for Computational Linguistics.

Kyle Wagner, James A. Reggia, Juan Uriagereka, and Gerald S. Wilkinson. 2003. Progress in the simulation of emergent communication and language. *Adaptive Behavior*, 11(1):37.

Gregory M Werner. 1991. Evolution of communication in artificial organisms, artifial life ii. In *Proceedings of the Second International Conference of Artificial Life*, pages 659–687.

Robert W White. 1959. Motivation reconsidered: the concept of competence. *Psychological review*, 66(5):297.

A Computational Study of Cross-situational Lexical Learning of Brazilian Portuguese

Pablo Faria
University of Campinas
R. Sérgio Buarque de Holanda, 571
Campinas, Brazil
pablofaria@gmail.com

Abstract

In this paper, a particular algorithm for lexical acquisition – taken as a problem of learning the mapping from words to meanings – is evaluated. The algorithm in Siskind (1996) is adapted to handle more complex input data, including data of Brazilian Portuguese. In particular, the input data in the present study covers a broader grammatical knowledge, showing both polysemy and higher inflectional and agreement morphology. Results indicate that these properties create difficulties to the learner and that more substantial developments to the algorithm are needed in order to increase its cross-linguistic capabilities.

1 Introduction

Computational modeling, as an empirical approach to theoretical problems, has the benefit of demanding clear and exhaustive specification of the problem under consideration (Pearl, 2010; Yang, 2011). In this paper, we consider a computational model of lexical acquisition by a child learning her native language. Lexical acquisition is taken here as a problem of learning the mapping from words to meanings based on a cross-situational strategy. Simply put, cross-situational lexical learning is the strategy by which word-to-meaning mappings are learned by assigning to a given word the meanings which are consistent across the situations where the word is heard. One computational modeling of this strategy is provided in Siskind (1996).

We present an implementation of Siskind's algorithm, which is part of a broader computational model of first language acquisition presented in Faria (2013). It is evaluated against informationally and morphologically more complex input data, including data of Brazilian Portuguese. As shown below, both aspects have an impact on the learner's performance. Consequently, a better understanding of them is necessary in order to progress towards learning models with wider grammatical and languages coverage.

The reader is referred to Siskind's (1996) arguments on the empirical plausibility of the model and for it being an approximation to the empirical problem of lexical acquisition through *cross-situational learning* which is taken in the psycholinguistic literature as a plausible learning strategy (Pinker, 1989; Fisher et al., 1994). Nonetheless, as stressed by Siskind, it is not claimed that the child employs the particular heuristics presented here. The main goal, instead, is to provide a proof of existence for an algorithm that solves approximations to the problem.

2 Lexical acquisition in the model

The lexical acquisition procedure presented in this paper is part of a broader first language acquisition model (Faria, 2013) which aims to simulate the acquisition of word to meaning mappings as well as syntactic knowledge. The model was also aimed at dealing with Brazilian Portuguese (BP) input data as well as with some issues of word order which were evaluated through an artificial corpus built with English vocabulary but displaying a strictly head-final order. Given its characteristics, the model can be included among somewhat similar studies found in the literature, such as Berwick (1985), Gaylard (1995), and Villavicencio (2002), among others.

The procedure is based on Siskind's (1996) heuristics, adapted in order to meet the goals of the modeling. One goal is to account for a greater variety of grammatical phenomena.[1] A second goal

[1] In Siskind's (1996) study, functional elements, such as articles, have no semantic-conceptual content, being acquired as lexical items that do not contribute to the meaning of sentences. This is a simplification not assumed in the model pre-

Proceedings of the Sixth Workshop on Cognitive Aspects of Computational Language Learning, pages 45–54,
Lisbon, Portugal, 18 September 2015.

is to account for a greater variety of languages which, in the present study, consists in extending learning to Brazilian Portuguese, a language which, for being of a different family (as compared to English), shows properties that pose difficulties to the original learning heuristics, as is shown in what follows.

2.1 Summary of Siskind's (1996) simulation

Siskind presents an algorithm consisting of a series of ordered heuristics. The heuristics were conceived to guarantee an efficient and successful learning under different conditions, that is, in the presence of noise (utterances paired with incorrect meanings), "referential uncertainty" (utterances paired with more than one partially correct meaning) and homonymy. The corpus used in the simulations was based on a simple context free grammar which randomly generated only simple declarative sentences, pre-segmented and without adjectives and other adjuncts.

Functional words, such as determiners, were assumed not to contribute meaning to sentences. The MLU of sentences varied from 4.99 to 6.29 and all sentences had between 2 and 30 words and no more than 30 conceptual symbols. Simulations evaluated different parameterizations for (i) the size of the vocabulary (1000 to 10,000), (ii) the degree of referential uncertainty (i.e., the number of meanings paired with an utterance), (iii) the noise rate (0 to 20%), (iv) the number of conceptual symbols (250 to 2,000), and (v) the mean rate of homonymy in the corpus (between 1 and 2).

Results showed that the parameters (ii) and (iv) seem not to affect the convergence of the learning process. Therefore, the apparent complexity of the discourse context and that the potentially infinite number of concepts we may entertain seem to be efficiently handled by a cross-situational learning strategy. All other parameters had an impact in the learning curve, but the rate of homonymy was crucial: while 10,000 words were sufficient for convergence given a rate of 1 (i.e., no homonymy), 900,000 words were necessary for convergence given a rate of 2. Learning is slow for the first 25 words and increases until most of the vocabulary is learned. In late stages, words can be learned even with one exposition.

Finally, Siskind emphasizes limitations of the algorithm. First, it assumes strict homonymy, that is, words may have completely distinct meanings, but not partially distinct. Thus, polysemy may pose difficulties to the author's heuristics. The semantic-conceptual representation is simplified, not only for leaving aside the semantic content of functional words, but also as a consequence of a restricted grammatical coverage.

sented here.

2.2 Lexical processing

In this model, lexical recognition and acquisition are part of the same process. At any given moment, the recognition of an utterance consists in obtaining the cross product of the sense sets of its words – Siskind names each combination as a "possible sense assignment" (PSA) – and, once the set of PSAs is obtained, identifying the PSA that is both consistent with the utterance (i.e., all words contribute to its meaning) and, in the case that more than one PSA is consistent, has the highest confidence factor (explained later).

2.3 The input data

The input data in this study is different from Siskind's (1996). First, it better reflects the distribution of types of utterances found in child directed data (Hoff-Ginsberg, 1986; Cameron-Faulkner et al., 2003). Second, by assumption, it more appropriately reflects the nature of the data that a child is exposed to.

2.3.1 Distribution

Hoff-Ginsberg (1986) studies the effects of functional and structural properties in the speech of mothers on the syntactic development of their children. Part of the author's findings is presented below, summarized in Table 1.

Measure	*M*
Measures of syntactic complexity	
MLU	4.47
VP/utterance	.95
NP/utternace	1.60
Auxiliaries/VP	.29
Words/NP	1.33
Frequencies of sentence forms (% of all utterances)	
Declaratives	25
Yes/no questions	15
Wh- questions	17
Imperatives	8
Interjections	17

Table 1: Structural Properties of Mothers' Speech in Hoff-Ginsberg (1986).

Cameron-Faulkner et al. (2003) provide a slightly more detailed description of these structural properties, as shown in Table 2. Fragments are utterances with one or more words, the latter consisting of NPs (43%), VPs (23%), PPs (10%) and other (24%). Complex constructions are sentences with sentential complements, as in "*I think it's going to rain*", and subordinate adverbial clauses introduced by *because*, *if* and *when*.

Type	Mean proportion	Tokens
Fragments	.20 (.13–.32)	3351
One word	.07	
Multi-word	.14	
Questions	.32 (.20–.42)	5455
Wh-	.16	
Yes/no	.15	
Imperatives	.09 (.05–.14)	1597
Copulas	.15 (.08–.20)	2502
Subject–predicate	.18 (.14–.26)	2970
Transitives	.10	
Intransitives	.03	
Other	.05	
Complex	.06 (.03–.09)	1028

Table 2: Survey of Child Directed Speech in Cameron-Faulkner et al. (2003).

By collapsing their findings, we arrived at the frequencies shown in Table 3, used in the generation of the input data for the model. Frequencies in the interior of each type are not controlled, that is, subtypes have random frequencies. With respect to similar models in the literature, the grammatical coverage is larger, although far from covering the full grammatical knowledge of a speaker.

Type	H-G	Cetal.	This study
Fragments	–	.20	.20
Questions	.32	.31	.32
Wh-	.17	.16	
Yes/no	.15	.15	
Imperatives	.08	.09	.09
Declaratives	.25	.39	.39
Total			1.00

Table 3: Types and frequencies of utterance types assumed in the present simulation. "H-G" stands for Hoff-Ginsberg (1986) and "Cetal." for Cameron-Faulkner et al. (2003).

2.3.2 Linguistic properties

This model embodies a richer diversity of word classes and utterance types. For a detailed view of these, I refer the reader to Faria (2013, p.154-155). A direct consequence is that polysemy in the input is higher. As one example, since inchoative uses of verbs are included in the input, it will have the learner dealing with potentially one extra (non-causative) sense for each verb of change of state. The verb "break", for instance, may appear in "John broke the car" and "The car broke", utterances which by assumption differ in terms of causativity. Thus, one of the goals of this modeling is to evaluate the learner's performance given more polysemy in the input.

2.4 The learning procedure

In the end of this section, an illustration of the functioning of the heuristics is provided. We refer the reader to Siskind (1996) for a lengthy discussion about the reasoning behind each heuristic. In what follows, the heuristics assumed are presented and the main adaptations to the original highlighted. As in the original procedure, for learning to be possible the lexicon LEX is organized in three tables:

1. Table N, which maps a sense to its *necessary* conceptual symbols;
2. Table P, which maps a sense to its *possible* conceptual symbols;
3. Table D, which maps each sense to its possible conceptual expressions.

Word symbols may have more than one *sense*, one for each of its meanings in cases of homonymy or polysemy. The following set of heuristics (rules 1 to 5) is applied to each of the PSAs generated for a given utterance, as explained in the previous section.

Rule 1. *Ignore a PSA when (i) at least one symbol from the meaning of the utterance is absent from all $P(w)$, and (ii) not all $N(w)$ contribute to the meaning of the utterance.*

Rule 2. *For each word w of the utterance, remove from $P(w)$ any symbol not included in the utterance meaning.*

Rule 3. *For each word w of the utterance, add to $N(w)$ any conceptual symbol exclusively in $P(w)$ (thus, absent from the P set of the remaining words).*

Rule 4. *For each word w in the utterance, remove from $P(w)$ any conceptual* *symbol that appears only once in the utterance meaning and is included in the N(w′) for some other word w′ of the utterance.*

Rule 5. *For each word w in the utterance, if w converged for its conceptual symbol set, that is, N(w) = P(w), remove from D(w) any expression that does not involve the conceptual symbols in N(w); if the word has not yet converged, remove from D(w) any expression that includes a symbol not in P(w).*

The original "Rule 1" in Siskind (1996, p.57) was conceived to deal with referential uncertainty. However, in the present study this parameter is not evaluated. Thus, the original rule being irrelevant, an alternative rule is conceived to deal with the possibility that the words of a sentence may never contribute the whole meaning of an utterance. In the present study, this is a consequence of including conceptual symbols for the utterance type, for instance, DECL for declarative sentences, which have no morphological realization in languages like English and Brazilian Portuguese. The original Rule 1 would discard relevant PSAs because at some point the symbol DECL would be absent from all P(*w*) (the set P for a word *w*), that is, at some point there would be no word in any utterance which could possibly contribute DECL.

Siskind proposes a sixth heuristic that is put aside here. Its task is to check if there is at least one combination of the subexpression for the words in the utterance that matches exactly the utterance meaning. Since in this study, words in a given utterance may not contribute all the conceptual symbols present in the utterance meaning, this rule would cause problems to the learner. Although acknowledging that a different version of this rule may still be useful, the learning procedure in the present study has only the five rules shown above.

Three situations may arise, after an utterance is processed: (i) the algorithm converges to an unique consistent PSA; (ii) it converges to a set of consistent PSAs; and (iii) no PSA is found to be consistent with the utterance meaning. In the first case, the confidence factors for the senses involved are incremented. In the second, the algorithm first identifies the PSA with the highest current confidence factor and then update the confidence factor of the senses involved. In the last case, the algorithm determines the least number of words to be updated in their P and D sets. If it identifies some, the utterance is processed again. Otherwise, the utterance is discarded. As we can see, the confidence factor is a simple measure that allows the learner to converge to more consistent senses while gradually eliminating incorrect lexical entries.

2.5 An illustration

Let us assume that at some given stage, the learner shows the following partial non-converged lexicon:

	N	P
John	{**John**}	**John**, **ball**
took	{CAUSE}	CAUSE, WANT, BECOME, **take**, PAST
the	{}	WANT, **arm**, DEF
ball	{**ball**}	**ball**, **take**

Now, suppose that the learner is presented with the input "John took the ball", paired with the meaning:

(1) DECL(PAST(CAUSE(**John**,
BECOME(DEF(**ball**), **take**))))

Since the N(*the*) is empty, the sole PSA for this input sentence (which includes **John**, CAUSE and **ball**) would be discarded given Rule 1. The algorithm then determines the minimum number of words to be updated in the lexicon, in this case, only the word *the*:

	N	P
John	{**John**}	**John**, **ball**
took	{CAUSE}	CAUSE, WANT, BECOME, **take**, PAST
the	{}	WANT, **arm**, DEF, DECL, PAST, CAUSE, **John**, BECOME, **ball**, **take**
ball	{**ball**}	**ball**, **arm**

Given the new lexicon and assuming the same input, Rule 1 would not filter out its PSA. Now, another inference becomes possible, captured by Rule 2: since the utterance meaning does not contain the symbols WANT and **arm**, they can be excluded from the P sets of the relevant lexical items. After this, a comparison between the P sets of the words is possible: exclusive symbols in the P sets of the words can be copied to their respective N sets, a task carried on by Rule 3. The updated lexicon shows the following configuration:

	N	P
John	{**John**}	**John**, **ball**
took	{CAUSE}	CAUSE, BECOME, **take**, PAST
the	{DEF}	DEF, DECL, PAST, CAUSE, **John**, BECOME, **ball**, **take**
ball	{**ball**}	**ball**

The fourth heuristic compares the necessary symbol sets of the utterance words. In the example, it will detect that **ball** and **John** appear (each) only once in the utterance meaning and that both are, respectively, in N(*ball*) and N(*John*). Thus, the conceptual symbol *ball* can be removed from P(*john*) and P(*the*), as shown below:

	N	P
John	{**John**}	**John**
took	{CAUSE}	CAUSE, BECOME, **take**, PAST
the	{DEF}	DEF, DECL, PAST, CAUSE, BECOME, **take**
ball	{**ball**}	**ball**

Some more input is necessary for a complete convergence. Suppose, now, that the learner receives the utterance "The kids" paired with DEF(**kids**). By applying Rules 1 to 4, the following updated lexicon would be obtained (the entry for *kids* is omitted):

	N	P
John	{**John**}	**John**
took	{CAUSE}	CAUSE, BECOME, **take**, PAST
the	{DEF}	DEF
ball	{**ball**}	**ball**

Note that *the* has totally converged. If exposed again to the utterance (1), Rules 1 to 4 would take the learner to the final partial state below:

	N	P
John	{**John**}	**John**
took	{PAST, CAUSE, BECOME, take}	PAST, CAUSE, BECOME, **take**
the	{DEF}	DEF
ball	{**ball**}	**ball**

The learner is ready for what Siskind (1996) calls "stage two": once the relevant conceptual symbols were discovered, a structured meaning is calculated for words that have more than one conceptual symbol. In the present model, instead, each sense starts with all possible valid subexpressions extracted from the utterance meaning as its D set. During the learning process, Rule 5 will remove all expressions that lack the necessary conceptual symbols of a sense. At the end of this process, only one subexpression should remain. This approach is simpler than the original calculations although it is not clear which one can be considered more plausible.

3 Simulations

Simulations were conducted for five corpora. Generation was controlled for the MLUw of each corpus (Parker and Brorson, 2005, for details) and for the distribution of types of utterances, as explained before.

3.1 Corpora

Table 4 summarizes the characteristics of the corpora used in the simulations. The MLUw measure takes the *mean number of words* instead of morphemes. The two measures are argued to be almost perfectly correlated (Parker and Brorson, 2005).

Corpora	Utter.	Words	MLUw	Lex.
Development	985	3065	3.11	52
"Head-final"	2071	10347	5.00	56
English	40863	245111	6.00	91
BP I	100000	575449	5.75	133
BP II	100000	577349	5.77	464

Table 4: Corpora used in the simulation.

Each corpus in the table above was conceived with a specific purpose. The "development" corpus was manually built in order to make learning easier and faster, such that the overall functioning of the model could be observed given a very favorable input. The vocabulary was smaller, as well as its MLUw, utterances were ordered from the simplest to the most complex and were also ordered to provide strong contrasts, making heuristics more effective.

The other corpora were all generated automatically. The "head-final" corpus also has a small vocabulary and had the intent of increasing the difficulty in the lexical acquisition task by eliminating the artificial simplicity and ordering of data of the development corpus. Finally, the English, the BP I and the BP II corpora, being much larger than the first two, had the goal of imposing a more substantial challenge to the learner. Given the richer morphology of Brazilian Portuguese, BP I and II corpora show the largest vocabularies and number of utterances, in order to ensure a sufficient exposition to all lexical items of BP.

3.2 General results

In this study, convergence means – as in Siskind (1996) – to acquire at least one meaning by word for 95% of the lexical items. For the development corpus, the learner fully converged to the target lexicon, without false positives. Convergence was also almost complete for the head-final corpus, but the learner's performance starts to fall down for the larger corpora. For these, the learner was successful in acquiring functional words in general (determiners, prepositions, etc.), nouns, adjectives, adverbs, copulas, auxiliaries and verbs in the imperative form. It also showed some success in acquiring passive verbs. However, in general, its performance was very poor for verbs either by converging to false positives or not converging at all. False positives were deviant cases where the meaning was partially correct, but not exactly. More specific details for each corpus and its respective simulation are provided in next subsection. Table 5 summarizes the learner's performance.

	Target	Acquired		
Corpus	Lex.	Lex.	False	Conv.
Development	52	52	0	100%
Head-final	56	54	0	96,4%
English	91	87	11	95,6%
BP I	133	70	2	52,63%
BP II	464	183	1	39,43%

Table 5: Summary of lexical acquisition for each corpus.

3.3 Specific results

As expected, the development corpus made it easy for the learner to converge. It consisted of 197 utterances which were iterated five times. Given the relative simplicity of the utterances (MLUw of 3.11), these iterations were meant to simulate multiple expositions to the same utterances while artificially excluding more complex utterances that could slower the learning process by creating too many concurrent senses for each word. Instead, this corpus favors higher contrasts between words thus leading to faster learning. The first iteration had a pre-specified order, starting with simple NP fragments, followed by NP with adjuncts, and finally clauses and yes/no questions. Consequently, almost all the target lexical items were acquired in the first iteration, the remainder being acquired in the second, as Figure 1 shows.

The head-final corpus is a small English corpus to which a strict head-final ordering was imposed. Although this property is not relevant for lexical acquisition, this corpus had the goal of removing the artificial restrictions of the development corpus. Thus, the behavior of the learner could

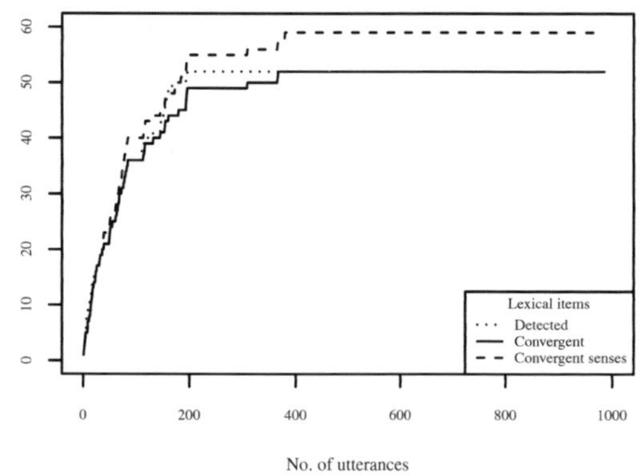

Figure 1: Lexical acquisition for the development corpus.

be evaluated given a slightly more complex input (which also included Wh- questions). Results, shown in Figure 2, show that in fact the learner is able to converge in the face of random exposition to data. Because of its small size, the corpus was insufficient for the learner to converge for all words.

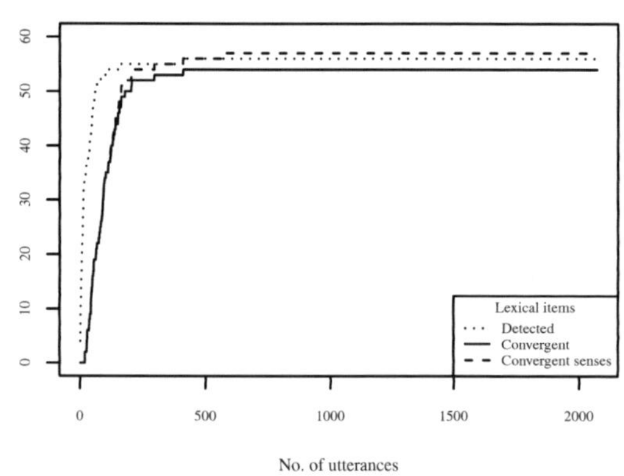

Figure 2: Lexical acquisition for the head-final corpus.

Starting with the English corpus, simulations tried to evaluate the performance of the learner given larger corpora with bigger vocabularies. The number of distinct verb stems was kept small with only two for each verb class (intransitive, unergative, etc.).

As Figure 3 shows, the learner converged almost fully, although it showed an interesting tendency of including definiteness as part of verb senses and excluding them from proper nouns. However, by inspecting the final lexical entries, it seemed possible that this tendency is temporarily

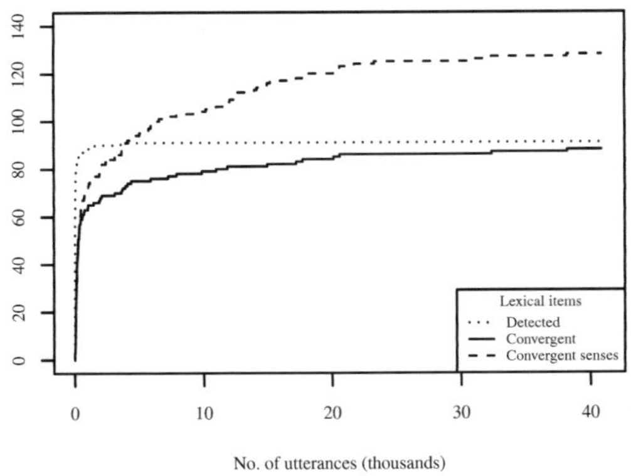

Figure 3: Lexical acquisition for the English corpus.

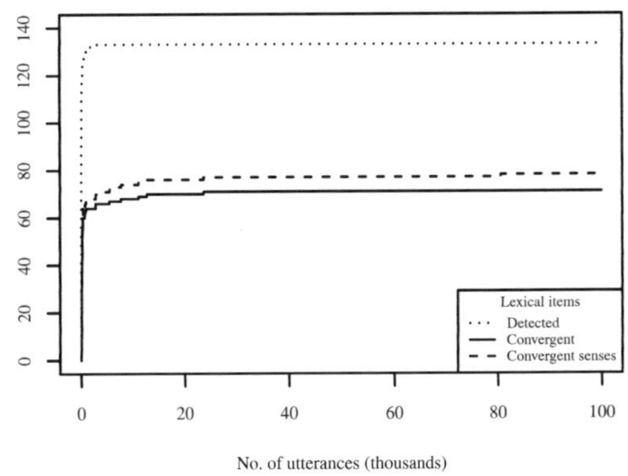

Figure 4: Lexical acquisition for the BP I corpus.

and could be overcome with more input data, as it did for some items. Related to this issue, we also see a strong tendency in this simulation for a high number of senses conjectured and converged to by the learner, as compared to other simulations. This is discussed in the next section.

The learner's performance drops drastically when exposed to Brazilian Portuguese data. The BP I corpus was also controlled for the number of verb stems, 1, by class of verbs. However, given the possible inflected verb forms of Brazilian Portuguese, the final vocabulary of BP I contained 42 more items when compared to the English corpus. As we can see in Figure 4, although the learner received more than twice the number of input utterances available in the English corpus, it acquired less words, consisting mostly of functional items, nouns, verbs in the imperative and passive forms, adjectives and adverbs. For almost all of the other inflected forms, the learner could not converge.

In the final simulation, with the BP II corpus, the learner followed the same tendency, with even lower proportional results (Figure 5). In this corpus, differently, there were more verb stems – up to 8 – per verb class.

3.4 Discussion

It was mentioned above a strong tendency, by the learner, of conjecturing and converging to a higher number of senses in the simulation for English. This is, in part, a direct consequence of the higher number of contexts in which the same word form appears with subtle meaning differences in English. However, for another part, the learner had a tendency of converging to senses

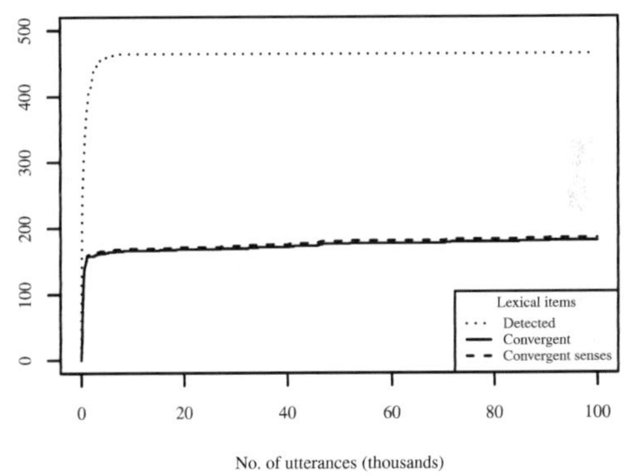

Figure 5: Lexical acquisition for the BP II corpus.

close to but divergent from the target ones. For instance, the learner had a tendency of converging to verb senses which included the definiteness feature, thus, showing at least two alternative senses for the same entry, one for definite and another for non-definite contexts. Sometimes it also included another sense along with these, now without the definiteness feature, thus closer to the target. This is a curious tendency and it is not yet clear whether it is temporarily and could be overcome by more data or if it may result from some inconsistency in the input data.

Apart from that, two main reasons seem to be involved in the learner's performances, in particular, for the lower performances for BP I and BP II corpora. First, it is possible that the learner could converge for Brazilian Portuguese if more data were available, given the sensitiveness of the heuristics to homonymy. As mentioned before, the polysemic nature of the input data in this model makes it likely that a corpus of up to a million words could be necessary for convergence. Unfortunately, technical issues prevented the learner to be exposed to such amounts of data. Thus, this can be taken as a first explanation for the learner's low performance for the BP corpora.

A second factor relates to morphological properties of the input language. Siskind's (1996) heuristics were only evaluated against English data, for which the present learner was also similarly successful. Thus, it is likely that the richer morphology of BP is causing problems to the heuristics as it leads to higher sparsity of data. It turns out that words show much lower frequencies in the BP corpora, when compared to the English corpora, as we can see in Figures 6 and 7.

As we see, there is a significant difference between frequencies for English and Brazilian Portuguese. Although they all lie below 10%, for BP the majority of the frequencies are close to zero. Consequently, occurrences of the correspondent lexical items will be dispersed through the corpus, probably distant from each other in terms of the number of utterances between them. This fact will not only make learning slower for these words, but will also lead the "garbage collection" procedure to discard non-convergent senses for these words before they have the chance to converge.

Conceived by Siskind both to discard wrong sense assignments caused by referential uncertainty and to keep the number of PSAs as low as possible (thus, increasing efficiency), the garbage collection, in cycles of 500 utterances, removes all "non-frozen" senses, that is, non-convergent ones or convergent ones that were not used successfully a predefined number of times. It is a way of having the learner "forgetting" unproductive senses. The problem is that for the BP data, given its sparseness, unfrequent words are reset again and again.

For this reason, in the simulations another strategy for garbage collection was also evaluated: instead of a cycle of 500 utterances, it assumed a cycle of 50 expositions to a given word. If a sense did not converge during the cycle, it was then discarded. However, this change did not have the desired effect. This indicates that, along with other adjustments, such simple garbage collection routines are not adequate. It is important to have in mind, nonetheless, that this model does not decompose words into morphemes. And this could be a way of overcoming the learning difficulty, since word stems would have higher frequencies and its affixes would fall into the category of functional words, for which the learner shows much better performance.

4 Conclusions

The study presented above had the goal of contributing to the understanding of lexical acquisition by children, by imposing conditions that, by assumption, can be considered as closer approximations to the ultimate complexities of the data available to the learner. As a consequence, Siskind's (1996) algorithm had to be adapted to be able to handle such input data. Two main aspects of the input are different. Informationally, more conceptual symbols are involved both to account for the meaning of functional words and to types of utterances. As a consequence, polysemy is added to the data. Morphologically, the input data shows higher sparsity – that is, words occur less frequently – caused by the various verb inflections and agreement morphology of Brazilian Portuguese.

Results indicate that both changes impose difficulties to the learning heuristics, although it is an open question whether the learner could overcome the challenge posed by polysemy if exposed to much more data. Nevertheless, sparseness seems to be more crucial to the learner's performance and it may demand a change in the "garbage collection" conceived in Siskind (1996). Another possibility, is to have the model being capable of decomposing words into stems and affixes, what by hypothesis could eliminate the problem of sparsity both by guaranteeing frequent expositions to the stems and by assigning affixes to the category of functional words for which the learner in the present study showed satisfactory performance.

Still, there are some more open issues to consider. First, although this study claims to be evaluating Siskind's (1996) heuristics, it is important to also guarantee that the implementation is at least equivalent to the original.[2] Therefore, a future

[2]In a recent work by Yu & Siskind (2013), the authors investigate a distinct approach, based on probabilistic methods, for learning "representations for word meanings from short clips paired with sentences". Given its perceptual grounding (on video clips), it covers only a toy grammar for some spacial relations and interactions. That particular study and the present one can be seen as complementary: as far as the probabilistic approach is able to model the cross-situational learning strategy successfully, studies like the present one provide knowledge about the kind of robustness the learner must have

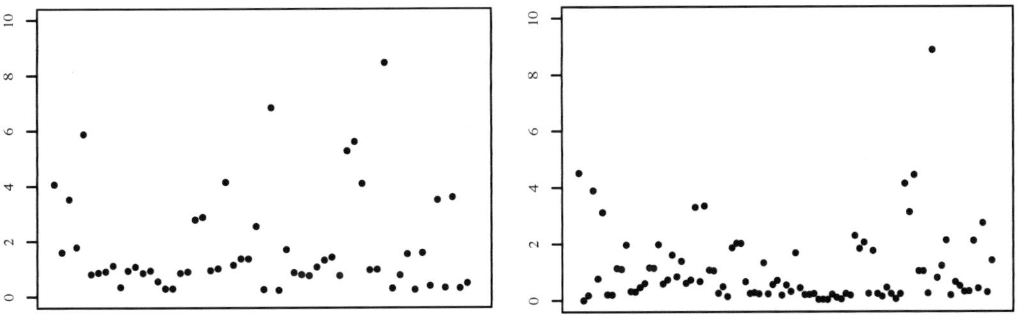

Figure 6: Word frequencies for the head-final and the English corpora.

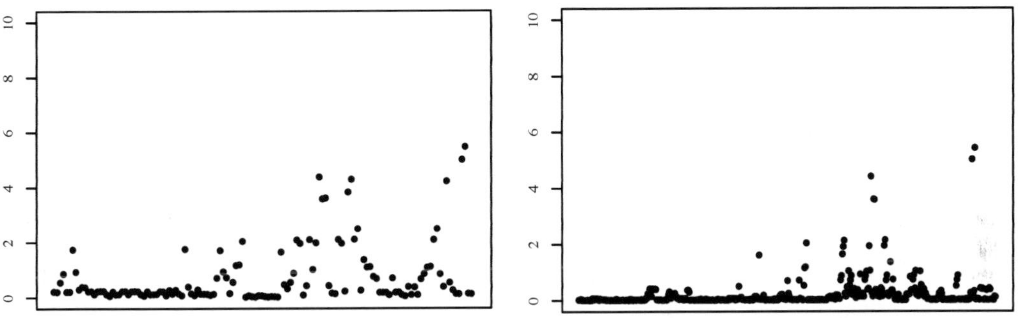

Figure 7: Word frequencies for the BP I and BP II corpora.

goal is to fully replicate Siskind's results, for all parameters (vocabulary size, rate of homonymy, etc.) involved. Such replication will not only add support to the results presented but will also make it possible to evaluate the same parameters for the kind of input data assumed here.

Apart from that, it is important to face the challenge of dealing with omitted words in utterances, such as argument omission (subject, object, etc.) and ellipsis phenomena. The present algorithm is a step in that direction as it is able to handle conceptual symbols – for instance, for utterance type – that lack morphological realization both in English and in Brazilian Portuguese. But the changes made to the original algorithm are probably not sufficient and have to be improved.

In somewhat the opposite direction, agreement morphology in languages cause the input to have two or more morphemes that share the same information. Thus, how is the algorithm to handle such cases? Certainly, it will have to allow some constrained meaning overlapping between morphemes in an utterance. However, the actual nature of the constraints needed in this case is still not clear. Adding Brazilian Portuguese to this simulation is a small but important step towards cross-linguistic coverage in this regard. Given that BP is from the family of Romance languages, being able to deal well with it makes it likely that the model will also be able to handle other languages of this family. Of course, it is important to keep adding languages from other families, specially those that show greater differences from English and BP.

Finally, although this model may be taken as reasonably plausible as a psychological model, it demands empirical support for the nature of the semantic-conceptual representation, as well as the learning heuristics, properties of the processor, etc. For all of these, it is necessary to state their empirical predictions and find ways of assessing them experimentally.

Acknowledgments

Thanks to Sao Paulo Research Foundation – FAPESP – for funding this research through grant no. 09/17172-3 and also thanks to the reviewers for their useful comments and suggestions.

in order to succeed in the face of distinct languages and more realistic grammars.

References

Robert C. Berwick. 1985. *The Acquisition of Syntactic Knowledge*. The MIT Press, Massachusetts.

Thea Cameron-Faulkner, Elena Lieven, and Michael Tomasello. 2003. A construction based analysis of child directed speech. *Cognitive Science*, 27:843—873.

Pablo Faria. 2013. *Um modelo computacional de aquisição de primeira língua*. Phd dissertation, University of Campinas (UNICAMP), Campinas, SP, Brasil, November.

Cynthia Fisher, D. Geoffrey Hall, Susan Rakowitz, and Lila Gleitman. 1994. When it is better to receive than to give: Syntactic and conceptual constraints on vocabulary growth. *Lingua*, 92:333–375.

Helen L. Gaylard. 1995. *Phrase Structure in a Computational Model of Child Language Acquisition*. Ph.D. thesis, University of Birmingham, March.

Erika Hoff-Ginsberg. 1986. Function and structure in maternal speech: Their relation to the child's development of syntax. *Developmental Psychology*, 22(2):155–163.

Matthew D. Parker and Kent Brorson. 2005. A comparative study between mean length of utterance in morphemes (mlum) and mean length of utterance in words (mluw). *First Language*, 25(3):365–376.

Lisa Pearl. 2010. Using computational modeling in language acquisition research. In E. Blom and S. Unsworth, editors, *Experimental Methods in Language Acquisition Research*. John Benjamins.

Steven Pinker. 1989. *Learnability and cognition: The acquisition of argument structure*. MIT press, Cambridge, Massachusetts.

Jeffrey M. Siskind. 1996. A computational study of cross-situational techniques for learning word-to-meaning mappings. *Cognition*, 61(1):39–91.

Aline Villavicencio. 2002. *The acquisition of a unification-based generalised categorial grammar*. Doctoral dissertation, University of Cambridge.

Charles Yang. 2011. Computational models of syntactic acquisition. *Wiley Interdisciplinary Reviews: Cognitive Science*.

Haonan Yu and Jeffrey M. Siskind. 2013. Grounded language learning from video described with sentences. In *Proceedings of the 51st Annual Meeting of the Association for Computational Linguistics*, pages 53–63.

Units in segmentation: a computational investigation

Çağrı Çöltekin
University of Tübingen
ccoltekin@sfs.uni-tuebingen.de

Abstract

This study investigates the use of syllables and phone(me)s in computational models of segmentation in early language acquisition. We results of experiments with both syllables and phonemes as the basic unit using a standard state-of-the-art segmentation model. We evaluate the model output based on both word- and morpheme-segmented gold standards on child-directed speech corpora from two typologically different languages. Our results do not indicate a clear advantage for one unit or the other. We argue that the computational advantage for the syllable suggested in earlier research may be an artifact of the particular language and/or segmentation strategy used in these studies.

1 Introduction

Segmentation is a prevalent problem in language processing. We process linguistic input as a combination of linguistic units such as words. However, spoken language does not include reliable cues to word boundaries that are found in many writing systems. The hearer needs to extract words, or lexical units, from a continuous stream of sounds using the information available in the input signal as well as his/her/its (implicit) linguistic knowledge. This makes segmentation a particularly challenging task for the early learners, since they need to discover the lexical units in the input without a lexicon and without much insight into the workings of the input language. The question of how early learners may accomplish this task has been an active area of research.

The problem have been studied extensively, through both psycholinguistic experiments and computational modeling. Experimental studies are mainly focused on particular cues that could help adults or children to solve the segmentation problem. Just to name a few, these cues include predictability statistics (Saffran, Aslin, and Newport, 1996), lexical stress (Cutler and Butterfield, 1992; Jusczyk, Houston, and Newsome, 1999), phonotactics (Jusczyk, Cutler, and Redanz, 1993), allophonic differences (Jusczyk, Hohne, and Bauman, 1999), *vowel harmony* (Kampen et al., 2008; Suomi, McQueen, and Cutler, 1997) and coarticulation (E. K. Johnson and Jusczyk, 2001). Computational models offer a complementary method to the psycholinguistic experiments. There have been an increasing number of computational models of segmentation in the literature, particularly within the last two decades (just to exemplify a few, Elman, 1990, Aslin, 1993, Cairns et al., 1994, Christiansen, Allen, and Seidenberg, 1998, Fleck, 2008, Brent and Cartwright, 1996, Brent, 1999, Venkataraman, 2001, Xanthos, 2004, Goldwater, Griffiths, and M. Johnson, 2009, M. Johnson and Goldwater, 2009, Monaghan and Christiansen, 2010, Çöltekin and Nerbonne, 2014).

In this paper, we investigate a recurring issue in the segmentation literature: the use of syllable or phoneme as the basic input unit in computational models of segmentation.[1] Most psycholinguistic research is based on syllable as the basic unit. The likely reason behind this choice is the early research pointing to syllable as a salient perceptual unit for adults (Cutler, Mehler, et al., 1986; Mehler et al., 1981; Savin and Bever, 1970), and infants (Eimas, 1999). However, these findings do not necessarily mean that infants are not sensitive to, and do not use, sub-syllabic units in speech segmentation. Although it is known that infants do not form adult-like phonetic categories until late

[1] Since the corpora used in majority of the computational studies of segmentation lack phonetic variation, the input unit in these models are effectively phonemes. We acknowledge that the input to the children exhibit phonetic variation, but this is not directly relevant to our results since the same applies to both units we compare.

Proceedings of the Sixth Workshop on Cognitive Aspects of Computational Language Learning, pages 55–64,
Lisbon, Portugal, 18 September 2015.

in the first year in life (Kuhl, 2004), they are sensitive to sub-syllabic changes in the input (Jusczyk and Derrah, 1987; Werker and Tees, 1984). Besides potential constraints due to young age, a logical reason for early learners not to have adult-like phonetic categories is the fact that learning these categories is largely mediated by their use in distinguishing lexical units from each other. For the purposes of segmentation, what really matters is not that infants are capable of classifying relevant phonetic segments into adult-like categories, but being able to detect the differences (and similarities) between such segments. Furthermore, it is also unrealistic to expect infants, who did not form phonetic categories, to perceive syllables categorically. Hence, whether the syllable or the phoneme is an earlier or better perceptual unit is still open to debate, and reality seems to be more complex than choosing one over the other (Dumay and Content, 2012; Foss and Swinney, 1973; Healy and Cutting, 1976; Morais and Kolinsky, 1994; Pallier, 1997).

A few exceptions aside (Gambell and Yang, 2006; Lignos and Yang, 2010; Phillips and Pearl, 2014; Swingley, 2005), most of the computational models in the literature take phonetic segments as the basic unit. For some of the models, the syllable is a natural choice as the basic unit because they are based on information associated with syllables rather than sub-syllabic units. For example both lexical stress (Gambell and Yang, 2006; Swingley, 2005), and vowel harmony (Ketrez, 2013) operates at the level of syllable. Even when such information, e.g., lexical stress, is used in phoneme-based models (e.g., by Christiansen, Allen, and Seidenberg, 1998, Çöltekin, 2011), the lexical stress is marked on all phonemes that span the stressed syllables, effectively informing the model about the syllable boundaries. For other models, the choice of basic unit does not alter the computations involved. However, the performance of the model may be affected by the choice of the basic unit.

Assuming syllables are the basic units, and evaluating the models based on gold-standard segmentation of words eases the learning task in general. However, syllabification of the input is not necessarily straightforward. In fluent speech, words are not uttered in isolation, hence, perceived syllables are likely to straddle lexical unit boundaries. For example the utterance [gɛt ɪt] will be syllabified as [gɛt.ɪt] if the word boundaries are given. However, the likely syllabification will be [gɛ.tɪt] when we do not assume word boundaries. Another problem with assuming that the syllable is an indivisible unit for lexical segmentation comes from the fact that some morphemes that learners eventually learn to extract out of continuous speech and use it productively are sub-syllabic. Hence, not only that the syllable is not the *only* unit of perception in early language acquisition, but it is also not necessarily the best basic unit for segmenting natural speech since some lexical unit boundaries may be syllable-internal.

This study contrasts the use of phoneme and syllable as the basic units in speech segmentation. To this end, we use a simple state-of-the-art segmentation model, and run a set of simulations on two typologically different languages, English and Turkish. We evaluate the results based on word- and morpheme-segmented gold standards.

The next section describes the model and the data used in this study, Section 3 presents results from a series of computational simulations, we discuss the results in Section 4 and conclude in Section 5.

2 Method and the data

2.1 Data

For the experiments reported in this paper, we use corpora of child-directed speech from English and Turkish. Both corpora used parts of the CHILDES (MacWhinney and Snow, 1985).

For English, we use the *de facto* standard corpus collected by Bernstein Ratner (1987) and processed by Brent (1999). The age range of children in our English data (the BR corpus) is between 0;6 and 0;11.29. Unlike earlier studies, we do not make use of phonemic transcriptions by Brent (1999) in our main experiments. Instead, we convert the orthographic transcriptions to transcriptions based on Carnegie Mellon University pronouncing dictionary (version 7b, Carnegie Mellon University, 2014). The main motivation for using an alternative (but more conventional) transcription has been to be able to apply the standard syllabification methods. The new transcription also avoids some of the arbitrary choices in phonemic transcriptions of Brent (1999).

Turkish child-directed corpus was formed by taking all child-directed utterances from the Aksu corpus (Slobin, 1982). The Aksu corpus contains 53 files (one for each recording session) with 33 target children between ages 2;0–4;4. Although

	English	Turkish
Utterances	9 790	10 206
MLU (word)	3.41	4.66
MLU (morph)	3.89	6.14
MLU (syl.)	4.00	7.86
MLU (phon.)	10.81	18.40
Word tokens	33 377	36 789
Word types	1 380	4 808
Word TTR	0.041 35	0.130 69
Morph tokens	38 081	62 612
Morph types	1 024	1 802
Morph TTR	0.026 89	0.037 89
Syllable tokens	39 150	80 178
Syllable types	1 165	1 044
Syllable TTR	0.029 76	0.013 02
Phone tokens	105 801	187 738
Phone types	37	29
Phone TTR	0.000 35	0.000 16

Table 1: General statistics about the corpora used. Besides type and token counts of each unit, type/token ratio (TTR) and mean length utterance (MLU) measured in different units are given.

the age range is not similar to the BR corpus, this corpus is currently the best option available for Turkish. We order the files by the age of the target child, and take all child-directed utterances. Similar to Brent (1999), onomatopoeia, interjections and disfluencies are removed. Turkish corpus was not converted to a phonetic/phonemic transcription as Turkish orthography follows the standard pronunciation rather closely (this practice is common in the literature, e.g., Göksel and Kerslake, 2005; Ketrez, 2013).

Table 1 presents some basic statistics about the corpora used. Although our corpora are similar in number of utterances, there are important differences due to differences between languages, and potentially due to the age of the target children.

2.1.1 Gold-standard syllabification and morpheme segmentation

Both corpora are syllabified and marked for morpheme boundaries for some of the experiments reported below. Most of the earlier studies rely on dictionaries or human judgments in syllabification of English. Since we do not only syllabify words, but also utterances, we do not use a dictionary-based method. For English, we use a freely available syllabification software that implements a few additional sub-regularities over the maximum-onset principle. English morpheme segmentation is done manually (Gorman, 2013). The morpheme boundaries are determined for each word type, and the same morpheme segmentation is used for all tokens of the same word. For syllabification and morpheme segmentation of Turkish, we use another set of freely available tools (Çöltekin, 2010, 2014).

Some statistics regarding morpheme-segmented and syllabified corpora are given in Table 1. Additionally, we note that the ratios of multi-syllabic word tokens are 16 % and 56 % in our English and Turkish input, respectively.

2.2 Evaluation

As with other models of language acquisition, evaluating models of segmentation is non-trivial. Not only we do not know our target, the early child lexicon, well, but it is also likely to differ substantially based on age, language and even the individual child. Furthermore, the linguistic units used by linguists may not necessarily match the units in a typical human lexicon. For the lack of a better method, we evaluate our model based on gold-standard word and morpheme segmentations. We acknowledge that early learners' lexicon is likely to contain multi-word units. To avoid arbitrary and corpus dependent decisions, however, we do not quantitatively evaluate the model's output based on a selection of multi-word expressions.

As in earlier studies, we report three types of *F_1-scores* (or F-scores). *Boundary* F-score (BF), measures the success of the model in finding boundaries. *Word*, or token, F-score requires both boundaries of a word to be found. Hence, discovering only one of the boundaries of a word does not indicate success for this measure. *Lexicon*, or type, F-score similar to token scores, however, the comparisons are done over the word types the model proposed and word types in the gold standard. F-score is the harmonic mean of precision and recall, and these three types of F-scores (also precision and recall) have conventional measures of success reported in the field (see e.g., Goldwater, Griffiths, and M. Johnson, 2009, for precise defintions).

Besides F-scores, we present oversegmentation (EO) and undersegmentation (EU) rates with the following definitions.

$$EO = \frac{FP}{FP + TN} \qquad EU = \frac{FN}{FN + TP}$$

where TP, FP, FN and TN stands for true positive, false positives, false negatives and true negatives, respectively. The error rates defined above are related to boundary precision and recall. Especially, the undersegmentation rate is equal to $1 - $ recall. The difference between the information conveyed by EO and boundary precision is more subtle. Unlike precision which measures the rate of the correct decisions over all boundary decisions made by the model, EO ranges over the word-internal positions in the gold-standard segmentation. For example, if the model admits one correct and one incorrect boundary, the precision will be 0.5. However, the EO depends on the number of word-internal positions in the gold standard. The smaller the number of potential false positives, the higher the EO will be for the same number oversegmentation errors. As a result, the error measures defined above give a more direct indication of how much room is left for improvement.

Similar to the earlier literature, we do not split our data as test and training set since we are using an unsupervised learning method.

2.3 The segmentation model

For the experiments reported below, we implement and use a well-known segmentation model.[2] The model assigns probabilities to possible segmentations as described in Equations 1 and 2.

$$P(s) = \prod_{i=1}^{n} P(w_i) \tag{1}$$

$$P(w) = \begin{cases} (1-\alpha)f(w) & \text{if } w \text{ is known} \\ \alpha \prod_{j=1}^{m} f(a_j) & \text{if } w \text{ is unknown} \end{cases} \tag{2}$$

where s is a sequence of phonemes (e.g., an utterance or a corpus), w_i is the ith word in the sequence, a_j is the jth basic unit in the word, $f(w_i)$ and $f(a_j)$ are the relative frequencies of word w_i or basic unit a_i respectively, n is the number of words in the utterance, m is the length of the word in input units, and $0 \leq \alpha \leq 1$ is the only parameter of the model. The parameter α can be interpreted as the probability of admitting novel lexical items, and it also affects how eager or the conservative the model is in inserting boundaries. In the simulations reported in this paper, we fix α at 0.5, and adopt an incremental learning method where learner processes the input utterance by utterance. Each utterance is segmented using the current model parameters (phoneme and word frequencies), and parameters are updated based on the segmented utterance before proceeding to the next.

[2]The source code of the implementation, the data files and utilities used in preprocessing the data are publicly available at `http://doi.org/10.5281/zenodo.27433`.

model	BF	WF	LF
Brent, 1999	82.3	68.2	52.4
Venkataraman, 2001	82.1	68.3	55.7
Goldwater, Griffiths, and M. Johnson (2009)	85.2	72.3	59.1
Blanchard, Heinz, and Golinkoff (2010)	81.9	66.1	56.3
Current model (incremental)	83.4	71.6	55.3
Current model (final)	86.6	76.3	70.7

Table 2: Performance scores of the present model in comparison to some of the models in the literature that are tested on the BR corpus.

One way to view this model is as an instance of minimum description length (MDL) principle (Rissanen, 1978). (Creutz and Lagus, 2007; Goldsmith, 2001; Marcken, 1996; Rissanen, 1978). Equation 1 imposes a preference for short utterances (in number of words). Assuming each word is represented by an index or pointer in the lexicon, this leads to a preference towards a representation that minimizes the corpus length. Let alone, this preference would result in no segmentation, and corpus size would be equal to the number of utterance types. Despite small corpus representation, this would lead to a large lexicon containing all the utterance types. The second part of Equation 2, on the other hand, imposes a preference for short words and, since shorter strings result in fewer word types, a shorter lexicon. In its limiting case, this preference would result in a lexicon containing the basic units. Resulting in a large corpus representation despite a very small lexicon. As a result, learning for this model is about finding a compromise (hopefully the best) between these two extremes.

The model as described above can also be seen as a generative model. At each step, the model either decides to produce a novel word with probability α, or pick a word from the lexicon with probability $1 - \alpha$. The probability of words from the lexicon is proportional to their empirical probability (relative frequency with which they are observed). If the model decides to generate a novel word, it produces a series of basic units. Choice of basic units is, again, proportional to their probability of occurrence (for completeness, one needs to either introduce a special end-of-word unit which terminates the sequence) With this description, the model is similar to the model suggested by Brent (1999), Venkataraman (2001, although he does not formulate his model as a generative model), and the unigram model of Goldwater, Griffiths, and M. Johnson (2009).

For simplicity, we use a fixed α and we do not consider word context (e.g., word bigrams). Despite these simplifications, the performance of the present model is competitive with the state-of-the-art models in the literature. To enable a rough comparison, we provide the performance scores of some of the similar models evaluated on the same corpus, together with result obtained using the present model in Table 2. Unlike the rest of the experiments reported in this paper, to increase the comparability of the results with the earlier literature, the result presented here are obtained using the phonemic transcription of the original BR corpus (the version transcribed by Brent, 1999). The row marked 'incremental' reflects the scores obtained by evaluating the segmentations on the whole corpus during a single pass. Although it is the common method of evaluating the incremental models in the literature, this leads to an unfair disadvantage when the model is compared with a batch model which would have already made many passes over the complete corpus at the time of evaluation. The row marked 'final' in Table 2 reports the final evaluation metrics obtained while they were calculated for each 1 000-utterance block. Hence, the 'final' results are obtained from a more 'learned state' of the model, providing a better comparison with batch models. In the rest of this paper, we present only the 'incremental' version of the performance score.

Although the results in Table 2 indicate that the model is comparable to (and better than on some counts) the state of the art, we note that our aim in this work is not to introduce another segmentation model, but compare two basic units using a model that shares many features with the earlier state-of-the-art models.

	BF	WF	LF	EO	EU
En (words)	89.1	77.6	55.1	3.2	0.0
En (uttr.)	71.9	56.7	42.4	5.8	19.3
Tr (words)	54.5	17.4	5.8	25.8	0.0
Tr (uttr.)	48.6	16.0	3.4	27.5	11.0

Table 3: Scores of 'syllable as word' baseline.

3 Experiments and results

3.1 'Syllable as word' baseline

For languages like (child-directed) English where most words are mono-syllabic, a potentially deceiving aspect of using syllable as the basic unit for segmentation is that the learner may learn single input units, syllables, as words. Hence, an interesting baseline can be obtained by segmenting at every syllable boundary. We segment both corpora trivially at syllable boundaries, and evaluate against the gold-standard word segmentation of these corpora. To approximate a possible syllabification when word boundaries are not given, we also preset results where syllabification algorithm is applied without marking the word boundaries. The evaluation results for both languages are presented in Table 3.

Not surprisingly, when syllabification is done at word boundaries, the model recovers all word boundaries, hence EU is 0 for both languages. The oversegmentation errors in this setting is the upper bound for EO when syllables are used as the basic unit. The F-scores of the syllable baseline on the BR corpus, where the words are predominantly monosyllabic, is similar to the state-of-the-art models presented in Table 2, while the numbers are substantially lower for Turkish.

To contrast with this 'syllable as word' baseline, it is also instructive to consider a 'phoneme as word' strategy. If one would segment at every phoneme, the error rates go up to 62.1 % and 89.7 % for English and Turkish respectively. This results in 0.4 % and 0.04 % lexical F-scores for English and Turkish. Clearly, the models considering syllable as the basic unit starts with a great advantage for English. While helpful, the results for Turkish is far from what we observe for English.

As expected, when syllabification is done without word boundaries, error rates increase for both languages. Undersegmentations are caused by syllables straddling the word boundaries, and oversegmentations increase because of increased number of word-internal syllable boundaries. However, the effect is not as drastic as the differences

	BF	WF	LF	EO	EU
En (phon)	80.9	68.2	51.0	5.7	20.3
En (syl/w)	48.5	29.4	23.5	0.01	67.9
En (syl/u)	55.5	36.1	25.0	0.2	61.3
Tr (phon)	65.7	42.1	29.0	9.4	24.3
Tr (syl/w)	69.8	50.7	39.1	2.6	38.5
Tr (syl/u)	68.5	49.6	38.2	2.8	39.3

Table 4: Segmentation scores using phonemes and syllables.

between the two languages in the same setting.

3.2 Syllables vs. phonemes

Table 4 presents segmentation performance of models that use phonemes or syllables as basic input units. We present results for syllabification with and without restricting syllable boundaries at word boundaries. We first note that the phonemic transcription we use seems to be harder to segment than the transcription by Brent (1999). The F-scores presented on the first row of Table 4 are all lower than the corresponding F-scores in Table 2.

For English, we observe an overall decrease in performance scores when the basic units are syllables. Despite the fact that model makes very few oversegmentation errors, the undersegmentation rate is even worse than a process that inserts boundaries at random. Given the overall conservative segmentation tendency of the model, this is not surprising. Surprisingly, however, when the syllabification is done based on whole utterances, the model seems to perform better. The decrease in EU seems to result in an improvement in all conventional F-scores.

The phoneme-based segmentation scores for Turkish is lower than English. This is in-line with earlier studies that compared English with other languages. As in English, the EO decreases, and the EU increases when syllables (rather than phonemes) are used as the basic units. However, unlike English, the effect of this is positive on all F-score measures. The surprising positive effect of syllabification of full utterances does not persist on the Turkish corpus. The utterance-based syllabification causes an increase on both EU and EO, resulting in a slight drop in all F-scores.

Although the overall performance/error scores presented are informative, the pattern of learning for the model is also important. To show how learning proceeds for both models, we plot over- and under-segmentation rates progressively for both languages, both for phoneme and syllable as basic units in Figure 1. As the description of the model in Section 2.3 indicate, all models start with a preference of undersegmentation. In the process, the EO increases, and EU decreases. In general, the models learn quickly. After a short initial period of the increase in EO and decrease in EU, the changes are rather small.

With syllables, the decrease in EU is very small, particularly for English. We observe a quicker drop of errors for phoneme-based models in general, and the expected trend of higher EU lower EO of the syllable-based model in comparison to phoneme based models holds in all settings. With respect to the differences between the languages, the undersegmentation curves for phoneme-based models are very similar, leading to similar error rates at the end of the learning. However, for Turkish we observe a higher rate of oversegmentation errors. The peak in EO for the phoneme-based segmentation just before the 1 000th utterance for English seems to be due to the particular ordering of the BR corpus. Multiple experiments with shuffling the sentences produce similar curves without abrupt changes.

3.3 Words vs. morphemes

Next, we use the same input described in Section 3.2, but evaluate on the morpheme-segmented gold standard corpora. The scores are presented in Table 5. Compared to the scores based on word segmentation in Table 4, we observe a slight increase in the performance scores in segmenting the BR corpus, since fewer of the model's segmentations are now marked as oversegmentation errors. The undersegmentation, on the other hand, increases slightly. The positive effect of reduced oversegmentation errors are more pronounced for Turkish. However, segmentation performance for Turkish with phonemes as the basic unit is still much lower than English. For both languages, the performance with syllables as basic unit is lower when tested against morpheme-segmented gold standard. Most of the morphemes being formed by sub-syllabic units, this is the expected result for English. However, syllabification does not help the model to find morphemes for Turkish either.

4 General discussion

Our main motivation in this study has been to gain further insight into usefulness of syllables or phonemes as the basic input units. We presented

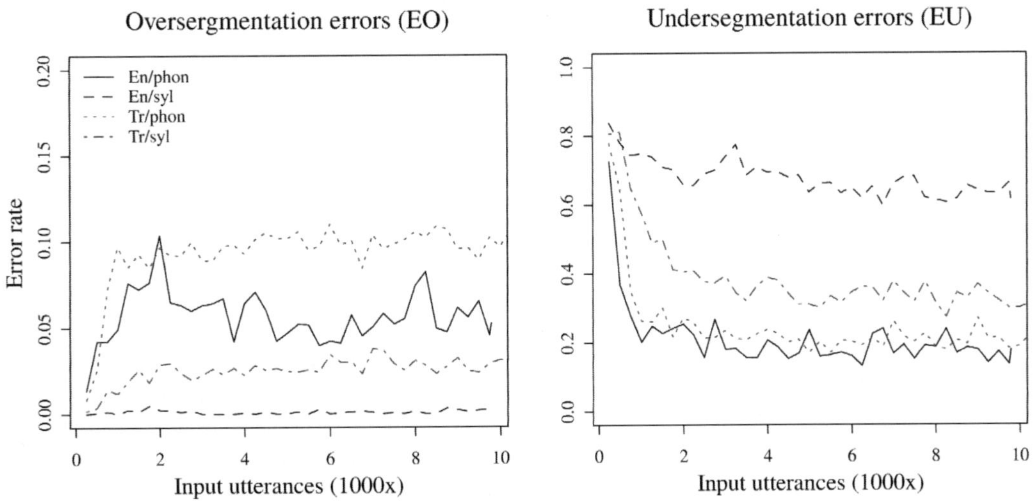

Figure 1: Oversegmentation (left) and undersegmentation (right) rate plotted incrementally during learning. Note that the y-axis ranges are not the same.

	BF	WF	LF	EO	EU
En (phon)	82.7	70.5	51.3	2.6	25.2
En (syl/w)	47.7	24.1	20.8	0.1	68.6
En (syl/u)	54.6	30.4	22.5	0.1	62.4
Tr (phon)	68.4	44.1	33.6	3.6	43.4
Tr (syl/w)	55.3	25.4	21.9	0.6	61.2
Tr (syl/u)	56.1	27.4	23.3	0.7	60.3

Table 5: Segmentation scores using phonemes and syllables with morph-segmentation as gold-standard segmentation.

results from experiments from two typologically different languages and two different settings for the gold-standard, one considering written words as the lexical units as in earlier studies, and the other with morphemes as lexical units.

Unlike earlier studies (e.g., Gambell and Yang, 2006; Phillips and Pearl, 2014), our results do not suggest a direct indication of the usefulness of the syllable (or the phoneme) as the basic input representation for segmentation. The syllable-based model performs worse than phoneme-based model on English, while it improves the segmentation performance on our Turkish corpus. For both languages, the invariant trend is that syllable-based models make fewer oversegmentation mistakes with the cost of higher undersegmentation rate. For English, where the words are rather short, the undersegmentation is severe, and syllable-based segmentation causes F-scores to drop drastically. For Turkish, since the average word length is much larger (see Table 1), the undersegmentation is less severe, and we see increase in the F-scores for segmentation.

The low oversegmentation is expected from the syllable-based models, simply because the models are restricted to insert boundaries in fewer locations. As the 'syllable as word' baseline results presented in Table 3 suggests, most of these locations are true word boundaries. If we allow a more eager segmentation strategy (through a different model, or different parameter settings), syllable-based models are expected to yield good segmentation scores for English. The success of the most eager segmentation strategy 'syllable as word' baseline is a clear example of this case. If such an eager strategy is constrained in the right direction, it is not surprising that one can get really good segmentation performance from a syllable-based segmentation model. This, probably, is also the reason for high segmentation scores of stress-based segmentation strategy presented by Gambell and Yang (2006). Since their model is restricted to insert word boundaries only at syllable boundaries and include some linguistically-informed constraints, the high segmentation F-socre is expected as the 'syllable as word' baseline already achieves a boundary F-score of 89 % (Table 3).

Besides the fact that syllables constrain the locations that one can insert boundaries, the success of syllable-based models are also related to some of the fine details of the model definition. As an example, consider the boundary decision involving a known word w consisting of basic units $a_1 \dots a_k$, and an adjacent unknown string s. With the model defined in Equations 1 and 2, the decision to insert a boundary between w and s in string ws (or sw) requires

$$(1-\alpha)P(w)\alpha P(s) > \alpha P(a_1)\dots P(a_k)P(s)$$
$$(1-\alpha)P(w) > P(a_1)\dots P(a_k)$$

In this setting, the probability of inserting a boundary decreases with the length of the known word. Since syllables reduce the lengths of lexical units, the model becomes more conservative.[3] This partially explains the low scores we obtain using syllable as the basic unit. A potential reason for the model to segment more eagerly (hence better) is high lexical word probabilities. Probably, this is part of the explanation for the better segmentation performance reported by Phillips and Pearl (2014) for syllable-based models only with bigram word probabilities. The probabilities of (real) words conditioned on the previous word will be higher if the words tend to cooccur. Hence, the model tends to segment more eagerly around the frequent bigrams, counteracting the conservative segmentation tendency introduced by using syllable as the basic unit.

Unlike our results on English, syllable-based model improves word segmentation of Turkish. Contrary to our expectations, however, the scores go down when evaluated on morpheme-segmented gold standard. There are at least three reasons for expecting the results to be even better with the syllable-based models when evaluated on the morpheme-based gold standard. First, on average, Turkish words are formed by longer sequences of morphemes. Second, Turkish morphemes are syllabic, our Turkish corpora does not contain any morpheme boundaries that are not syllable boundaries. Third, similar to the English function words, frequent affixes are more frequent than frequent roots/stems. Hence they should be more likely to be picked as lexical units. However, for both languages, syllable based model performs worse when evaluated against morpheme-based gold standard. Looking closer to the errors suggests that the syllable-based models exhibit a similar behavior on morpheme-based gold standard as the English syllable-based model evaluated on word-based gold standard. The model is precise, but misses many of the boundaries.

Besides missing the morphemes that may be formed by sub-syllabic sequences, another potential problem with the syllable-based models when evaluated against morpheme segmented gold-standard is that the syllables perceived from fluent speech may straddle word boundaries. As a result, we expect worse segmentation scores if the syllabification does not consider word boundaries as absolute syllable boundaries. However, the results are surprising for English, at least. It seems syllabification of complete utterances causes a decrease in undersegmentation errors. Despite a small increase in oversegmentation errors, the overall effect of this on the F-scores reported in Table 4 is positive. The reason for this seems to be the change in the syllable distribution resulting in smaller syllable probabilities on average, and hence, more eager segmentation. In general, it seems both problems mentioned above regarding syllable-based models do not cause serious difficulties. However, in general, we did not find a clear computational benefit of one unit or the other as the basic unit for both languages.

5 Conclusions

In this paper, we compared the effects of syllables or phonemes as the basic unit for segmentation using child-directed speech corpora from two typologically different languages. The simulations reported in this paper do not favor one unit over another. In different settings, the success of models based on syllables or phonemes seems to differ. A reasonable explanation for these differences is the relative lengths of lexical and basic units, and their distributions. In other words, the differences observed are likely to be an artifact of the modeling practice. This is not necessarily a disadvantage if the model in question matches the way humans perform the task. Otherwise, the conclusions that may be drawn from these models regarding whether syllable or phoneme is a better choice as the basic unit for early segmentation may be misleading.

In this paper, we investigated the behavior of a single family of models. It would be interesting to observe the difference between syllables and

[3]Also note the model's unintuitive preference for low-probability basic unit sequences as known lexical units. If word length is fixed, right side of the inequality will be higher if the probabilities of the basic units forming the word are higher.

phonemes in other modeling approaches, such as the ones that use local cues, possibly using more distributed representations for the basic units. Although our aim here was to contrast these two potential basic units, it is likely that humans make use of multiple units at different levels. Hence, another interesting question for the future work is whether these units play complementary roles in segmentation.

References

Richard N. Aslin 1993. Segmentation of fluent speech into words: Learning models and the role of maternal input. In *Developmental Neurocognition: Speech and Face Processing in the First Year of Life*. Ed. by B. De Boysson-Bardies et al. Kluwer Academic Publishers pp. 305–315.

Nan Bernstein Ratner 1987. The phonology of parent-child speech. In *Children's language*. Ed. by K. Nelson and A. van Kleeck. Vol. 6. Hillsdale, NJ: Erlbaum pp. 159–174.

Daniel Blanchard, Jeffrey Heinz, and Roberta Golinkoff 2010. Modeling the contribution of phonotactic cues to the problem of word segmentation. *Journal of Child Language* 37(Special Issue 03):487–511.

Michael R. Brent 1999. An Efficient, Probabilistically Sound Algorithm for Segmentation and Word Discovery. *Machine Learning* 34(1-3):71–105.

Michael R. Brent and Timothy A. Cartwright 1996. Distributional regularity and phonotactic constraints are useful for segmentation. *Cognition* 61(1-2):93–125.

Paul Cairns et al. 1994. Modelling the acquisition of lexical segmentation. In *Proceedings of the 26th Child Language Research Forum*. University of Chicago Press.

Carnegie Mellon University 2014. *CMU pronouncing dictionary version 7b*. URL: `http://www.speech.cs.cmu.edu/cgi-bin/cmudict` (visited on 04/01/2015).

Morten H. Christiansen, Joseph Allen, and Mark S. Seidenberg 1998. Learning to Segment Speech Using Multiple Cues: A Connectionist Model. *Language and Cognitive Processes* 13(2):221–268.

Çağrı Çöltekin 2010. A freely available morphological analyzer for Turkish. In *Proceedings of the 7th International Conference on Language Resources and Evaluation (LREC 2010)*. Valetta, Malta pages 820–827.

Çağrı Çöltekin 2011. *Catching Words in a Stream of Speech: Computational simulations of segmenting transcribed child-directed speech*. PhD thesis. University of Groningen.

Çağrı Çöltekin 2014. A set of open source tools for Turkish natural language processing. In *Proceedings of the Ninth International Conference on Language Resources and Evaluation (LREC-2014)*. Reykjavik, Iceland: European Language Resources Association (ELRA).

Çağrı Çöltekin and John Nerbonne 2014. An explicit statistical model of learning lexical segmentation using multiple cues. In *Proceedings of EACL 2014 Workshop on Cognitive Aspects of Computational Language Learning*.

Mathias Creutz and Krista Lagus 2007. Unsupervised models for morpheme segmentation and morphology learning. *ACM Trans. Speech Lang. Process.* 4(1):3.

Anne Cutler and Sally Butterfield 1992. Rhythmic cues to speech segmentation: Evidence from juncture misperception. *Journal of Memory and Language* 31(2):218–236.

Anne Cutler, Jacques Mehler, et al. 1986. The syllable's differing role in the segmentation of French and English. *Journal of Memory and Language* 25(4):385–400.

Nicolas Dumay and Alain Content 2012. Searching for syllabic coding units in speech perception. *Journal of Memory and Language* 66(4):680–694.

Peter D. Eimas 1999. Segmental and syllabic representations in the perception of speech by young infants. *The Journal of the Acoustical Society of America* 105(3):1901–1911.

Jeffrey L. Elman 1990. Finding structure in time. *Cognitive Science* 14:179–211.

Margaret M. Fleck 2008. Lexicalized phonotactic word segmentation. In *Proceedings of the Annual Meeting of the Association of Computational Linguistics (ACL-08)* pages 130–138.

Donald J. Foss and David A. Swinney 1973. On the psychological reality of the phoneme: Perception, identification, and consciousness. *Journal of Verbal Learning and Verbal Behavior* 12(3):246–257.

Timothy Gambell and Charles Yang 2006. *Word segmentation: Quick but not dirty*. Unpublished manuscript.

Aslı Göksel and Celia Kerslake 2005. *Turkish: A Comprehensive Grammar*. London: Routledge.

John Goldsmith 2001. Unsupervised learning of the morphology of a natural language. *Computational Linguistics* 27(2):153–198.

Sharon Goldwater, Thomas L. Griffiths, and Mark Johnson 2009. A Bayesian framework for word segmentation: Exploring the effects of context. *Cognition* 112(1):21–54.

Kyle Gorman 2013. *syllabify.py: Automated English syllabification*.

Alice F. Healy and James E. Cutting 1976. Units of speech perception: Phoneme and syllable. *Journal of Verbal Learning and Verbal Behavior* 15(1):73–83.

Elizabeth K. Johnson and Peter W. Jusczyk 2001. Word segmentation by 8-month-olds: When speech cues count more than statistics. *Journal of Memory and Language* 44(4):548–567.

Mark Johnson and Sharon Goldwater 2009. Improving nonparameteric Bayesian inference: experiments on unsupervised word segmentation with adaptor grammars. In *Proceedings of Human Language Technologies: The 2009 Annual Conference of the North American Chapter of the Association for Computational Linguistics* pages 317–325.

Peter W. Jusczyk, Anne Cutler, and Nancy J. Redanz 1993. Infants' preference for the predominant stress patterns of English words. *Child Development* 64(3):675–687.

Peter W. Jusczyk and Carolyn Derrah 1987. Representation of speech sounds by young infants. *Developmental Psychology* 23(5):648–654.

Peter W. Jusczyk, Elizabeth A. Hohne, and Angela Bauman 1999. Infants' sensitivity to allophonic cues for word segmentation. *Perception and Psychophysics* 61(8):1465–1476.

Peter W. Jusczyk, Derek M. Houston, and Mary Newsome 1999. The Beginnings of Word Segmentation in English-Learning Infants. *Cognitive Psychology* 39:159–207.

Anja van Kampen et al. 2008. Metrical and statistical cues for word segmentation: The use of vowel harmony and word stress as cues to word boundaries by 6- and 9-month-old Turkish learners. In *Language Acquisition and Development: Proceedings of GALA 2007*. Ed. by Anna Gavarro and M. Joao Freitas pages 313–324.

F. Nihan Ketrez 2013. Harmonic cues for speech segmentation: a cross-linguistic corpus study on child-directed speech. *Journal of Child Language* 41:1–23.

Patricia K. Kuhl 2004. Early language acquisition: cracking the speech code. *Nature Reviews Neuroscience* 5(11):831–843.

Constantine Lignos and Charles Yang 2010. Recession segmentation: simpler online word segmentation using limited resources. In *Proceedings of the fourteenth conference on computational natural language learning* pages 88–97.

Brian MacWhinney and Catherine Snow 1985. The child language data exchange system. *Journal of Child Language* 12(2):271–269.

Carl de Marcken 1996. Linguistic structure as composition and perturbation. In *Proceedings of the 34th annual meeting on Association for Computational Linguistics*. Santa Cruz, California: Association for Computational Linguistics pages 335–341.

Jacques Mehler et al. 1981. The syllable's role in speech segmentation. *Journal of Verbal Learning and Verbal Behavior* 20(3):298–305.

Padraic Monaghan and Morten H. Christiansen 2010. Words in puddles of sound: modelling psycholinguistic effects in speech segmentation. *Journal of Child Language* 37(Special Issue 03):545–564.

José Morais and Régine Kolinsky 1994. Perception and awareness in phonological processing: the case of the phoneme. *Cognition* 50(1–3):287–297.

Christophe Pallier 1997. Phonemes and Syllables in Speech Perception: size of the attentional focus in French. In *Proceedings of Eurospeech '97*. Vol. 4 pages 2159–2162.

Lawrence Phillips and Lisa Pearl 2014. Bayesian inference as a viable cross-linguistic word segmentation strategy: It's all about what's useful. In *Proceedings of the 36th Annual Conference of the Cognitive Science Society*. Quebec City, CA: Cognitive Science Society pages 2775–2780.

Jorma Rissanen 1978. Modeling by shortest data description. *Automatica* 14(5):465–471.

Jenny R. Saffran, Richard N. Aslin, and Elissa L. Newport 1996. Statistical learning by 8-month old infants. *Science* 274(5294):1926–1928.

H.B. Savin and Thomas G. Bever 1970. The nonperceptual reality of the phoneme. *Journal of Verbal Learning and Verbal Behavior* 9(3):295–302.

Dan I. Slobin 1982. Universal and particular in the acquisition of language. In *Language acquisition: the state of the art*. Ed. by Eric Wanner and Lila R. Gleitman. Cambridge University Press. Chap. 5 pp. 128–170.

Kari Suomi, James M. McQueen, and Anne Cutler 1997. Vowel Harmony and Speech Segmentation in Finnish. *Journal of Memory and Language* 36(3):422–444.

Daniel Swingley 2005. Statistical clustering and the contents of the infant vocabulary. *Cognitive Psychology* 50(1):86–132.

Anand Venkataraman 2001. A statistical model for word discovery in transcribed speech. *Computational Linguistics* 27(3):351–372.

Janet F. Werker and Richard C. Tees 1984. Cross-language speech perception: Evidence for perceptual reorganization during the first year of life. *Infant Behavior and Development* 7(1):49–63.

Aris Xanthos 2004. An incremental implementation of the utterance-boundary approach to speech segmentation. In *Proceedings of Computational Linguistics in the Netherlands (CLIN) 2003* pages 171–180.

Estimating Grammeme Redundancy by Measuring Their Importance for Syntactic Parser Performance

Aleksandrs Berdicevskis
UiT The Arctic University of Norway
Department of Language and Linguistics
aleksandrs.berdicevskis@uit.no

Abstract

Redundancy is an important psycholinguistic concept which is often used for explanations of language change, but is notoriously difficult to operationalize and measure. Assuming that the reconstruction of a syntactic structure by a parser can be used as a rough model of the understanding of a sentence by a human hearer, I propose a method for estimating redundancy. The key idea is to compare performances of a parser on a given treebank before and after artificially removing all information about a certain grammeme from the morphological annotation. The change in performance can be used as an estimate for the redundancy of the grammeme. I perform an experiment, applying MaltParser to an Old Church Slavonic treebank to estimate grammeme redundancy in Proto-Slavic. The results show that those Old Church Slavonic grammemes within the case, number and tense categories that were estimated as most redundant are those that disappeared in modern Russian. Moreover, redundancy estimates serve as a good predictor of case grammeme frequencies in modern Russian. The small sizes of the samples do not allow to make definitive conclusions for number and tense.

1 Introduction

Explanations of historical language change often involve the concept of redundancy, especially grammatical (morphological) redundancy.

One important example is a family of recent theories about linguistic complexity (Sampson et al., 2009), including those known under the labels "sociolinguistic typology" (Trudgill, 2011) and "Linguistic Niche Hypothesis" (Lupyan and Dale, 2010). The key idea behind these theories is that certain sociocultural factors, such as large population size or a large share of adult learners in the population can facilitate morphological simplification, i.e. increase the likelihood that the language will lose some morphological features, which are often described as "complex" and "redundant".

It is, however, often difficult to determine (and provide empirical evidence in favour of the chosen decision) whether a certain feature is indeed redundant, or to what extent it is redundant and to what extent it is functional. Some conclusions can be drawn from indirect evidence, e.g. typological (cf. Dahl's (2004) notion of *cross-linguistically dispensable* phenomena). For modern languages, redundancy can be studied and measured by means of psycholinguistic experiments (e.g. Caballero and Kapatsinski, 2014), but this approach is not applicable to older language stages and extinct languages.

I propose a computational method to estimate the functionality (and, conversely, redundancy) of a grammeme (that is, a value of a grammatical/morphological category) that can potentially work for any language for which written sources are available or can be collected.

I describe the philosophy behind the proposed method and its relevance to cognitive aspects of language evolution in section 2. Section 3 provides the necessary background for a particular instance of language change that will be used as a case study. Section 4 describes how the experiment was performed, section 5 provides the results. Section 6 discusses possible interpretations of the results, and section 7 concludes.

2 Using parsers to measure morphological redundancy

In the most general terms, morphological redundancy can be described as follows: if a message contains certain morphological markers that are not necessary to understand the message fully and correctly, then these markers can be considered (at least to some extent) redundant.

The problem with operationalizing this intuition is that it is unclear how to model *understanding* (that is, the reconstruction of the semantic structure) of a message by human beings.

Proceedings of the Sixth Workshop on Cognitive Aspects of Computational Language Learning, pages 65–73,
Lisbon, Portugal, 18 September 2015.

In the method I propose, syntactic structure is taken as a proxy for semantic structure, and a reconstruction of syntactic structure by an automatic parser is taken as a model of how a human hearer understands the meaning.

The assumption that these processes have enough in common to make the model adequate is bold, but not unwarranted. It is generally agreed that a correct interpretation of syntactic structure is necessary to understand the meaning of a message, and that humans use morphological cues to reconstruct syntactic structure. Parsers, obviously, do the latter, too. Crucially, the model does not require the assumption that parsers necessarily process the information in exactly the same way as humans. It is enough that they, using the same input, can approximate the output (i.e. syntactic structures) well enough, and modern parsers usually can. Furthermore, parsers also rely heavily on the morphological information, not unlike humans.

The key idea is then to take a morphologically tagged treebank of a language in question and parse it with an efficient parser, *artificially removing* morphological features (either grammemes or categories) one by one. Changes in the parser's performance caused by the removal of a feature can serve as a measure of its redundancy. In other words, if the removal of a feature causes a significant decrease in parsing accuracy, the feature can be considered important for extracting syntactic information and thus functional. If, however, the decrease is small (or absent), the feature can be considered redundant.

Obviously, it is not necessary that this approach will provide an exact and comprehensive measure of morphological redundancy; there are numerous potential sources of noise and errors. We can, however, expect that at least some real redundancy will be captured. The method can then be applied to make rough estimates and thus be useful, for instance, in large-scale typological studies, or in language change studies, or any studies aiming at understanding why languages need (or do not need) redundancy. Understanding that, in turn, will help to reveal the cognitive biases that influence language learning.

It has been shown by means of computational modelling and laboratory experiments that strong biases which affect the course of language change can stem from weak individual cognitive biases, amplified by iterated learning over generations (Kirby et al., 2007; Reali and Griffiths, 2009; Smith and Wonnacott, 2010) and communication within populations (Fay and Ellison, 2013). Thus, if it is shown that there is a diachronic bias towards eliminating redundant grammemes, it will be possible to hypothesize that this bias stems from individual speakers' preference to avoid overloading their speech with excessive complexity.

Importantly for diachronic studies, the method can be applied to extinct languages, provided that large enough treebanks exist.

In the following sections, I will exemplify the method by applying it to a particular case of language change (Proto-Slavic —> Contemporary Standard Russian). I also use the case study to test whether the resulting redundancy estimates are plausible. Following a common assumption that more redundant grammemes are in general more likely to be lost (Kiparsky 1982: 88–99, see also references above), and that Russian has been under considerable pressure to shed excessive complexity (see section 3), I make the prediction that the grammemes that did disappear were on average more redundant than those that were kept, and that the "remove-and-reparse" method should be able to capture the difference.

In order to be explicit about the assumptions behind the current study and its limitations I want to highlight that the study attempts to test two independent hypotheses at once: first, that redundant grammemes are more likely to disappear or become less frequent; second, that parsing is an adequate model of human language perception, since what is redundant for a parser is redundant for a human as well. This can be problematic, since we do not really know whether either of these hypotheses is true.

Let us look at the experiment from the following perspective: if it turns out that there is a strong correlation between importance of the grammeme for parser performance and grammeme survivability, then this fact has to be explained. A plausible explanation which fits well with the existing linguistic theories would be the one outlined above in the form of the two hypotheses: under certain sociocultural conditions speakers tend to abandon redundant grammemes; grammemes that are not important for the parser are redundant. If there is no correlation, however, this absence would not tell us whether both hypotheses are false or only one of them (and which one) is.

In addition to the main prediction, I make a secondary one: assuming that more redundant grammemes will tend to become less frequent, and more functional grammemes will tend to become more frequent, we can expect that the functionality of grammemes in Proto-Slavic should serve as a good predictor of their frequency in modern Russian. I will test this prediction as well, though the possibilities for this test offered by the current study are limited. In addition, the prediction itself relies on stronger assumptions (redundancy is not necessarily the only, nor even the most important predictor of frequency).

3 From Proto-Slavic to Russian

In this section, I briefly describe the relevant morphological changes that occurred in the period from Proto-Slavic (alias Common Slavic, a reconstructed protolanguage that existed approx. from the 5th to 9th centuries AD) to Contemporary Standard Russian (CSR). Old Church Slavonic is used as a proxy for Proto-Slavic (see section 4.1).

CSR has been chosen for the pilot study for the following reasons. First, Russian is the largest Slavic language with a total of about 166 million speakers (Lewis et al., 2015). Second, its contact with other languages has been quite intense. Bentz and Winter (2013) use 42% as an estimate for the ratio of L2 speakers to the number of all speakers of CSR (their absolute estimate is 110 million). According to the linguistic complexity theories cited in section 1, these factors make pressure towards simplification stronger, i.e. redundant morphological features are more likely to be lost.

Russian has not lost any Proto-Slavic morphological category completely, though many have been very significantly restructured. Some grammemes, however, did disappear.

Proto-Slavic had seven nominal cases: **n**ominative, **a**ccusative, **g**enitive, **d**ative, **i**nstrumental, **l**ocative and **v**ocative. Russian has preserved the former six, but lost the vocative and is now using the nominative in its place. It should be noted that some scholars do not consider the vocative a real *case* (Andersen, 2012: 139–143). In addition, the vocative was relatively infrequent, and often coincided with the nominative already in Proto-Slavic. Still, there is a clear distinction between Proto-Slavic (where a separate obligatory vocative form existed) and CSR (where there is no such form). The fact that CSR developed several novel marginal cases, including the so-called "new vocative", does not affect the general picture in any relevant way.

Proto-Slavic had three numbers: **s**ingular, **d**ual and **p**lural, of which the dual is not present in CSR: the plural is used instead (the dual, however, left visible traces in the morphosyntax of the numerals and the formation of plural forms).

Proto-Slavic had five basic verbal tenses: present (also called *non-past*), aorist, imperfect, perfect and pluperfect.[1] The perfect and pluperfect were analytical forms, consisting of resp. present and imperfect[2] forms of an auxiliary ('be') and a so-called resultative participle. Later, the aorist, imperfect and pluperfect went out of use, while the former perfect gradually lost the auxiliary verb. As a result, in CSR the only means to express indicative past tense is the former resultative, which has lost most of its participial features and is treated on a par with other finite forms. In the current study, I will consider four morphologically distinct tenses: **p**resent, **a**orist, **i**mperfect and re**s**ultative. The label "resultative" will cover all uses of the resultative participle, both in the perfect and pluperfect, both with and without an auxiliary. Non-indicative verbal forms (except for the resultative) will be ignored (i.e. the present and past tense of participles, imperatives, infinitives and subjunctive). To sum up: we will focus on the four tenses listed above, of which two (aorist and imperfect) disappeared, replaced by the resultative.

Finally, a Proto-Slavic verbal grammeme called supine also disappeared, but it will ignored in the current study, partly since its frequency in Old Church Slavonic is very low, partly since it is not entirely clear what grammatical category it belongs to.

4 Materials and methods

4.1 Language data

The oldest Slavic manuscripts were written in Old Church Slavonic (OCS), a literary language based on a South Slavic dialect of late Proto-Slavic. OCS is not a direct precursor of CSR (nor of any other modern Slavic language), but it is the best available proxy for Proto-Slavic, and is commonly used in this role.

4.2 Treebank and parser

I extracted OCS data from the Tromsø Old Russian and OCS Treebank,[3] limiting myself to one document, the Codex Marianus, which has been thoroughly proofread and submitted to compre-

[1] The verb 'be' also has a separate synthetic future tense, which is ignored here.

[2] Sometimes also aorist or perfect.

[3] https://nestor.uit.no/

hensive consistency checks (Berdicevskis and Eckhoff, 2015). The Codex Marianus is dated to the beginning of the 11th century. The TOROT file contains 6350 annotated sentences.

The TOROT is a dependency treebank with morphological and syntactic annotation in the PROIEL scheme (Haug, 2010, Haug et al., 2009). For the purposes of the experiment, I converted the native PROIEL format to the CONLL format (see Table 1).

For the parsing experimens I used MaltParser (Nivre et al., 2007), version 1.8.1.[4] The Codex Marianus was split into a training set (first 80% of sentences) and a test set (last 20% of sentences). The parser was optimized on the training set using MaltOptimizer (Ballesteros and Nivre, 2012), version 1.0.3.[5] Optimization had been performed before any grammemes were merged or any morphological information was deleted (see section 4.3).

Parsing the TOROT with MaltParser faces several difficulties. First, the PROIEL scheme uses secondary dependencies – for external subjects in control and raising structures, and also to indicate shared arguments and predicate identity. Since MaltParser cannot handle secondary dependencies, all this information was omitted. Second, the PROIEL scheme also systematically uses empty verb and conjunction nodes to account for ellipsis, gapping and asyndetic coordination. Since MaltParser cannot insert empty nodes, they were explicitly marked in both the training and test sets (with form and lemma having the value *empty*; part-of-speech marked as resp. verb or conjunction, and morphological features having the value *INFLn* 'non-inflecting', see Table 1, token 14).

The LAS (labelled attachment score) for parsing the test set was 0.783. Parsing took place before merging grammemes, but after removing person and gender information from verbs (see section 4.3).

4.3 Merging grammemes

When linguists say that a grammeme *disappeared*, they usually mean that the grammeme merged with another one, or that another grammeme expanded its functions, replacing the one that *disappeared*. As described in section 3, disappearances that occurred in the (pre)history of Russian were actually mergers: vocative > nominative; dual > plural; aorist and imperfect > resultative.

I will illustrate how I model grammeme mergers using the example of the number category. The category has three values: **s**ingular, **p**lural, and **d**ual, their absolute frequencies in the Codex Marianus are resp. 28004, 10321 and 942. Every grammeme is consecutively merged with the other grammemes in the same category. When, for instance, the s>p merger takes place, the string *NUMBs* in the FEATURE column (see Table 1) is replaced with *NUMBp* (see below about the number of occurrences that are replaced). After that, the original values are restored, and s>d merger follows: *NUMBs* is being replaced with *NUMBd*. Later, p>s, p>d, d>s and d>p mergers take place in the same way.

After every merger, the Codex Marianus is split into the same training and test sets, and parsed anew, using the same optimization settings. The difference between the original LAS and the resulting LAS (delta) shows how strongly the merger affected parser performance. For every grammeme, the sum of deltas for all its mergers (for s, that would be the sum of deltas for the mergers s>p, s>d) is taken as a measure of its functionality, or non-redundancy. The higher this number is, the more important the grammeme is for parser, and the less redundant it is.

The frequency of grammemes can vary greatly, as the number category illustrates. It can be expected that if we always merge all the occurrences of every grammeme, then the deltas will tend to be higher for more frequent grammemes, because the larger number of occurrences is affected. On the one hand, frequency is an important objective property of any linguistic item, and it is legitimate to take it into account when estimating redundancy and functionality. On the other hand, very high frequencies can skew the results, making the functionality estimate a mere correlate of frequency, which is undesirable. In order to test whether redundancy/functionality is a useful measure, we need to disentangle it from potential confounding factors. To address this issue, the experiment was run in two conditions.

In condition 1, all occurrences of every grammeme are merged (that is, the s>d merger results in 28946 *NUMBd* strings and 0 *NUMBs* strings, while the d>s merger results in 28946 *NUMBs* strings and 0 *NUMBd* strings). It is reasonable to expect that this condition will have a bias for more frequent grammemes: they will get higher functionality scores.

[4] http://www.maltparser.org/

[5] http://nil.fdi.ucm.es/maltoptimizer/index.html

1	2	3	4	5	6	7	8
1	i *and*	i	C	C-	INFLn	10	aux
2	aŝe *if*	aŝe	G	G-	INFLn	10	adv
3	k″to *anyone*	k″to	P	Px	NUMBs|GENDq|CASEn	4	sub
4	poimet″ *forces*	pojati	V	V-	NUMBs|TENSp|MOODi|VOICa	2	pred
5	tja *you*	tja	P	Pp	PERS2|NUMBs|GENDq|CASEa	4	obj
6	po *by*	po	R	R-	INFLn	4	adv
7	silě *force*	sila	N	Nb	NUMBs|GENDf|CASEd	6	obl
8	pop′riŝe *mile*	pop′riŝe	N	Nb	NUMBs|GENDn|CASEa	14	adv
9	edino *one*	edino	M	Ma	NUMBs|GENDn|CASEa	8	atr
10	idi *go*	iti	V	V-	PERS2|NUMBs|TENSp|MOODm|VOICa	0	pred
11	s″ *with*	s″	R	R-	INFLn	10	obl
12	nim′ *him*	i	P	Pp	PERS3|NUMBs|GENDm|CASEi	11	obl
13	d′vě *two*	d″va	M	Ma	NUMBd|GENDn|CASEa	10	adv
14	empty *(go)*	empty	V	V-	INFLn	4	xobj

Table 1. Example sentence (Matthew 5:41, 'If anyone forces you to go one mile, go with them two miles') from the Codex Marianus in the PROIEL scheme and CONLL format. OCS words are transliterated using the ISO 9 system (with some simplifications). Columns: 1 = token ID; 2 = form; 3 = lemma; 4 = coarse-grained POS tag; 5 = fine-grained POS tag; 6 = features; 7 = head; 8 = dependency relation. For the reader's convenience, an English gloss is added under every form (in italics). Note the absence of the *PERS3* feature for token 4. While it had originally been there, it was removed in order to facilitate the mergers of indicative and participial forms (see main text). It is, however, kept for those verb forms which will not be affected by any mergers (e.g. token 10, which is in the imperative).

In condition 2, the number of merged occurrences is *constant for all grammemes* in the category, and equal to *the frequency of the least frequent grammeme*. For number, that would be dual with its frequency of 942. Here, the s>d merger results in 1884 *NUMBd* strings (942 original + 942 merged) and 27062 *NUMBs* strings (28004 original - 942 merged), while the d>s merger results in 28946 *NUMBs* strings (28004 original + 942 merged) and 0 *NUMBd* strings (942 original - 942 merged). This condition can potentially create a bias for less frequent grammemes: while the absolute number of the affected occurrences is always the same, their share in the total occurrences of the grammeme that is being merged can be very different. The d>s merger, for instance, empties the dual grammeme fully, while the s>d merger removes only a small share of the singular occurrences. This potential bias can, however, be expected to be weaker than the reverse bias in condition 1, and the results can then be expected to be more reliable.

The occurrences to be merged are selected randomly. Since the resulting change in parser performance may depend on the sample of selected occurrences, the process is repeated 10 times on 10 random samples, and the average of 10 functionalities is taken as the final measure.

Note that in both conditions, mergers always affect two grammemes: the source (i.e. the one that is being merged) and the target one. However, I consider only the former effect and ignore the latter: for instance, the change of LAS after s>d merger is added to the functionality of s, but not of d. Technically, it is possible to take into account the respective delta when calculating the functionality of d, too, but it is not quite clear whether this is theoretically justified. The rationale behind adding the delta to the functionality of s is that s has been (partially) removed, and we are investigating how this removal affected the possibility to restore syntactic information. No instances of the target value, however, have been removed, and while the grammeme has been somewhat changed by its expansion, it is not clear how to interpret this change. Besides, I assume that the influence of the expansion of the target grammeme is small (compared to that of the removal of the source one) and ignore it in the current study.

Case is processed in exactly the same way as number (each case is consecutively merged with the six others), but tense represents an additional substantial problem. Remember that the present, imperfect and aorist are typical finite forms, which means that they have the features person, number, tense, mood (the value is always **i**ndicative) and voice, while the resultative is a participle (the mood[6] value is always **p**articiple), and does not have the feature person, but does have the features gender, case and strength.[7] By the OCS period, however, the resultative has already lost most of its original participial properties, and case is always nominative, while strength is always **s**trong. The problem is that when we merge, for instance, the present with the resultative, we have a feature mismatch: the present has one extra feature (person) that the resultative never has, but lacks the three other features (gender, case, strength); in addition, the mood feature is different. Obviously, the merger in the other direction faces the inverse obstacle.

I solve this problem in the following way. Since there is no means to reconstruct information about person when merging resultative to the three indicative tenses and no means to reconstruct information about gender when merging in the other direction, I remove person and gender features from all relevant verbal forms. This is done prior to any other operations. The initial LAS (0.783) is calculated after this removal. Without it, LAS would have been 0.785. When a resultative > {present | aorist | imperfect} merger occurs, information about case and strength is removed, and mood is changed from **p** to **i**. When a merger in the other direction occurs, information about case and strength is added (resp. **n** and **s**), and mood is changed from **i** to **p**. While these changes are pretty artificial, they do ensure that we perform a full merger that affects all relevant properties of a grammeme, and not only changes its label.

5 Results

Results of the experiment for both conditions are presented in Table 2. Grammemes within each category are first sorted in descending order by their functionality in the condition 2 (which is supposed to be a more reliable measure), then by their functionality in condition 1.

Zero values for vocative in columns 3 and 4 do not mean that merging vocative with other cases never affects the parser performance at all, but that the changes are negligibly small, represented as 0 after rounding to three decimal places. Negative functionality values (for number grammemes) mean that merging this grammeme with others on average leads to *increase* of the LAS, not decrease. These results can be interpreted in the same way as positive and zero values: lower functionality (which in this case means larger increase in parsing accuracy) implies higher redundancy (so high that its removal facilitates the restoration of the syntactic structure instead of inhibiting it).

Absolute frequencies of every grammeme are provided for OCS (the Codex Marianus) and CSR. The CSR frequencies were calculated using the manually disambiguated part (≈6 million words) of the Russian National Corpus[8] (RNC). While it is known that ranking the CSR grammemes by frequency may sometimes provide different results depending on the chosen corpus (Kopotev 2008), the general picture can be assumed to be adequate and stable, since the RNC is a relatively large and well-balanced corpus.

6 Discussion

As can be seen, in both conditions the vocative gets identified as the most redundant case. This fits nicely with the fact that CSR lost it, while preserving the other six cases.

[6] The mood category in the PROIEL scheme for OCS has broader coverage than the traditional mood category. It has the grammemes indicative, imperative, subjunctive, infinitive, participle, gerund and supine (i.e. covers both mood and finiteness).

[7] Strength here refers to the distinction between long and short forms of Slavic adjectives and participles, remotely similar to the Germanic distinction between weak and strong adjectives.

[8] http://ruscorpora.ru/

Category	Grammeme	Functionality (condition 1)	Functionality (condition 2)	Frequency (OCS)	Frequency (CSR)
CASE	n	0.039	0.009	9812	1026131
	g	0.017	0.008	4470	731435
	a	0.017	0.006	7657	539768
	d	0.006	0.004	3694	180131
	l	0.008	0.001	1671	265701
	i	0.005	0.001	1050	271531
	v	0	0	400	0
NUMBER	s	-0.004	0	28004	2861455
	p	-0.004	-0.001	10321	886420
	d	-0.002	-0.002	942	0
TENSE	s	0.009	0.009	199	458820
	p	0.009	0.001	4452	231946
	a	0.007	0.001	3772	0
	i	0.003	0.001	1121	0

Table 2. Results of the merging experiment for the two conditions.

Moreover, most modern Indo-European languages have lost the original Proto-Indo-European vocative. Most Slavic languages, however, have retained it. Outliers here are Bulgarian and Macedonian, which have lost all the cases but the vocative. These two Slavic languages, however, are exceptional in many respects (possibly due to the influence of the Balkan Sprachbund).

Importantly, the functionality ranking of cases does not seem to be a mere reflection of their frequency ranking in OCS. In condition 1, the genitive and the accusative[9] have the same functionality (while the accusative is noticeably more frequent), and the dative is less functional than the locative, while being more frequent). In condition 2, the genitive is more functional than the accusative, despite lower frequency.

As regards the second prediction, functionality scores do turn out to be a good predictor for CSR frequency. Pearson correlation coefficients[10] are 0.96 ($p < 0.001$) in condition 1, and 0.92 ($p = 0.004$) in condition 2. Importantly, in both conditions functionality is a better predictor than plain OCS frequency. The Pearson coefficient for the OCS and CSR frequencies is 0.86 ($p = 0.012$).

Absolute differences between the functionality of cases are larger in condition 1, which can probably be explained by a frequency effect.

For number, the situation is different. In condition 2, the singular gets the highest functionality score and the dual the lowest, which again fits with the historical development of the Slavic languages: all except Slovene and Sorbian have lost the dual form (the same holds for most other Indo-European languages). In condition 1, however, the results are opposite: the dual is the most functional grammeme, while the singular and the plural are the most redundant ones.

Functionality is a poor predictor for CSR frequency in condition 1 ($r = -0.73$, $p = 0.471$). It is better correlated (though still insignificant) in condition 2 ($r = 0.98$, $p = 0.14$), but loses out to OCS frequency ($r = 1$, $p = 0.026$). The extremely small sample size, however, makes the Pearson test unreliable.

Within the tense category, the resultative is at the most functional end of the scale, while the aorist and the imperfective are at the least functional end in both conditions. The absolute values, however, differ, as does the position of the present: in condition 1, it has the same value as the resultative (slightly higher than the aorist), whereas in condition 2, its functionality is equal to that of the aorist and the imperfect. Importantly, the least frequent tense (the resultative) gets the highest functionality score in both conditions.

For tense, OCS frequency is the worst predictor of CSR frequency ($r = -0.39$, $p = 0.611$). Functionality has larger coefficients and smaller p-values, though they do not reach significance (in condition 1 $r = -0.74$, $p = 0.259$; in condi-

[9] Both in OCS and CSR the accusative case of some animate nouns is identical to the genitive. In the TOROT, these genitive-accusatives are annotated as genitives. For consistency's sake, I coded them as genitives when calculating the CSR frequencies as well.

[10] It can be questioned whether it is legitimate to use Pearson product-moment correlation, or a non-parametric method like Spearman rank correlation should be preferred. Given that the data are on the interval scale and that they answer the Shapiro-Wilk normality criterion, I opt for Pearson.

tion 2 $r = -0.87$, $p = 0.132$). Again, small sample size prevents any definitive conclusions.

It is not quite clear why the present scores so low in the condition 2: it is frequent enough, it has survived in all Slavic languages, and can be expected to be quite functional. It can be a consequence of the complicated corrections that were performed to compensate for the morphological mismatch between participle and indicative (see section 4.3).

It is remarkable that the two tenses that get the lowest scores in both conditions are those that have disappeared in CSR: the aorist and the imperfect. They have not survived in other Slavic languages either, with the exception of Bulgarian, Macedonian and partly Bosnian-Serbo-Croatian, where its use is restricted to certain genres and dialects (Dahl 2000: 101). The decline of the imperfect usually happens before the decline of the aorist in Slavic languages (including the East Slavic group, to which the CSR belongs), and, remarkably, the imperfect gets lower functionality score in condition 1.

The difference between the scores of the most and the least functional grammemes is largest for case and lowest for number in both conditions. This fits with the functionality values of the categories themselves measured in a separate experiment, where the changes of LAS were measured after deleting all information about a particular category (for instance, removing all strings *NUMBs*, *NUMBd* and *NUMBp* from the FEATURE column). Case turned out to be the most functional category (0.030), which is unsurprising, given that cases are typically assumed to mark the syntactic role of an argument in a sentence, and hence can be expected to be crucial for the reconstruction of the syntactic structure. Tense got second place (0.014) and all other categories scored noticeably lower, from 0.004 to 0 (for number the value is 0.003). This difference can account for the contradictory results that the two conditions return for number: given that the total functionality of the category (from parser's perspective) is relatively small, the proposed method can be less sensitive to real performance changes caused by mergers and more vulnerable to random fluctuations.

7 Conclusion

While the results vary across categories and conditions, the general trend is quite clear: grammemes that did disappear in the course of language history tend to get lowest functionality scores in the present case study, in other words, the main prediction holds. If we follow the assumption that the most redundant morphological features tend to disappear first, especially under conditions that facilitate morphological simplification (see section 1), then the results confirm the validity of the proposed method.

The secondary prediction holds for case grammemes, where functionality allows to make better predictions about the frequencies that the grammemes will have after almost a thousand years than plain frequency. It does not hold for number and tense, but small sample sizes (i.e. the number of grammemes within a given category) can be the reason.

The fact that the functionality scores for case correlated with the CSR frequencies suggests that the method can predict grammeme development, at least in some cases. It seems to be able to capture the "functional potential" of a grammeme, which can influence its frequency in the future: the lower it is, the more likely the frequency is to decrease. However, given the small differences in correlation coefficients, the small number of datapoints and the problematic situation with number and tense, the support for this hypothesis at the moment is rather weak.

It is not quite clear which of the two conditions gives better predictions. It is possible that the best way to calculate functionality is to combine the results of both conditions in some way. The method should be tested on larger language samples in order to solve this and other potential issues and find its strengths and limitations. One immediate development of this study would be to take into account *all* modern Slavic languages to find out how likely a given Proto-Slavic grammeme (or category) was to disappear or to stay. Intermediate language stages (Old Russian, Old Bulgarian etc.) can, of course, also be considered. Given that some amount of noise (for instance, peculiarities of a specific treebank, specific document or a chosen parser) will always affect the performance of the method, larger language samples can also lead to more stable and more interpretable results.

Looking from another perspective, this study is an attempt to model how human speakers process linguistic information and which features are least informative for them. While the processing itself is not expected to be entirely isomorphic to what happens in a human mind (and the model in general is somewhat of a black box, unless we use a fully deterministic parser), the output gives us some information about human cognition and existing learning and usage biases.

The method can be applied not only to language change or older stages of language, but also to modern languages, and the results can be tested against existing psycholinguistic or typological evidence about redundancy.

Obviously, it is necessary to test how robust the results are with respect to the choice of the parser, annotation scheme, merging procedures and languages.

The results can have some practical value, too, as they provide information about which features are most and least useful for parsers.

Acknowledgments

I am grateful to Hanne Eckhoff, Laura Janda and three anonymous reviewers for their valuable comments, and to Ilya German for technical assistance. This work has been supported by the Norwegian Research Council grant 222506.

References

Henning Andersen. 2012. The New Russian Vocative: Synchrony, Diachrony, Typology. *Scando-Slavica*, 58(1):122–167.

Miguel Ballesteros and Joakim Nivre. 2012. MaltOptimizer: A System for MaltParser Optimization. *Proceedings of the Eighth International Conference on Language Resources and Evaluation (LREC), Istanbul, Turkey, 23–27 May 2012*. European Language Resources Association.

Christian Bentz and Bodo Winter. 2013. Languages with More Second Language Learners Tend to Lose Nominal Case. *Language Dynamics and Change*, 3:1–27.

Aleksandrs Berdicevskis and Hanne Eckhoff. 2015. Automatic identification of shared arguments in verbal coordinations. *Computational linguistics and intellectual technologies. Papers from the annual international conference "Dialogue"*, 14:33–43.

Gabriela Caballero and Vsevolod Kapatsinski. 2014. Perceptual functionality of morphological redundancy in Choguita Rarámuri (Tarahumara). *Language, Cognition and Neuroscience*, DOI: 10.1080/23273798.2014.940983

Östen Dahl (ed.) 2000. *Tense and Aspect in the Languages of Europe*. Mouton de Gruyter, Berlin, Germany.

Östen Dahl. 2004. *The growth and maintenance of linguistic complexity*. John Benjamins, Amsterdam, The Netherlands.

Nicolas Fay and T. Mark Ellison. 2013. The cultural evolution of human communication systems in different sized populations: usability trumps learnability. *PLoS ONE* 8(8):e71781.

Dag Haug. 2010. PROIEL guidelines for annotation. http://folk.uio.no/daghaug/syntactic_guidelines.pdf

Dag Haug, Marius Jøhndal, Hanne Eckhoff, Eirik Welo, Mari Hertzenberg and Angelika Müth. 2009. Computational and Linguistic Issues in Designing a Syntactically Annotated Parallel Corpus of Indo-European Languages. *Traitement Automatique des Langues* 50(2):17–45.

Simon Kirby, Mike Dowman and Thomas L. Griffiths. 2007. Innateness and culture in the evolution of language. *Proceedings of the National Academy of Sciences* 104(12):5241–5245.

Mikhail Kopotev. 2008. K postroeniju chastotnoj grammatiki russkogo jazyka: padezhnaja sistema po korpusnym dannym. *Slavica Helsingiensia* 34:136–151.

M. Paul Lewis, Gary F. Simons and Charles D. Fennig (eds.). 2015. *Ethnologue: Languages of the World, Eighteenth edition*. SIL International, Dallas, Texas.
Online version: http://www.ethnologue.com.

Gary Lupyan and Rick Dale. 2010. Language structure is partly determined by social structure. *PLoS ONE* 5(1):e8559.

Daniel Nettle. 2012. Social scale and structural complexity in human languages. *Phil. Trans. R. Soc. B* 367:1829–1836.

Joakim Nivre, Johan Hall, Jens Nilsson, Atanas Chanev, Gülşen Eryigit, Sandra Kübler, Svetoslav Marinov and Erwin Marsi. 2007. MaltParser: A language-independent system for data-driven dependency parsing. *Natural Language Engineering* 13(2):95–135.

Florencia Reali and Thomas L. Griffiths. 2009. The evolution of frequency distributions: Relating regularization to inductive biases through iterated learning. *Cognition* 111:317–328.

Geoffrey Sampson, David Gil and Peter Trudgill (eds.) 2009. *Language complexity as an evolving variable*. Oxford University Press, Oxford, UK.

Kenny Smith and Elizabeth Wonnacott. 2010. Eliminating unpredictable variation through iterated learning. *Cognition* 116:444–449.

Peter Trudgill. 2011. *Sociolinguistic typology: social determinants of linguistic complexity*. Oxford University Press, Oxford, UK.

Improving Coordination on Novel Meaning through Context and Semantic Structure

Thomas Brochhagen
Institute for Logic, Language and Computation
University of Amsterdam
P.O. Box 94242, 1090GE Amsterdam, The Netherlands
t.s.brochhagen@uva.nl

Abstract

Meaning conveyance is bottlenecked by the linguistic conventions shared among interlocutors. One possibility to convey non-conventionalized meaning is to employ known expressions in such a way that the intended meaning can be abduced from them. This, in turn, can give rise to ambiguity. We investigate this process with a focus on its use for semantic coordination and show it to be conducive to fast agreement on novel meaning under a mutual expectation to exploit semantic structure. We argue this to be a motivation for the cross-linguistic pervasiveness of systematic ambiguity.

1 Introduction

Semantic heterogeneity is an inherent aspect of human communication. Nevertheless, successful communication relies on mutual intelligibility. That is, an expression's meaning has to be assumed to be jointly known, or at least be abducible provided other information. Here, the latter communication strategy is addressed. In particular, we focus on the repurposing of an expression to convey novel meaning, derived from the expression's conventional meaning and the context it appears in.[1] As a consequence, single forms may come to be associated with multiple meanings.

We argue such repurposing motivated ambiguity to be driven by two main forces: the predictive power of semantic structure and potential for confounding. On the one hand, using the same expression to convey similar yet non-identical meanings in different contexts allows for the interpretation of one in terms of the other, modulo context. On the other hand, if the contexts these meanings appear in are either too similar, or too dissimilar, the intended interpretation may fail, leading to suboptimal communication.

Ambiguity in cooperative communication has been argued to be motivated by effort and cost minimization. Santana (2014) shows that ambiguity is evolutionarily advantageous when disambiguating contexts are available and cost is associated with a larger vocabulary size. In a similar spirit, Piantadosi et al. (2012) argue ambiguity to enable a reuse of forms that are easy to produce and comprehend (for example, shorter, phonotactically unmarked, expressions). Thus, according to this view, ambiguity's advantage mainly lies in effort reduction in production while safeguarding comprehension through contextual information.

More generally, the argument is that if context is (at least partially) shared, informative, and cheap, less information needs to be carried by signals. Following Piantadosi et al. this can readily be illustrated by comparing the amount of information required to disambiguate a meaning $t \in T$ with and without context K using Shannon entropy (Shannon, 1948). If K is informative about T, then $H(T) > H(T|K)$. That is, context can alleviate the need for distinct forms for distinct meanings. However, this ignores the subtler issue of how the information of K relates to that of T. In structured domains not all elements are equal: similarity can introduce noise to meaning discriminability or, conversely, emphasize the contrast between dissimilar meanings. Crucially, there are many alternatives ranging from inefficient to efficient contextual exploitation. In turn, this depends on the meaning-form associations of a language and their relation to the contexts they appear in. Other things being equal, an ambiguous language that colexicalizes contextually distinguishable meanings will be more effi-

[1] In the following, context is construed broadly as any source of information beyond an expression's literal meaning. It is understood as a condensed prior of the association strength with which an interpretation comes to mind (Franke, 2009).

Proceedings of the Sixth Workshop on Cognitive Aspects of Computational Language Learning, pages 74–82,
Lisbon, Portugal, 18 September 2015.

cient, compression-wise, than one that colexicalizes contextually indistinguishable ones.

The tacit prediction of past research is that languages maximize the utility of ambiguity when colexicalizing meanings that appear in contexts as distinct as necessary to avoid misunderstanding. Thus, if compression and ease of transmission are ambiguity's main driving force, it is not expected for related meanings to be expressed by a single form, as this could make them more prone to be confused. In the following, we argue that ambiguity also has motivations at the semantics-pragmatics interface, where interlocutors may exploit semantic structure to coordinate on novel meaning.

2 Regularities in semantic structure and their relation to context

Assessing the relation between novel meaning, conventional meaning, and the contexts they appear in, presents many difficulties. We begin by considering already conventionalized ambiguous expressions as a proxy for form coexistence of distinct meanings. We do this to support two claims. First, that (at least) some cases of ambiguity in natural language are motivated by semantic relatedness (Apresjan, 1974; Nunberg, 1979; Pustejovsky, 1995).[2] Second, that context and semantic relatedness interact. An in-depth discussion of either claim is outside the scope of the present contribution. However, albeit often presupposed and of certain intuitive appeal, it should be stressed that neither is innocuous.

Semantic relatedness. First evidence for semantic regularities in ambiguity comes from the wide range of genealogically unrelated languages that colexify the same meaning pairs. For instance, the CLiCS corpus (List et al., 2014) lists 297 English noun pairs whose meaning is expressed by a single form in at least 10 languages from three or more language families. For example, 106 languages from 40 families express 'flesh' and 'meat' by a single form. Such cross-linguistic regularities are not expected should an expression's form be ambiguity's main driving force. On a more general level, a number of systematic meaning alternations, such as producer-product, as in *Rembrandt*, or material-artifact, as in *glass*, have also been attested across multiple languages (Srinivasan and Rabagliati, 2015), although with notably less cross-linguistic coverage.

[2]A more differentiated classification of ambiguity is not required for the present purpose. Thus, we purposefully avoid referring to polysemy, metonomy, or metaphor explicitly.

Furthermore, a body of experimental evidence suggests that the processing of forms that conflate related meanings is distinct from that of unrelated ones (for an overview see Simpson (1984) and Eddington and Tokowicz (2015)). More specifically, semantic relatedness is generally judged as facilitatory for semantic access in comparison to both monosemous and homonymous expressions.

The experiments of Rodd et al. (2012) on the acquisition of novel meaning through the use of forms already associated with conventional meaning are of particular relevance for the claim that reuse of semantic material is conducive to agreement on non-conventionalized meaning. Their results suggest that non-conventionalized meanings are recalled better if they are related to the conventional meaning of a known expression. Similarly, in lexical decision tasks, subjects exhibited increased performance for novel ambiguous words with related meanings but not for unrelated ones. More generally, Srinivasan and Snedeker (2011) show that four-year olds generalize semantic alternations of ambiguous expressions to novel monosemous forms that lexicalize a meaning participating in such alternations. In other words, human interlocutors appear to expect semantic relations to be exploited and generalize known alternations.

Context, disambiguation, and prediction. Contextual information not only has a facilitatory effect on the interpretation of ambiguous expressions (Frazier and Rayner, 1990; Klepousniotou and Baum, 2007). It can furthermore be employed to predict the number of distinct meanings a form has (Hoffman et al., 2013). In particular, distributional semantic models have been shown to provide well-performing context-dependent vectorial representations for the meanings of ambiguous expressions by clustering an expression's co-occurrence counts. Using such methodology, Reisinger and Mooney (2010) found a negative correlation between the variance of cluster similarities and that of human sense annotations: The more similar co-occurrence clusters of an ambiguous form were, the less human raters agreed on their distinct meanings, suggesting an inverse relationship between distributional similarity and semantic discriminability. Boleda et al. (2012) show how distributional models can be used to predict regular meaning alternations for novel words. Here, the similarity of a form's co-occurrence vector to the centroid of two alternation's representations is used to assess whether the form participates in the alternation. As above, this research provides some support to the idea that natural languages do not solely maximize contextual contrast between meanings but that there are regularities between semantic relations and context, reflected in regular colexification patterns.

3 Improving coordination

Taken together, the preceding survey provides indirect evidence for the claim that semantic relatedness plays a role for (at least some types of) ambiguity, as well as for an interplay between interpretation, context, and meaning-multiplicity. In the following, we show that a joint expectation to exploit semantic relations and context leads to improved coordination on novel meaning.

We assume the information provided by context to be shared and noiseless, i.e. interlocutors have access to the same contextual information.[3] Furthermore, we restrict our analysis to cooperative communication. As a consequence, context is taken to be informative about a speaker's intended meaning. The set of meanings compatible with a context k_i, the support of the meaning distribution conditioned on k_i, is denoted by $K_i^\star$, $K_i^\star := \{t|p(t|k_i) > 0\}$. As we are interested in novel use of conventionalized expressions, a fixed message inventory M is considered, where $p(t|m, k_i) = 1$ for exactly one $m \in M$ provided that $t \in K_i^\star$. That is, the messages in M are already conventionally associated with some meanings, guaranteeing communicative success for those meanings. $I(m)$ is the conventional interpretation of a message, $I(m) := \arg\max_t p(t|m, K)$.[4]

So far, when communicating about conventional meaning, interlocutors need not make use of contextual information. Things are different, however, when conveying novel meaning. In such cases, the best a receiver can do is to guess intended t based on the contextual information provided; $p(t|m, k_i) \propto p(t|k_i)$ if $I(m) \notin K_i^\star$. That is, if a message's conventional meaning is ruled out, the best a literal receiver can do is to interpret based on the contextually conditioned meaning distribution. We refer to this communicative strategy as S_l.

Languages that enable strategies akin to S_l are at the stage at which Santana (2014) and Piantadosi et al. (2012) predict ambiguity to be advantageous: whenever T can be partitioned to allow a message to be associated with two contextually disjoint meanings. However, this sidesteps the ad hoc interpretation of such 'surprise' messages in a conventionally incongruent context, as well as the regularities surveyed above. Particularly, it's unclear how meaning can come to be associated with disjoint contexts and whether there are ways to improve this process beyond best guesses.

Under the assumption that there are regularities interlocutors may exploit them to coordinate. The conventional meaning associated with a message can be repurposed in such a way that, in unison with context, a receiver can abduce the intended non-conventional meaning. In accord with the preceding discussion, we assume two factors to play a key role in this process: the relation between the conventionalized and non-conventionalized meanings, as well the information context provides about them. The former indicates the ease to predict or derive one meaning from the other. The latter is a factor for potential equivocation. We call this strategy S_m.

The above can be summarized as follows: Given a context k_i, a meaning to convey t, and a message m, if $I(m) \in K_i^\star$ and $I(m) = t$, then

$$p(t|m, k_i) = 1 \quad (1)$$

If $I(m) \notin K_i^\star$, then

$$p(t|m, k_i) \propto w_1 p(t|R(I(m), t)) + w_2 p(t|k_i) \quad (2)$$

where $R(x, y)$ stands for a relation between x and y, and w_1 and w_2 are weights, $w_1 + w_2 = 1$. The weights control how much import relations have for the non-conventionalized interpretation of a message based on its conventional meaning. S_l corresponds to $w_1 = 0$ and S_m to $w_1 > 0$. Crucially, for a message m, and all meanings t and t' compatible with context k, if $p(t|R(I(m), t)) \geq p(t'|R(I(m), t')) > p(t|k)$, then coordination on t improves for any value of w_1 greater than zero.

[3] This assumption is made mainly for expository convenience. As shown by Juba et al. (2011), ambiguity also provides an efficient solution for uncertainty about the degree to which the contextual prior of interlocutors matches.

[4] The conventional interpretation of a message is, generally speaking, independent of a particular context k_i as long as $I(m) \in K_i^\star$.

Thus, S_m can aid coordination on non-conventionalized meaning if (i) there is a relation that appropriately captures the structure of T, and (ii) interlocutors have a mutual expectation to exploit this relation in both production and comprehension. Put differently, S_m has an advantage over S_l in cases where the relation is more informative about the intended meaning than the meaning distribution conditioned on the context. In all other cases performance depends on the value of the weights and the information provided by context.

3.1 Coordination without prior expectation of a particular relation

Prima facie, the above hinges not only on a mutual expectation to use semantic relations to guide coordination, but on the mutual expectation to exploit a particular relation. To see whether coordination improves without this assumption we compare the performance of S_l and S_m in adaptive two-player Lewisian signaling games.

A Lewisian signaling game (Lewis, 1969), $\langle T, M, A, p^*, u_S, u_R \rangle$, consists of a set of meanings T, signals M, and acts A. p^* is a probability distribution over T, and u_S and u_R are the sender's and receiver's respective utility functions. In cooperative signaling sender and receiver have a joint payoff. Thus, a single utility function u can be considered, $u\colon T \times M \times A \rightarrow \mathbb{R}$. Meanings are assumed to be equiprobable, $p^*(t) = \frac{1}{|T|}$, and for each t_i there is exactly one a_j such that $u(t_i, m, a_j) = 1$ if $i = j$. Otherwise, the players receive no payoff. Note as well that a receiver's correct interpretation of a sender's intended meaning is the sole factor influencing the game's outcome. In this sense, meaning-signal associations are arbitrary.

A game iteration begins with a stochastically determined meaning for the sender to convey. To this end, the sender sends a signal. Upon reception of the signal, the receiver selects an act, which in turn determines the players' payoff. Before interacting, sender and receiver have no, or only a partial set of conventions to draw from. Thus, the players' task is to establish a meaning-signal mapping that maximizes their expected utility, i.e. to establish an efficient communication system. To this end, we adopt a common choice for learning in signaling games; Roth-Erev reinforcement learning (RL) (Roth and Erev, 1995). RL provides a good fit to the behavior of human subjects in comparable tasks (Roth and Erev, 1995; Erev and Roth, 1998; Bruner et al., 2014), is a well-understood learning mechanism, and has convenient convergence properties (Beggs, 2005; Catteeuw and Manderick, 2014). Furthermore, given its simplicity, RL presupposes little sophistication from players.

As with other reinforcement learning algorithms, successful actions in a state of affairs increase a player's propensity for the same action given the same state. More specifically, a player's actions are informed by her accumulated rewards. These are values associated with state-action pairs and represent the success of an action in a given state. In signaling games, states are meanings for the sender and signals for the receiver, and their respective actions are signals and acts. Given a state p, a player will select an action q with a probability proportional to its accumulated rewards, $p(q|p) = \frac{ar(p,q)}{\sum_{q \in Q} ar(p,q)}$. After a game iteration, the accumulated rewards of selected state-action pairs are updated by the players' payoff. As a consequence, a successful meaning-signal-act triple $\langle t_i, m_j, a_k \rangle$ makes a sender more propense to send m_j given t_i in future interactions. Analogously, the receiver is more propense to select a_k given m_j. In this way, players (ideally) learn to communicate efficiently through iterated interactions.

We expand this setup by adding structure to the set of meanings, a set of contexts, as well as two types of players corresponding to S_l and S_m. To add structure, T is modeled as a n-dimensional grid of natural numbers, $T = [o, r]^n$. The relations in T are given by the Manhattan distance between two elements; $R(x, y) := \sum_{i=1}^{n} |x_i - y_i|$. For example, $R((1,1),(3,4)) = 5$. These choices were made to accommodate the simple learning and selection mechanisms of the players. In particular S_l receivers proceed by best guesses and only learn through positive feedback. If T were large or continuous it could take a prohibitive amount of time until the first successful action is performed.

The set of contexts K corresponds to all convex subsets of T. That is, if x and y are elements of a context, then either $R(x, y) = 1$ or there is a third element z in the context such that $R(x, y) = 1$ and $R(y, z) = 1$. Consequently, the information about meaning conveyed by a context can be represented by the points it contains. The more elements a context has, the less informative it is. Two extremes in K are its singletons and the set containing all points in T. The former are contexts where only one meaning is probable and thusly jointly known to be the intended meaning, $p(t|k) = 1$ if $t \in k$ and $|k| = 1$. The latter context is not informative about meaning, $p(t|k) = p(t)$ if $T = k$. More generally, this means that $p(t|k) = \frac{1}{|k|}$ if $t \in k$ and 0 otherwise.

In contrast to classic signaling games, a game iteration now beings with both a meaning to convey, as well as with the determination of a context. While the meaning is a sender's private information, the context is public and shared across all players. In line with the preceding discussion the only restriction we impose is that sampled t has to be an element of sampled k. That is, context never rules out a speaker's intended meaning.

In what follows, we compare the performance of two types of players; S_l and S_m. Both receivers act in accordance to (1) to interpret conventionalized meaning, and (2) for non-conventionalized meaning. They differ in that S_l is given by $w_1 = 0$, whereas S_m corresponds to any value of w_1 greater than zero. The same applies to S_l and S_m senders, mutatis mutandis.

3.2 Simulations

We compare the iterations needed for S_l and S_m players to achieve reasonably efficient communication by means of signals already associated with conventional meaning. Their task is to employ these signals to convey novel meaning. Crucially, players employing S_m begin the game with no bias towards a particular relation to exploit. This means that, while exploration for S_l involves only coordinating on new form-meaning associations, S_m players additionally explore different potential relations.

On the one hand, we expect that once a suitable relation, i.e. one that holds pairwise between all conventionalized and novel meanings, is found, coordination is faster. On the other hand, considering multiple relations, or settling on a relation that does not hold between all pairs, may lead to suboptimal communication and prolong exploration. (Recall that the degree to which relations affect players' choices is controlled by the value of w_1.) Furthermore, it is clear that once a new convention for the (now) ambiguous signals is established, high values of w_1 will interfere with – rather than aid – coordination.

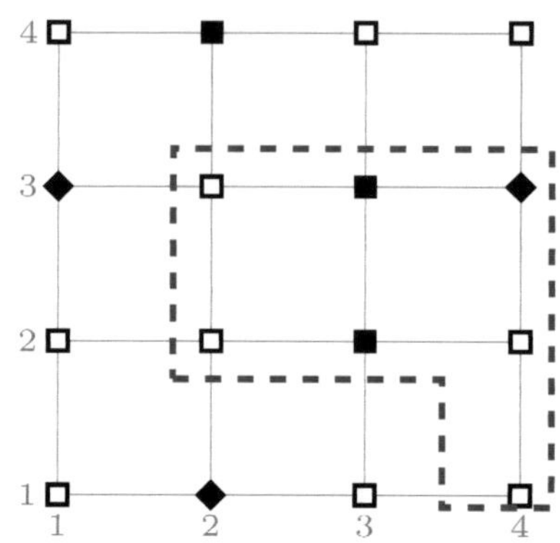

Figure 1: Exemplary instance of an iteration in $[1, 4]^2$. Shapes correspond to meanings. Diamonds are conventionalized and squares are not. Filled out squares are meanings for which players need to establish conventions. The dashed line encloses contextually probable points in this particular iteration.

We compare the effect of different weight values in 100 games of 2000 iterations per value. As mentioned above, $w_1 = 0$ corresponds to S_l. For S_m we consider values for $w_2 \in [.8, .98]$. The set of meanings T is $[1, 4]^2$, yielding 16 potential meanings to choose from, as well as seven distinct relations. Each game is initialized with three randomly sampled meanings taken to be conventionalized and three novel meanings to coordinate on.

The players' performance depends on how many iterations they require to reach an expected utility greater than 0.66 for the latter set of meanings. This corresponds to a better performance than the best suboptimal pooling equilibrium in a signaling game with three meanings, signals, and acts (ignoring the added listener-uncertainty about which three meanings could possibly be intended in the present setup). Reaching this threshold indicates substantial learning as this task is complex for unsophisticated agents. In principle, any element in T could be the intended meaning and learning with RL is slow until at least some successful interactions have transpired. In the worst case, the probability of guessing the right meaning for a receiver using S_l is $\frac{1}{15}$. Figure 1 illustrates an exemplary instance of a single game iteration.

To make the exploitation of relations viable, we ensure that at least one value of the Manhattan distance holds between conventionalized and novel elements. For instance, if points $(1, 3), (2, 1)$ and $(4, 3)$ are conventionalized, and $(3, 3), (3, 2)$ and

w_2	mean	SD	Cohen's d
0.95	792	294	3.34
0.90	1238	286	1.34
0.85	1474	289	0.26
0.80	1569	324	-0.08

Table 1: Iterations needed to reach an expected utility greater than 0.66. Cohen's d indicates the difference to the mean of $w_2 = 1$; 1533 (SD = 140).

w_2	mean	SD	Cohen's d
0.95	0.70	0.047	0.49
0.90	0.64	0.054	1.88
0.85	0.60	0.051	2.69
0.80	0.56	0.061	3.19

Table 2: Expected utility after 2000 iterations. Cohen's d indicates the difference to the mean of $w_2 = 1$; 0.73 (SD = 0.04).

$(2, 4)$ are novel meanings to convey, then a distance of 3 allows for their pairwise association. In general, multiple relations hold between conventionalized and novel elements, allowing for more than one relation to be considered. As a consequence, an advantage of S_m over S_l is not certain.

Results & evaluation. In the following, two results are reported. First, the mean of the iterations both types of signalers needed to reach an expected utility greater than 0.66. Second, their mean expected utility after 2000 iterations, indicating long term effects of different w_1-values.

Detailed excerpts of the results, showcasing general trends and the effect size between values of $w_2 = 1$ (S_l) and $w_2 < 1$ (S_m), are shown in Tables 1 and 2, for iterations required and expected utility after 2000 iterations, respectively. Figures 2 and 3 depict plots for all weight values. In the former figure points below the horizontal uninterrupted line show values for which S_m performed better than S_l. In the latter figure points above this line indicate better performance.

Generally, our expectations were met. The higher w_1, the less efficient a communicative system was after a game's conclusion. However, even with respect to expected utility after 2000 iterations, the mean of S_m players was higher than that of S_l players for low w_1-values. For instance, players with $w_1 = 0.02$ reached a mean of 0.76 (SD = 0.023), which is significantly higher than

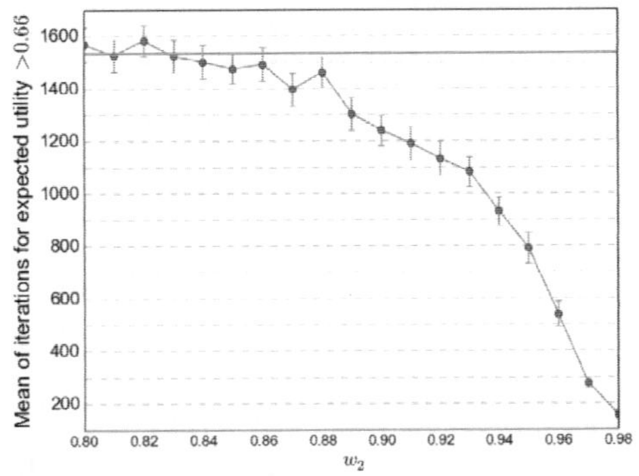

Figure 2: Mean of iterations needed to reach an expected utility greater than 0.66 with 95% confidence intervals. The horizontal uninterrupted line indicates the mean of $w_2 = 1$; 1533 $[1505, 1561]$.

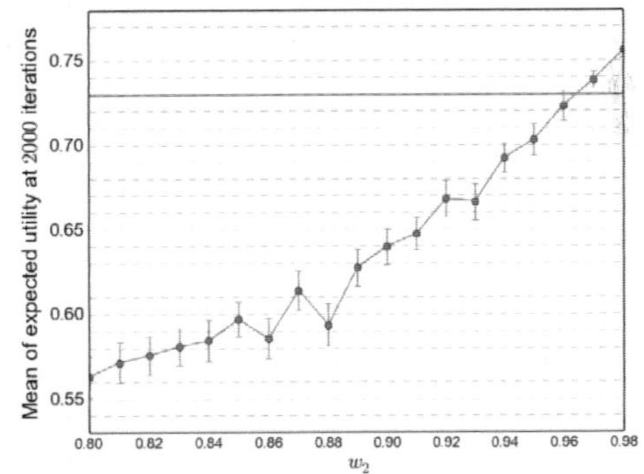

Figure 3: Mean of expected utility after 2000 iterations with 95% confidence intervals. The horizontal uninterrupted line indicates the mean of $w_2 = 1$; 0.73 $[0.717, 0.735]$.

that of $w_1 = 0$ (Cohen's d = -1.11). Crucially, these results show that prior agreement on a single relation is not necessary to uphold the advantage of exploiting semantic relations over best guesses. This is evinced by the range of values that reached the imposed threshold in significantly less iterations than S_l.

In this setup low values of w_1 performed best with respect to learning speed, as well as longer term communicative efficiency. This adds to our previous assumption in that low yet positively valued w_1 improves early exploration without interfering with exploitation. Put differently, a slight bias towards relation exploitation is useful both in short and long term, whereas a major reliance on this mechanism can have negative effects in the long run, at least when multiple relations are viable candidates.

Overall, even when multiple relations are available, S_m can nevertheless be conducive to fast agreement on novel meaning. This, however, comes at a cost when weights are static. After improving the search for novel meaning, high values of w_1 interfere with further interactions. This is due to the present setup allowing for the "right" relation to hold between more than one of the meanings to convey. As a consequence, S_l generally fared better over time.

4 General discussion

To recapitulate, we argued that repurposing expressions in novel contexts improves coordination when interlocutors exploit semantic regularities. Moreover, our simulations show this advantage to hold without prior agreement on a particular as well. The generality of the latter result, however, is constrained by the setup considered. On the one hand, only a small set of meanings and relations was used. Furthermore, simplifying assumptions were made to model context and its relation to meaning. On the other hand, human agents are able to learn and reason about their interlocutors in more sophisticated ways than our agents, and draw from more information sources. Thus, while its relation to natural language structure and reasoning is tentative, on a more general level the present analysis applies to systems where coder and encoder share an expectation to repurpose information through regular means.

Returning to natural language, our argument partially resembles Grice's modified Occam's razor: "senses should not be multiplied beyond necessity" (Grice, 1978). In a nutshell, Grice argues that, should it be predictable that a speaker would use a particular expression to convey something in a given context, then there is no need to assume this to be a separate meaning of the expression. Without dwelling on the issue whether the meanings considered here constitute novel meanings in their own right – as done so far – the crucial point is that exploiting relations enables predictable interpretation-multiplicity. In this sense, players using S_m can be seen as learning to predict and convey meaning based on the structure of semantic space.

Having a way to predict interpretations, in turn, was shown to lead to faster coordination on non-conventionalized meaning. Furthermore, the longer term comparisons between S_l and S_m suggest that, should the information provided by relations be insufficient to tease apart meaning alternations throughout varying contexts, interlocutors perform best when their choices are only weakly influenced by them. This aligns well with recent research on learning through generalization (O'Connor, forthcoming). O'Connor's results add strength to the claim that generalization speeds up learning whilst paying a cost in precision. Communicatively efficient meaning alternations need to be frequent, and the participating meanings discriminable by the contexts they appear in. In the long run, when potential for confounding exists and high precision is required, interlocutors fare better when coining a new signal for a novel meaning or by drawing from additional information to reduce communicative uncertainty.

We see two main venues for future research. First, there is a need for further analysis involving differently sized and structured meaning spaces, different relations, the addition of noise to the information provided by context, as well as an analysis of population dynamics in larger agent communities.[5] Second, our general proposal requires empirical validation. Here, one possibility is to test its performance on corpus data to predict unwitnessed meaning alternations in a similar spirit to the work of Reisinger and Mooney (2010) and Boleda et al. (2012) surveyed above.

A further issue left undiscussed is that of the cost of ambiguity. In the current proposal cost implicitly came into play as equivocation potential when multiple relations are available for exploitation. Other sources of cost may relate to lexical storage, as assumed by Santana (2014), or processing cost. In particular the latter requires a more detailed treatment. Past experiments suggest ambiguous words with related meanings to be processed faster than monosemous or homonymous words (Rodd et al., 2002; Klepousniotou and Baum, 2007), as well as finer-grained distinctions within their class (Klepousniotou et al., 2008). These aspects relate to issues of lexical storage, lexical representation and lexical access,

[5]As noted by an anonymous reviewer, the simplicity of Lewisian signaling games may have to be abandoned to fully explore and expand this proposal. A potentially suitable alternative is given by the language game paradigm as laid out in, for example, Steels (2012).

neither of which were addressed here.

Our overall proposal is based on relations of unspecified nature. To conclude this discussion, we submit that one possibility to model semantic relatedness in a more concrete but framework-independent way is to equate it to transformational complexity between representations, given by the Kolmogorov complexity of one representation conditioned on the other (Chater and Hahn, 1997). Informally, $K(x|y)$ is a complexity measure given by the shortest program that takes y as input and returns x. Kolmogorov complexity is well-understood and widely applicable. Chiefly, it is independent of the representations required for particular applications and provides a good fit for human similarity judgments (see Hahn et al. (2003) for details). Lastly, it addresses the problems of metric-based similarity relations raised by Tversky (1977), who shows that neither triangle inequality nor symmetry need hold for human similarity judgments. The same is true of transformational complexity, as it is compatible with both symmetric and asymmetric relations.

5 Conclusion

Conveying and comprehending novel meaning relies on the interlocutors' mutual reasoning about what is contextually relevant. Among others, meaning can be expressed by composing conventionalized forms, coining new expressions, or by exploiting semantic relations by scaffolding on conventionalized meaning. The present investigation focused on the latter as a communication strategy for fast coordination. We showed that, if a specific relation is mutually expected to be exploited, this mechanism provides a robust solution for reliable and fast coordination. However, when multiple relations are likely candidates, repurposing comes at a risk of lower precision. As a consequence, its advantage depends on the relations available, their regularity across semantic space, previous successful exploitation thereof, and the contexts in which the relevant meanings appear in.

Our analysis draws its main motivation from the cross-linguistic pervasiveness of ambiguous expressions that lexicalize related meanings. In a sense, it is not surprising that certain meaning clusters exhibit systematic alternations. Without risk for confounding, they provide a safe and efficient expansion of a language's expressive range. In other words, relation exploitation provides a partial solution to lexical bottlenecks. Learning and predicting alternations is not only important for our understanding of human communication, but also to overcome analogous bottlenecks faced by computational systems (Navigli, 2009).

More generally, we argued that natural language ambiguity is motivated by more than form-based considerations. When members of a linguistic community are biased towards regularities, repurposing conventionalized material provides an efficient means to convey novel meaning.

Acknowledgments

I thank Robert van Rooij, Michael Anslow, Inés Crespo, and three anonymous reviewers for helpful comments and discussion. This research has been funded by the European Community's Seventh Framework Programme (FP7/2007-2013) under grant agreement no. 567652 */ESSENCE: Evolution of Shared Semantics in Computational Environments/*.

References

Juri Derenick Apresjan. 1974. Regular polysemy. *Linguistics*, 12(142).

Alan W. Beggs. 2005. On the convergence of reinforcement learning. *Journal of Economic Theory*, 122(1):1–36.

Gemma Boleda, Sebastian Padó, and Jason Utt. 2012. Regular polysemy: A distributional model. In *Proceedings of the First Joint Conference on Lexical and Computational Semantics*, pages 151–160. Association for Computational Linguistics.

Justin Bruner, Cailin O'Connor, Hannah Rubin, and Simon M. Huttegger. 2014. David Lewis in the lab: experimental results on the emergence of meaning. *Synthese*.

David Catteeuw and Bernard Manderick. 2014. The limits and robustness of reinforcement learning in Lewis signaling games. *Connection Science*, 26(2):161–177.

Nick Chater and Ulrike Hahn. 1997. Representational distortion, similarity and the universal law of generalization. In *SimCat97: Proceedings of the Interdisciplinary Workshop on Similarity and Categorization*.

Chelsea M. Eddington and Natasha Tokowicz. 2015. How meaning similarity influences ambiguous word processing: the current state of the literature. *Psychon Bull Rev*, 22(1):13–37.

Ido Erev and Alvin E. Roth. 1998. Predicting how people play games: Reinforcement learning in experimental games with unique, mixed strategy equilibria. *American economic review*, 88(4):848–881.

Michael Franke. 2009. *Signal to Act: Game Theoretic Pragmatics*. Ph.D. thesis, University of Amsterdam.

Lyn Frazier and Keith Rayner. 1990. Taking on semantic commitments: Processing multiple meanings vs. multiple senses. *Journal of Memory and Language*, 29(2):181–200.

Herbert P. Grice. 1978. Some further notes on logic and conversation. *Syntax and Semantics*, 9:113–128.

Ulrike Hahn, Nick Chater, and Lucy B. Richardson. 2003. Similarity as transformation. *Cognition*, 87(1):1–32.

Paul Hoffman, Matthew A. Lambon Ralph, and Timothy T. Rogers. 2013. Semantic diversity: A measure of semantic ambiguity based on variability in the contextual usage of words. *Behavior Research Methods*, 45(3):718–730.

Brendan Juba, Adam Tauman Kalai, Sanjeev Khanna, and Madhu Sudan. 2011. Compression without a common prior: An information-theoretic justification for ambiguity in language. In *Proceedings of the 2nd Symposium on innovations in computer science*.

Ekaterini Klepousniotou and Shari R. Baum. 2007. Disambiguating the ambiguity advantage effect in word recognition: An advantage for polysemous but not homonymous words. *Journal of Neurolinguistics*, 20(1):1–24.

Ekaterini Klepousniotou, Debra Titone, and Carolina Romero. 2008. Making sense of word senses: The comprehension of polysemy depends on sense overlap. *Journal of Experimental Psychology: Learning, Memory, and Cognition*, 34(6):1534–1543.

David Lewis. 1969. *Convention: A Philosophical Study*. Harvard University Press, Cambridge.

Johann-Mattis List, Thomas Mayer, Anselm Terhalle, and Matthias Urban. 2014. CLiCs – database of cross-linguistic colexifications. Version 1.0.

Roberto Navigli. 2009. Word sense disambiguation. *CSUR*, 41(2):1–69.

Geoffrey Nunberg. 1979. The non-uniqueness of semantic solutions: Polysemy. *Linguistics and Philosophy*, 3(2):143–184.

Cailin O'Connor. forthcoming. Evolving to generalize: Trading precision for speed. *British Journal for the Philosophy of Science*.

Steven T. Piantadosi, Harry Tily, and Edward Gibson. 2012. The communicative function of ambiguity in language. *Cognition*, 122(3):280–291.

James Pustejovsky. 1995. *The Generative Lexicon*. MIT Press, Cambridge, MA.

Joseph Reisinger and Raymond J. Mooney. 2010. Multi-prototype vector-space models of word meaning. In *Human Language Technologies: The 2010 Annual Conference of the North American Chapter of the Association for Computational Linguistics*, pages 109–117. Association for Computational Linguistics.

Jennifer Rodd, Gareth Gaskell, and William Marslen-Wilson. 2002. Making sense of semantic ambiguity: Semantic competition in lexical access. *Journal of Memory and Language*, 46(2):245–266.

Jennifer M. Rodd, Richard Berriman, Matt Landau, Theresa Lee, Carol Ho, M. Gareth Gaskell, and Matthew H. Davis. 2012. Learning new meanings for old words: effects of semantic relatedness. *Memory & Cognition*, 40(7):1095–1108.

Alvin E. Roth and Ido Erev. 1995. Learning in extensive-form games: Experimental data and simple dynamic models in the intermediate term. *Games and Economic Behavior*, 8(1):164–212.

Carlos Santana. 2014. Ambiguity in cooperative signaling. *Philosophy of Science*, 81(3):398–422.

Claude E. Shannon. 1948. A mathematical theory of communication. *Bell System Technical Journal*, 27(3):379–423.

Greg B. Simpson. 1984. Lexical ambiguity and its role in models of word recognition. *Psychological Bulletin*, 96(2):316–340.

Mahesh Srinivasan and Hugh Rabagliati. 2015. How concepts and conventions structure the lexicon: Cross-linguistic evidence from polysemy. *Lingua*, 157:124–152.

Mahesh Srinivasan and Jesse Snedeker. 2011. Judging a book by its cover and its contents: The representation of polysemous and homophonous meanings in four-year-old children. *Cognitive Psychology*, 62(4):245–272.

Luc Steels. 2012. *Experiments in Cultural Language Evolution*. John Benjamins.

Amos Tversky. 1977. Features of similarity. *Psychological Review*, 84(4):327–352.

Perceptual, Conceptual, and Frequency Effects on Error Patterns in English Color Term Acquisition

Barend Beekhuizen
Leiden University Centre for Linguistics
Leiden University
barendbeekhuizen@gmail.com

Suzanne Stevenson
Department of Computer Science
University of Toronto
suzanne@cs.toronto.edu

Abstract

Children's overextension errors in word usage can yield insights into the underlying representation of meaning. We simulate overextension patterns in the domain of color with two word-learning models, and look at the contribution of three possible factors: perceptual properties of the colors, typological prevalence of certain color groupings into categories (as a proxy for cognitive naturalness), and color term frequency. We find that the perceptual features provide the strongest predictors of the error pattern observed during development, and can effectively rule out color term frequency as an explanation. Typological prevalence is shown to correlate strongly with the perceptual dimensions of color, and hence provides no effect over and above the perceptual dimensions.

1 Overextensions in word learning

When learning their language, children often overextend a word by erroneously using it to refer to concepts similar to its actual meaning – e.g., a child learning English might refer to all round things as *ball*. We can learn much about the mechanisms and representations the child uses to arrive at an adult level of understanding by exploring whether the proposed mechanisms lead to observed patterns of such errors over the course of development.

Several factors have been named as potential influences on early overextensions in word meaning acquisition, including underspecification of semantic representations (Clark, 1973), as well as word frequency (mostly invoked as a zero-hypothesis to be rejected; Gülzow and Gagarina (2007), Goodman et al. (2008)).

Another possible factor is conceptual prior biases. Bowerman (1993) suggests that some semantic features (or values of features) may be cognitively more readily available than others, and argues that (crosslinguistic) semantic typology can shed light on the degree of cognitive naturalness of features in a domain. This idea was further articulated by Gentner and Bowerman (2009), who proposed the Typological Prevalence Hypothesis. This proposal states that the more frequently languages make a certain semantic grouping – i.e., collect together a certain set of situational meanings under a single term – the more likely this is a cognitively natural grouping. The reasoning is that if some conceptual categorization comes naturally, languages are more likely to develop linguistic categorization systems that follow these biases. Gentner and Bowerman (2009) further argue that, other things being equal, linguistic terms referring to such cognitively more natural groupings will be acquired more readily by children than terms in a language that do not follow the typical conceptual category boundaries.

The Typological Prevalence Hypothesis explains the error pattern Gentner and Bowerman (2009) observed in the acquisition of Dutch topological spatial markers. Whereas English uses the preposition *on* for all sorts of conceptual relations of support between a figure object and a ground object, Dutch distinguishes *op* 'surface support', *aan* 'tenuous support', and *om* 'surrounding (support)'. Gentner and Bowerman (2009) found experimentally that Dutch children overgeneralize *op* to situations where adults would use *aan* or *om*, but not vice versa. Gentner and Bowerman (2009) note that it is crosslinguistically very common to have a term like *op* that reflects a semantic grouping of various surface support relations, whereas terms such as *aan* that denote 'tenuous support' are typologically rare. They suggest that this pattern reflects a difference in cognitive naturalness (surface support being the more prototypical case of support than tenuous support), which in turn

Proceedings of the Sixth Workshop on Cognitive Aspects of Computational Language Learning, pages 83–92,
Lisbon, Portugal, 18 September 2015.

makes *aan* harder to acquire than *op*.

Beekhuizen et al. (2014) operationalized the Typological Prevalence Hypothesis within a word-learning model by creating a semantic representation for topological situations that used the words themselves from across a number of languages as the features for representing spatial relations. In such a representation, commonalities and differences in the way languages carve up the space of topological relations is reflected in the way the terms within each language group together various situations. This approach yields a semantic representation that can capture crosslinguistic naturalness of the underlying spatial relations, without the need for explicit identification of appropriate semantic features. Situations that, within many languages, are expressed with the same word are closer in this semantic space than those that are more often labelled by different terms within a language. Beekhuizen et al. (2014) simulated the above experimental results on Dutch children by using this semantic space within a computational model for learning Dutch prepositions, whose developmental trajectory displayed the same trends as children.

Here we extend the method of Beekhuizen et al. (2014) to the acquisition of color terms, another domain in which children are known to make overextension errors. Color terms form an interesting test of the Typological Prevalence Hypothesis, because we know reasonably well what the perceptual dimensions of color are, and can test if there is any effect of typological prevalence on top of this. Specifically, we ask if crosslinguistic consistency provides a good basis for the representation of color in word learning, and if such a semantic representation adds information beyond the perceptual properties of color.[1]

Note that other work, such as Regier et al. (2007) among others, has reasoned from the perceptual features of color as well as general considerations concerning category structure to propose an explanation for the observed tendencies across color lexicons. Instead, we explore whether the typological tendencies among color lexicons reflect semantic information relevant to word learning, and especially whether that information goes beyond that provided by perceptual features. We refer to the typologically-based semantic representation as 'conceptual' features (in contrast to perceptual ones) because they refer to the way color concepts are (preferably) structured in the lexicons of the various languages.[2]

Thus, here we explore three potential influences on the error patterns observed in learning of color terms: perceptual factors, conceptual factors, and word frequency effects. We also take the opportunity to strengthen the evaluation method of Beekhuizen et al. (2014) by here using a quantitative measure of model deviation from the observed pattern of word use in order to arrive at more complete insights into the role of these factors.

2 Data on the acquisition of color terms

Across languages, children overextend certain color terms at the cost of others, and there has been a long tradition of research into this domain (Bateman, 1915; Istomina, 1960; Harkness, 1973; Bartlett, 1978; Davies et al., 1994; Davies et al., 1998; Roberson et al., 2004). The case used for our current study is Bateman (1915), who studied 591 English-speaking children in the age range 6-11. Eight color chips of the 'best' examples[3] of the colors BLACK, BLUE, BROWN, GREEN, ORANGE, PURPLE, RED, YELLOW were presented to the subjects, who were then asked to name the color.[4] We use Bateman's elicitation data in the initial application of our approach to this domain because, despite being a century old, it remains the most comprehensive published error data on color terms.

Bateman found that BLACK, WHITE, RED and

[1]For the latter question, the hypothesis is that a color c may be at the same perceptual distance to c' as it is to c'', but for some other reason, languages categorize c and c' with the same term more often than c and c''. There could be various reasons for this difference, such as a preference for certain category structures, or communicative pressures concerning disambiguation. We do not investigate here what those factors might be, but rather explore whether the typologically-derived semantic space provides information in addition to the perceptual features.

[2]A reviewer noted that 'conceptual' may be an inaccurate term, since factors beyond strictly the conceptual biases of language users might influence color lexicons and their crosslinguistic similarities and differences. In adopting the Typological Prevalence Hypothesis as a working hypothesis, we consider that crosslinguistic patterns reflect cognitively natural conceptual groupings, while acknowledging that other factors need to be investigated as well.

[3]"Each color was of the purest tone and strongest saturation obtainable", p. 476.

[4]We adopt the convention of denoting the stimuli with small capitals and the words with italics. The responses contain all eleven English basic color terms (Berlin and Kay, 1969): *black, white, red, yellow, green, blue, orange, purple, pink, brown* and *grey*.

BLUE were learned (nearly) error-free ($\leq 2\%$ erroneous responses at age 6), but YELLOW (7% at age 6), GREEN (6% at age 6), ORANGE (6% at age 6), and especially PURPLE (11% at age 6) displayed errors. For YELLOW, the term *orange* is the most frequent error. For ORANGE various errors are found (*yellow, red, blue, purple, brown, pink*). GREEN displays mostly errors in which *blue* is used. For PURPLE, *blue* is the most frequent erroneous term. Whereas the errors for YELLOW and GREEN have disappeared at age 7, the errors for ORANGE and PURPLE are somewhat more persistent, and are found until age 11 and 9 respectively.

In summary, this data yields the following five phenomena that must be explained:

- BLACK, WHITE, BLUE, and RED display hardly any errors;
- GREEN and YELLOW display some errors at age 6 but none afterwards;
- ORANGE displays (somewhat haphazard) persistent errors;
- PURPLE displays persistent errors, mostly *blue*;
- However, *purple* is not overextended to BLUE.

While previous accounts of the error patterns have mainly focused on perceptual closeness of the various colors (Bartlett, 1978; Pitchford and Mullen, 2003), this cannot be the full explanation: If the overextension of *blue* to PURPLE stimuli was solely due to color similarity, we would expect (contrary to observation) that *purple* would also be incorrectly overextended to BLUE stimuli.

Here, we explore three potential factors that might lead to the observed pattern of color errors: perceptual features of color, conceptual/typological prevalence factors, and/or frequency of the color terms.

3 Operationalizing the Three Factors

We simulate the acquisition of color terms by training a word-learning model on a generated input stream, in which each input item pairs a semantic representation $s \in S$ of a color, with a color term $t \in T$ used to refer to it. S is drawn from the 330 chips of the Munsell color chart, and T contains the eleven basic color terms that comprised the responses in Bateman (1915). We explore the impact of perceptual and/or conceptual (typological) factors by varying the representation of s, using one or both of the feature sets described in Sections 3.1 and 3.2.[5] The role of frequency of t is examined by varying the way the input items are generated, as in Section 3.3.

3.1 Perceptual features

As the perceptual dimensions, we use the CIELab color space. The CIELab space describes all colors visible to the human eye, and consists of three dimensions, lightness (L^*), a red-green scale (a^*) and a yellow-blue scale (b^*). Importantly, the Euclidean distance between any pair of coordinates in CIELab is thought to directly reflect the perceptual similarity between colors. Since color perception is thought to be adultlike before age two (Pitchford and Mullen, 2003), we can assume these perceptual features to be stable over development.

3.2 Conceptual features

The conceptual dimensions reflect the crosslinguistic biases in categorizing the color space. To capture these, we use the World Color Survey data of Kay et al. (2009), which contains elicitations for each of the 330 chips of the Munsell color chart, for 110 typologically diverse languages, with on average 24 participants per language. From this data, we extract an n-dimensional conceptual space by using the first n dimensions of a Principal Component Analysis (PCA, Hotelling (1933)) over the elicited color terms for a number of color stimuli following the method of Beekhuizen et al. (2014), as described below.

The elicitations for each language give us a count matrix C containing a set of color stimuli S on the rows, and a set of color terms T in that language on the columns. Every cell is filled with the count of participant responses to stimulus s that use color term t. Matrix C captures the way that the language carves up the space of color: stimuli s and s' are treated similarly in the language to the extent that the labels used to express them are similar, reflected in rows s and s' of C. As we want to know how often stimuli are co-categorized *across* languages, the procedure of Levinson et al. (2003) is adapted: for every language l, an $|S| \times |S|$ distance matrix D^l containing the Euclidean distances between all pairs of situations is extracted. By summing the distance matrices for all languages, we arrive at a distance matrix D^{all}

[5]The values for the 330 chips on the two feature sets are available from the first author upon request.

whose elements d_{ij} are the summed distances between s_i and s_j across all languages. A PCA was applied to D^{all}, from which we use the 4 components with an Eigenvalue ≥ 1 (Kaiser's rule) as our conceptual space to represent color semantics.

3.3 The role of frequency

In the input generation procedure, a pair of a color term $t \in T$ and a stimulus $s \in S$ is sampled from the distribution $P(t, s) = P(s|t)P(t)$. The likelihood $P(s|t)$ is the relative frequency of a specific color chip given a term (as given by the data for English of Berlin and Kay (1969)):

$$P(s|t) = \frac{n(t, s)}{\sum_{s' \in s} n(t, s')} \tag{1}$$

where $P(s|t) = 0$ for s not included in the elicitation data.

To explore the role of term frequency in color errors, we base the prior probability $P(t)$ on the relative frequency of t among the 11 primary color terms in the Manchester corpus of child-directed speech (Theakston et al., 2001). We then compare this to holding frequency constant, i.e. with $P(t)$ a uniform distribution over T.

4 The Experimental Approach

4.1 The learning models

We model word-learning as a categorization problem by considering the 11 color terms as the "categories" to be learned over the various color semantics (the representations of the color chips) each is associated with in the input. Extending Beekhuizen et al. (2014), we try two different categorization models: a Gaussian Naïve Bayes learner (GNB, as in their work), and a Generalized Context Model (GCM, Nosofsky (1987)), for two reasons. First, if the same effects are found with multiple models, the effect is more robust, and not an effect of the model per se. Second, GCM is an exemplar-based categorization model that has been shown to simulate human categorization behavior well.

In the GNB approach, for a given amount of input data of color-semantics/color-term pairs, the model estimates Gaussian distributions over each of the perceptual and/or conceptual feature dimensions. The model is then presented with each of Bateman's 8 color stimuli as the test phase, and it outputs the color term with the Maximal A Posteriori probability as the predicted category for each color.

In the GCM model, the probability of categorizing a color stimulus s_i with category J (response R_J, a color term) is given as the summed similarity η between s_i and all instances of category J (all colors referred to by the color term), divided by the summed similarity between s_i and all exemplars (colors) in the data set.

$$P(R_J|s_i) = \frac{b_J \sum_{j \in C_J} \eta_{ij}}{\sum_K (b_K \sum_{k \in C_K} \eta_{ik})} \tag{2}$$

where b is the category bias, here set to uniform for categories. η_{ij} is given by:

$$\eta_{ij} = e^{-d_{ij}^{\delta}} \tag{3}$$

where δ is the decay function, here set to 1 (exponential). For d we use the Euclidean distance between the coordinate vectors of i and j.

4.2 Experimental set-up

Each model is trained on successively larger amounts of data, in blocks of 10 input pairs. Every 10 input items, the model is presented with the 8 colors of Bateman (1915) and predicts the most likely category label from the set of 11 color terms. As Bateman does not give values in a color space for his stimuli, we assume that the focal colors, as described by Berlin and Kay (1969), were used.[6] For each of the 12 parameter settings ($\texttt{features} = \{\texttt{perc}, \texttt{conc}, \texttt{perc\&conc}\} \times \texttt{frequency} = \{\texttt{relative}, \texttt{uniform}\} \times \texttt{model} = \{\texttt{GCM}, \texttt{GNB}\}$), we run 30 simulations of 1000 input items each, each of which yields 100 test points.

4.3 Evaluating the model predictions

Assessing the accuracy of the model in simulating the observed error data requires us to align the predictions P at the 100 test moments of the model with Bateman's observed data O in the 5 age bins (6-, 7-, 8-, 9-, and 10-to-11-year-olds). We represent O as a 5×8 matrix in which each element o_{ij} is the distribution of responses over the children at age bin i to color stimulus j (where j is one of the 8 stimulus colors). The matrix P contains the

[6] If multiple tokens were named as focal in the data of Berlin and Kay (1969), we set coordinates of a test item to the mean of each coordinate for all focal instances of that category.

models responses under a given parameter setting; it is a 100×8 matrix in which each element p_{kj} is the distribution of responses over the 30 simulations at test point i to color stimulus j. For example, p_{kj} for j the RED stimulus might look like:

$$p_{kj} = [\ \textit{red} : 0.8, \textit{orange} : 0.1, \textit{purple} : 0.1, ...\ ]$$

indicating that of the 30 simulations at test point k, 24 predicted *red*, 3 *orange*, and 3 *purple*, to the stimulus j=RED (and 0 responses for all other color terms). To recap, each row of O and P is a vector of 8 elements, each of which is a distribution over the 11 color terms that comprises the responses of the children/model at that age/test point, respectively, to the 8 color stimuli.

To determine the degree to which the predictions of the model given in P mimic the error data in O, we need to map each row i of O (the responses for that age bin) to some row k in P, such that each o_{i+1} maps to a higher k than o_i. (This constraint ensures that older age bins map to later test points of the model.) To find this mapping between observed and predicted data, we find the series of 5 (possibly discontiguous) rows in P that minimize the average distance between those 5 rows and the 5 rows of O.

To compare rows o_i and p_k, we find (and average) the distance d between each paired distribution (e.g., RED in o_i and RED in p_k):[7]

$$\Delta(o_i, p_k) = \sum_{s \in S_{\text{test}}} d(o_i^s, p_k^s) \times \frac{1}{|S_{\text{test}}|} \quad (4)$$

where S_{test} is the set of 8 test colors. Using $\Delta(o_i, p_k)$, we compare all o_i and p_k (subject to the ordering constraint on k) and find the series of 5 p_{k_i}'s with the lowest distance to the o_i's they are mapped to.

Now we can calculate the overall **error** of the model's predictions P with respect to the observed data O as:

$$\textbf{error}(O, P) = \left(\frac{\sum_{i \in [1...5], k_i} \Delta(o_i, p_{k_i})}{5} \right) \quad (5)$$

where the indices k_i are given by the mapping that minimizes the **error**, as explained above.

[7]The experiments reported below use Euclidean distance for d, but the pattern of results is the same under cosine or Canberra distance.

5 Results and discussion

5.1 Global fit and effect of parameters

In order to study the effect of the various parameters ($\texttt{features} = \{\texttt{perc}, \texttt{conc}, \texttt{perc\&conc}\} \times \texttt{freq} = \{\texttt{relative}, \texttt{uniform}\} \times \texttt{model} = \{\texttt{GCM}, \texttt{GNB}\}$), we enter the **error** for the output for each setting into a two-way ANOVA. As we can see in Table 1, there are two main effects: the `features` and the `model`. A post-hoc test (Tukey HSD) shows that for the `features` variable, the difference between `perc` and `conc` ($p < 0.001$) as well as between `perc&conc` and `conc` ($p < 0.001$) are statistically significant, but not the difference between `perc&conc` and `perc` ($n.s.$). For the `model` parameter, we observe a slightly better fit for GCM than for GNB. For the `freq` parameter, there is no difference between `relative` and `uniform`.

The analysis shows that the perceptual features perform better than the conceptual features, and adding the conceptual features to the perceptual ones gives no improvement. It seems that perceptual features play an important role in explaining the overextensions and lack thereof in the development of color terminology, but that the conceptual features explain little on top of this.

The lack of an effect of the conceptual features is unexpected, given that Beekhuizen et al. (2014) found that using their typological conceptual space explained the errors in the acquisition of Dutch spatial relation terms. One could argue that the domain of color is conceptually simpler than space (pertaining to properties of entities rather than relations between them, cf. Gentner (1982)), which is supported by the finding of Majid et al. (2015) that, at least among Germanic languages, space lexicons vary more crosslinguistically than color lexicons. However, the fact that children acquire color terms relatively late (compared to spatial terms) goes against this analysis, but then again, the late acquisition of color may also be due to other factors (e.g., the difficulty of disentangling color from other properties, cf. Soja (1994)). Understanding the lack of an effect of the conceptual features here ultimately requires us to analyze the crosslinguistic data further, which we plan to do in future work.

We also found no significant effect of the frequency manipulation, suggesting that the observed errors are not influenced by the varying frequencies of color terms. This is surprising because

parameter	F	p	parameter setting	mean **error**
features	$F(2) = 2790.070$	$p = 0.000$	perc&conc	$\mu = 0.015$
			perc	$\mu = 0.020$
			conc	$\mu = 0.354$
frequency	$F(1) = 0.026$	$p = 0.887$	relative	$\mu = 0.130$
			uniform	$\mu = 0.130$
model	$F(1) = 11.208$	$p = 0.044$	GCM	$\mu = 0.120$
			GNB	$\mu = 0.139$

Table 1: Results of the ANOVA; see Section 5.1 for post-hoc analyses.

Beekhuizen et al. (2014) found that an interaction of frequency and typological factors contributed to the errors they modeled. Moreover, frequency has been shown to correlate with acquisition of color terms (Yurovsky et al., 2015), albeit for younger children than the ones in the Bateman data.

This suggests that a possible explanation for the lack of both frequency and typological prevalence effects is that the error data we are modeling are from older children (ages 6–11). Perhaps effects of frequency and/or conceptual factors (on the basis of typological prevalence) are only found in younger children. It may be that, by age 6, the young language user has organized her semantic space in accordance with her native language, thus no longer displaying effects of typological prevalence. In the future we will need to look at earlier error data to explore whether the factors involved vary in their importance during the development of a vocabulary: frequency and conceptual biases may have certain effects early on, but factors pertaining to perceptual dimensions leading to the overextension of category boundaries may be more persistent.

5.2 Findings per color

Here we look at the results of the model per test color, considering the role of the different feature spaces, `perc` and `conc`, and of the different frequency settings, `uniform` and `relative`, used for calculating the prior probability of the color terms. In addition to looking at the overall **error** of the model's predictions (Table 2), we also look at the actual responses in some of the interesting cases. Even though the `frequency` setting made no difference overall in the amount of **error**, we show results for both settings, since it affects the pattern of responses for some individual colors. All these results use the GCM model, since it performed slightly (but statistically significantly) better than the GNB model.

Recall that the first two observed error patterns to be explained (see Section 2) are that there are no overextensions for BLACK, WHITE, RED, and BLUE, and few, non-persistent overextensions for YELLOW and GREEN. Regarding these color stimuli, we find that the model provides a good fit under all settings for `features` and `frequency`. In all cases, the **error** is caused by underestimation of the model of the few overextensions that are there, that is: the model predicts no overextensions for these six stimuli, whereas there are some.

The next two phenomena concern the persistent errors for ORANGE and PURPLE, where other color terms are overextended by even older children to these stimuli. For these two stimuli, the model fit is slightly worse than for the other colors when using the **perc** features, but the setting of **conc** features alone worsens the fit with a dramatic increase in the model **error**.

For ORANGE, the model behaves similarly as with the previous 6: it predicts no overextensions (for `perc&conc` and `perc`) or a complete overextension of *red* (for `conc`). As such, we cannot explain the observed overextension pattern for ORANGE well at this point. However, we can exclude term frequency as an explanation: under both settings for `frequency`, the model has the same fit with the observed pattern.

The results for PURPLE, the other color with persistent overextensions, display a number of noteworthy effects. Here, in addition to the model **error** in Table 2, we also show figures with the proportion of responses to PURPLE over time, for both the child data and for the model under several interesting settings; see Figure 1.

First, the model under all settings does predict overextensions of other color terms to PUR-

	BLACK	BLUE	GREEN	ORANGE	PURPLE	RED	WHITE	YELLOW
perc&conc, uniform	0.000	0.005	0.013	0.029	0.024	0.003	0.000	0.011
perc, uniform	0.000	0.005	0.013	0.029	0.026	0.003	0.000	0.011
conc, uniform	0.000	0.019	0.030	1.000	0.854	0.003	0.000	0.011
perc&conc, relative	0.000	0.005	0.013	0.029	0.036	0.003	0.000	0.011
perc, relative	0.000	0.005	0.013	0.029	0.015	0.003	0.000	0.011
conc, relative	0.000	0.028	0.013	1.000	0.852	0.003	0.000	0.011

Table 2: Mean **error** per stimulus, in the GCM model.

PLE. Focussing on the settings with a good fit (perc&conc and perc), we find that the term *blue* is in all cases persistently overextended to PURPLE. However, the various settings do provide different overextension patterns, as can be seen in Figure 1. The setting with the closest fit (**error** = 0.014) is pred, relative (Fig. 1d): here we see a pattern most similar to that found in child data (Fig. 1a). From the fact that the model **error** for this setting is about twice as low as the settings with uniform frequency and with conceptual dimensions we can infer two things. First, we do find a frequency effect: *blue* being more frequent than *black* in child-directed speech explains why there are more overtextensions of *black* given the setting perc, uniform (Fig. 1c) than given perc, relative. Second, the conceptual dimensions hurt the prediction of the overextension pattern. Including the conceptual dimensions correctly predicts *blue* to be the most frequent overextension, but underestimates the total amount of errors (Fig. 1b).

The final phenomenon concerns the asymmetry in overextensions between PURPLE and BLUE. Whereas *blue* is overextended to the PURPLE stimulus, *purple* is not overextended to BLUE. We can rule out the frequency difference between *blue* and *purple* as an explanation, despite that *purple* is much less frequent: Under both frequency settings, *purple* is not overextended to BLUE. Given that the conceptual features do not help the model fit, it is likely that the source of the asymmetry is to be found in the perceptual feature space.

Looking more closely at the color stimuli and the perceptual feature space, we can identify that the reason for the observed asymmetry is the location of the focal colors within each color category. As Figure 2 shows, the BLUE and PURPLE categories form a sphere in the three perceptual dimensions. The focal exemplars of each category, however, are located at different values for L^*, the luminance dimension. Focal PURPLE is darker than focal BLUE, and hence closer (on the dimensions a^* and b^*) to BLUE exemplars with a lower luminance. Focal BLUE is more luminant, and hence further away from PURPLE exemplars with the same luminance.

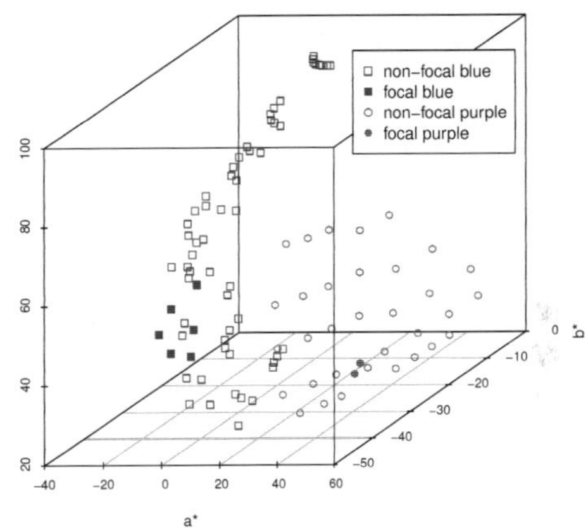

Figure 2: Positions of the various BLUE and PURPLE exemplars in the CIELab space.

On the assumption that Bateman's test items were focal exemplars of the categories, this means that the lack of overextension of *purple* to BLUE can be attributed to the lay-out of the perceptual dimensions, and to the position that the focal exemplars have in that space. Thus, the model's results suggest a new explanation for the asymmetry in overextensions that goes beyond simple perceptual closeness and frequency of color terms.

5.3 The role of the conceptual features

If the conceptual dimensions have little additional predictive power over the perceptual ones, two

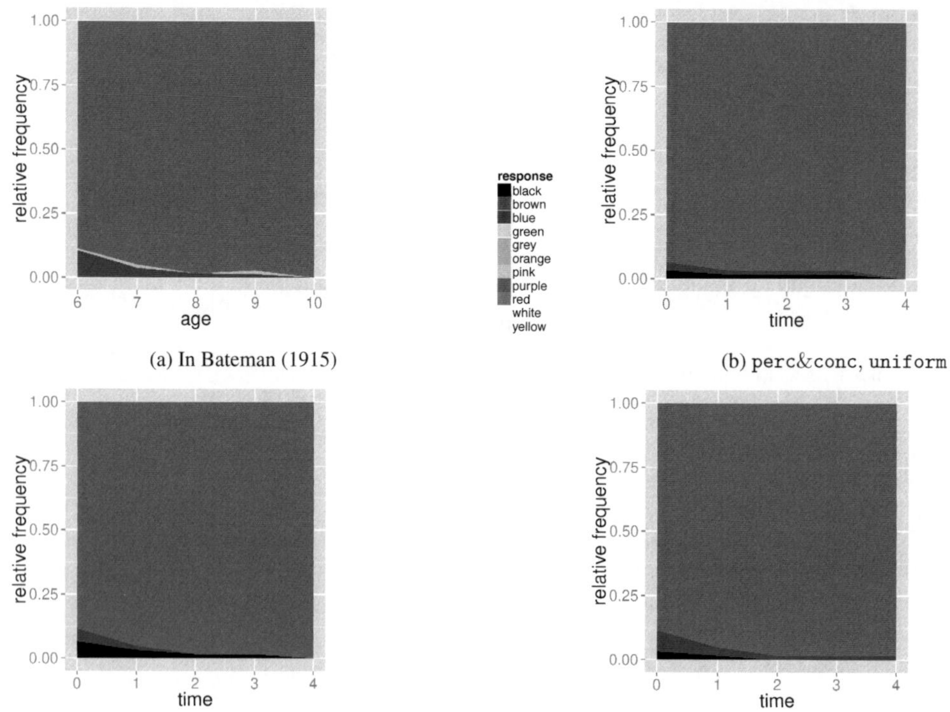

(a) In Bateman (1915)

(b) `perc&conc`, `uniform`

(c) `perc`, `uniform`

(d) `perc`, `relative`

Figure 1: Observed and predicted responses to PURPLE over time.

	L^*	a^*	b^*
PCA1	-0.01	0.80^*	-0.01
PCA2	-0.97^{***}	0.40	-0.08
PCA3	0.16	-0.03	-0.88^{**}
PCA4	0.60	-0.86^*	0.70

Table 3: Correlation matrix for the four used PCA components and the three perceptual dimensions. Stars indicate level of significance of the correlation (* = $p < .05$, ** = $p < .01$, *** = $p < .001$).

scenarios are possible. The conceptual dimensions may correlate with the perceptual ones, or they may be independent from them. In the former case, it means that the crosslinguistic commonalities in structuring the domain of color mirror the perceptual biases. This would mean that adding the conceptual dimensions can be expected to have no explanatory effect on top of the perceptual dimensions. In the latter scenario, it means that there are other biases causing the commonalities in the crosslinguistic data, but that these biases do not affect language acquisition. This scenario would imply a negative assessment of the Typological Prevalence Hypothesis.

As we can see in Table 3, the former scenario of correlated features seems closer to the truth than the latter. The luminance dimension L^* displays an almost perfect negative correlation with component 2 of the PCA, whereas the red-green scale a^* has a strong positive correlation with component 1 and a strong negative one with component 4. The yellow-blue scale, finally, has a strong negative correlation with component 3. That is: all four features of our `conc` space (i.e., those PCA components with Eigenvalues greater than 1) have correlating perceptual dimensions. This means that they can be seen as symptoms of these dimensions and that the category structure of color terms across languages depends to a large extent on the perceptual dimensions of color.

What this means is that using crosslinguistic data does lay bare an important part of the conceptual structure of the domain. If we did not know of the perceptual properties of color, a Principal Component Analysis on the basis of crosslinguistic data would provide us with an insight in all three dimensions of the perceptual space.

One concern remains, however. Even though

the perceptual feature space by itself constitutes a good predictor of the error terms, the use of only conceptual dimensions does not explain as much of the error pattern.

6 Conclusion

In this paper, we looked at overextensions in the acquisition of the meaning of color terms. For this initial study, we focused on the English data of Bateman (1915) – the most comprehensive published error data on color terms – in which we identified five phenomena that characterize the pattern of children's errors, and that must be explained by a theory of word meaning acquisition. We considered three factors that might play a role in this domain: (1) the identified perceptual dimensions relating to the various exemplars of the color terms; (2) the effect of typological prevalence (i.e., the more frequently a certain grouping of color exemplars is crosslinguistically, the more cognitively natural it is thought to be, and hence the more readily/robustly acquirable, Gentner and Bowerman (2009)); and (3) the frequency of color terms.

We used an extension of the modeling approach taken in Beekhuizen et al. (2014). In that work, the effects of typological prevalence and frequency were studied in the domain of spatial relations. In this paper, we applied the same technique to the crosslinguistic elicitation data of the World Color Survey (Kay et al., 2009) to arrive at a set of features (the 'conceptual' space) reflecting typological frequency of semantic groupings. We considered in addition the possible impact of a perceptual representation of color.

We find several notable effects within our setup. First, the perceptual influence provides the best explanation of the errors: Including the perceptual features gives the model a very good fit with the developmental overextension pattern for all five phenomena observed in the Bateman data, and adding either or both of the conceptual (typological) features and the frequency information does not improve the fit. This last finding is revealing, as it means that the overextensions cannot be ascribed to the frequencies of the color terms.

We argued that the reason the conceptual features do not improve the model fit is that the perceptual and conceptual spaces are strongly correlated. This suggests that the typological prevalence patterns in the crosslinguistic data follow the perceptual dimensions. However, the model fit is actually worse when only using the conceptual features, an issue that we must explore further.

Furthermore, it may be that the conceptual features do help for the acquisition of color words in other languages. The lack of an effect of the conceptual space on top of the perceptual features may also be due to the (older) age of the children in the data. Overextension patterns in younger children may display effects of the conceptual dimensions, as well as frequency. We are currently planning to extend this research to a variety of error data sets, both in English and other languages, to see if similar results are found and to further evaluate the role of the various perceptual, typological, and frequency factors.

Another issue we plan to work on is the fact that the model performs 'too well': It predicts no overextensions for 6 out of the 8 color stimuli, despite children displaying a few errors on 4 of these colors. Using our typologically-derived semantic space within a fuller model of word learning, such as that of Fazly et al. (2010) or Nematzadeh et al. (2012), rather than using a simple categorization model as we do here, might further our insight into potential sources of overextensions.

Given our general methodological approach, reviewers noted other interesting possibilities and suggested that alternative design choices are possible as well for the dimensionality reduction technique, the alignment method between predicted model data and observed experimental data, and the statistical evaluation procedure. We plan to follow up on these suggestions in future research, in addition to the exploration of a wider set of crosslinguistic error patterns, the consideration of earlier developmental stages, and the use of a more realistic word-learning model.

Acknowledgments

We gratefully acknowledge NSERC of Canada for the funding of both authors, as well as the four anonymous reviewers for their comments and suggestions.

References

Elsa Jaffe Bartlett. 1978. The acquisition of the meaning of colour ters: a study of lexcal development. pages 89–108.

W. G. Bateman. 1915. The Naming of Colors by

Children the Binet Test. *The Pedagogical Seminary*, 22(4):469–486, December.

Barend Beekhuizen, Afsaneh Fazly, and Suzanne Stevenson. 2014. Learning Meaning without Primitives: Typology Predicts Developmental Patterns. In *Proceedings of the 36th annual meeting of the Cognitive Science Society*.

Brent Berlin and Paul Kay. 1969. *Basic color terms: Their universality and evolution*. University of California Press, Berkeley, CA.

Melissa Bowerman. 1993. Typological perspectives on language acquisition: Do crosslinguistic patterns predict development? In Eve V. Clark, editor, *Proceedings of the Twenty-fifth Annual Child Language Research Forum*, pages 7–15, Stanford, CA. CSLI Publications.

Eve V. Clark. 1973. What's in a word? On the child's acquisition of semantics in his first language. In Timothy E. Moore, editor, *Cognitive Development and the Acquisition of Language*, pages 65–110. New York: Academic Press.

Ian R. L. Davies, Greville Corbett, Harry McGurk, and David Jerrett. 1994. A developmental study of he acquisition of colour terms in Setswana. *Journal of Child Language*, 21:693–712.

Ian R. L. Davies, Greville Corbett, Harry McGurk, and Catriona MacDermid. 1998. A developmental study of the acquisition of Russian colous terms. *Journal of Child Language*, 25:395–417.

Afsaneh Fazly, Afra Alishahi, and Suzanne Stevenson. 2010. A probabilistic computational model of cross-situational word learning. *Cognitive Science*, 34(6):1017–1063.

Dedre Gentner and Melissa Bowerman. 2009. Why some spatial semantic categories are harder to learn than others. The Typological Prevalence Hypothesis. In J. Guo, E. Lieven, N. Budwig, S. Ervin-Tripp, K. Nakamura, and S. Ozcaliskan, editors, *Crosslinguistic approaches to the psychology of language. Research in the tradition of Dan Isaac Slobin*, chapter 34, pages 465–480. Psychology Press, New York, NY.

Dedre Gentner. 1982. Why Nouns are Learned Before Verbs : Linguistic Relativity versus Natural Partitioning. In Stan Kuczaj, editor, *Language Development. Volume 2: Language, Thought, and Culture*, volume 2, chapter 11, pages 301–334. Lawrence Erlbaum Associates, Hillsale, New Jersey.

Judith C Goodman, Philip S Dale, and Ping Li. 2008. Does frequency count? Parental input and the acquisition of vocabulary. *Journal of child language*, 35(3):515–31, August.

Insa Gülzow and Natalia Gagarina, editors. 2007. *Frequency Effects in Language Acquisition. Defining the Limits of Frequency as an Explanatory Concept*. De Gruyter Mouton, Berlin.

Sara Harkness. 1973. Universal Aspects of Learning Color Codes: A Study in Two Cultures. *Ethos*, pages 175–200.

H. Hotelling. 1933. Analysis of a complex of statistical variables into principal components. *Journal of Educational Psychology*, 24:417–441,498–520.

Z.M. Istomina. 1960. Perception and naming of color in early childhood. *Izvestiia Akademii Pedagogicheskikh*, 113:37–45.

Paul Kay, Brent Berlin, Luisa Maffi, William R. Merrifield, and Richard Cook. 2009. *World Color Survey*. CSLI Publications, Stanford, CA.

Stephen C. Levinson, Sergio Meira, The Language Group, and Cognition. 2003. 'Natural Concepts' in the Spatial Topological Domain – Adpositional Meanings in Crosslinguistic Perspective: An Exercise in Semantic Typology. *Language*, 79(3):485–516.

Asifa Majid, Fiona Jordan, and Michael Dunn. 2015. Semantic systems in closely related languages. *Language Sciences*, 49:1–18.

Aida Nematzadeh, Afsaneh Fazly, and Suzanne Stevenson. 2012. A computational model of memory, attention, and word learning. In *Proceedings of the Third Workshop on Cognitive Modeling and Computational Linguistics*.

Robert M Nosofsky. 1987. Attention and Learning Processes in the Identification and Categorization of Integral Stimuli. *Journal of Experimental Psychology*, 13(1):87–108.

Nicola J. Pitchford and Kathy J. Mullen. 2003. The development of conceptual colour categories in preschool children: Influence of perceptual organization. *Visual Cognition*, 10(1):51–57.

Terry Regier, Paul Kay, and Naveen Khetarpal. 2007. Color naming reflects optimal partitions of color space. *PNAS*, 104:1436–1441.

Debi Roberson, Jules Davidoff, Ian R L Davies, and Laura R Shapiro. 2004. The development of color categories in two languages: a longitudinal study. *Journal of experimental psychology. General*, 133(4):554–71, December.

Nancy N. Soja. 1994. Young Children's Concept of Color and Its Relation to the Acquisition of Color Words. *Child Development*, 65:918–937.

Anna L. Theakston, Elena V.M. Lieven, Julian M. Pine, and Caroline M. Rowland. 2001. The role of performance limitations in the acquisition of verb-argument structure: An alternative account. *Journal of Child Languages*, pages 127–152.

Daniel Yurovsky, Katie Wagner, David Barner, and Michael C. Frank. 2015. Signatures of Domain-General Categorization Mechanisms in Color Word Learning. In *Proceedings CogSci*.

Motif discovery in infant- and adult-directed speech

Bogdan Ludusan[1], Amanda Seidl[2], Emmanuel Dupoux[1], Alejandrina Cristia[1]
[1]Laboratoire de Sciences Cognitives et Psycholinguistique (ENS, EHESS, CNRS)
Département d'Études Cognitives, École Normale Supérieure, PSL Research University, France
[2]Department of Speech, Language, and Hearing Sciences
Purdue University, USA
bogdan.ludusan@ens.fr, aseidl@purdue.edu
{emmanuel.dupoux, alecristia}@gmail.com

Abstract

Infant-directed speech (IDS) is thought to play a key role in determining infant language acquisition. It is thus important to describe how computational models of infant language acquisition behave when given an input of IDS, as compared to adult-directed speech (ADS). In this paper, we explore how an acoustic motif discovery algorithm fares when presented with speech from both registers. Results show small but significant differences in performance, with lower recall and lower cluster collocation in IDS than ADS, but a higher cluster purity in IDS. Overall, these results are inconsistent with a view suggesting that IDS is acoustically clearer than ADS in a way that systematically facilitates lexical recognition. Similarities and differences with human infants' word segmentation are discussed.

1 Introduction

The ability to learn words from continuous speech is a crucial skill in language acquisition, since only about 7% of words occur in isolation, and thus infants must be able to segment, i.e. pull out words from running speech. It has been proposed that infant-directed-speech (IDS), the particular register that parents use when addressing their infant, could facilitate word segmentation when compared to adult-directed-speech (ADS) (Singh et al., 2009; Thiessen et al., 2005). Even though a number of acoustic and linguistic studies have documented systematic differences between these registers (Cristia, 2013; Fernald and Morikawa, 1993), there is little computational work assessing how precisely word segmentation performance is affected by these differences. The present report takes one step in this direction.

1.1 Computational model of word segmentation

We model infant word learning using MODIS (Catanese et al., 2013), a computational system which attempts to discover spoken terms from the raw speech signal. We think that this system is cognitively plausible for several reasons. First, the algorithm does not rely on labeled or pre-segmented data. Instead, it takes as input spectral features and looks for repetitions inside of a short signal buffer (which thus resembles a short-term memory). When the first repetition is found, two acoustic stretches that are judged to be matched are stored together as a cluster (represented as a kind of average of the acoustic items it contains) inside the library. Clusters can be thought of as 'lexical entries' in the context of this project and the library as its long-term memory. It then continues parsing the speech looking for matches with respect to the clusters in the long-term memory as well as other close repetitions in the buffer. If a match to an existing cluster is found, the cluster model is updated, in order for it to also contain information about the latest token.

Given its general features, this algorithm appears to be a reasonable approximation of word segmentation strategies used by a naïve learner (a learner who has not yet extracted abstract phonemic categories). It is very likely that infants begin to segment words before they have learned their language's phoneme inventory since, in certain situations, infants as young as 4 months of age can recognize words in fluent speech (Johnson et al., 2014), but there is little evidence that infants this young have converged upon their native phonemes (Tsuji and Cristia, 2014). Moreover, since young infants can more easily recognize word tokens that are similar acoustically, than tokens which are dissimilar (Bortfeld et al., 2005; Singh et al., 2012), it follows that an acoustic motif discovery algorithm is not an unreasonable first approach.

Proceedings of the Sixth Workshop on Cognitive Aspects of Computational Language Learning, pages 93–102,
Lisbon, Portugal, 18 September 2015.

It is also very plausible that the patterns infants discover in running speech will be constrained to a short-term memory window, although we do not know of evidence directly addressing this (most work has investigated the limits of long-term memory, e.g. (Houston and Jusczyk, 2003), rather than how close in time two subsequent repetitions must occur to be detectable). Finally, we know that infants can store repeated words in some form of long-term memory because this is precisely the type of design that typical word segmentation studies have, whereby the child is familiarized with a word repeated and later tested with novel instances of those wordforms.

1.2 Influencing factors and general predictions

Properties of IDS compared to ADS	Predictions for word learning
Not tested in this paper	
prosodic boundaries easier	IDS>ADS
clearer referential situation	IDS>ADS
simpler vocabulary	IDS>ADS
more attention grabbing	IDS>ADS
Tested in this paper	
acoustically more variable	IDS<ADS
more repetitions	IDS>ADS
more bursty	IDS>ADS

Table 1: Differences between IDS and ADS and potential effects for word learning.

IDS is characterized by an array of properties (Cristia, 2013, see Table 1), some of which could facilitate or hinder word segmentation. IDS has been reported to contain shorter utterances and clearer *prosodic boundaries* than ADS. To test this would require a learner that extracts and uses prosodic cues from the speech signal, which is not the case in the current implementation of MODIS (see also the Conclusions). The same would also be true for *referential and contextual cues*. The effect of *vocabulary* is neutralized in our experiment, because the corpus used contained the same keywords in both registers, and only these keywords were considered for the evaluation of word learning. Regarding *attention*, since MODIS works by finding acoustic matches in the speech signal, it does not have a cognitive component that models the attention process.

Therefore, none of first 4 differences in Table 1 are tested here. Instead, our corpus and computational model allows us to look at differences in performance related to three other properties of IDS: *acoustic variability*, *repetitions*, and *burstiness*.

First and foremost, mounting evidence suggests that sounds and words are more variable in IDS than ADS. For instance, Martin and colleagues have documented that phonemic categories are significantly *harder* to classify in IDS than in ADS (Martin et al., 2015). This may be due to an increase in variability, which has been documented in several studies (Cristia and Seidl, 2014; Kuhl et al., 1997; McMurray et al., 2013). If the acoustic implementation of phonemes is more variable in IDS than ADS, it is possible that other linguistic levels that build on sounds, such as words, might also be significantly different across the registers.

To our knowledge, there is only one modelling study that partially investigated this question, although it was not a model of word learning, but rather of phoneme learning. Kirchhoff and Schimmel (2005) trained a speech recognizer with human-segmented and labeled tokens of three minimally different target words (sheep, shoe and shop) drawn either from IDS or ADS, and tested the performance on a new set of IDS and ADS tokens. Results revealed a lower performance overall in the IDS-trained classifier, but a smaller generalization cost (i.e., the loss in performance in switching from IDS to ADS was smaller than vice versa). These results are consistent with the idea that words are more variable in IDS, and suggest that there could be learnability differences across the two registers. It remains to be seen whether such effects would also emerge in a model of word learning in which there is no explicit human-obtained segmentation and labels.

It is to be expected that acoustic variability could be problematic to learners who find wordforms using acoustic pattern matching, leading them to posit too many or too few types (e.g., the word *dog* is so variable that the learner posits two different types, dog1 and dog2; or confuses them with similar words such that *dog* and *dock* are clustered together). Laboratory work in infancy demonstrates that early on infants have difficulty matching wordforms that are acoustically variable (Bortfeld et al., 2005; Singh et al., 2012), as if infants create separate lexical entries for e.g., the word *dog* spoken by two different speakers. This is precisely what occurs with word segmentation models that operate on the basis of acoustic motif discovery, and thus we predict that our the model would perform more poorly in IDS than ADS, because of its greater variability.

The second property of IDS that we address is *repetition*. It has been reported that IDS is more repetitive than ADS (Daland, 2013). We suspect repetition is perceptually relevant to infants because most word segmentation experiments use very repetitive stimuli, and this feature has even been found to draw infants' attention (McRoberts et al., 2009). Some repetition is necessary for our model learner, as this is a condition for incorporating an item into the lexicon (words that are not repeated cannot be found). However, once the second token of the same type is detected, it is unclear whether any benefit is derived from additional repetitions. MODIS will decide whether a pattern encountered matches one in the lexicon, by comparing the new pattern to an average or prototype of all the other patterns in that cluster. Hence, it is possible that additional tokens of the same type will simply compound the negative effects of increased segmental variation.

A third property of IDS that we address is *burstiness*, which characterizes the likelihood of a word to re-appear in the same conversation once it has been used. Thus, registers where one tends to stay longer on a given topic will be more bursty - for instance, news reports are more bursty than spontaneous phone conversations. Daland has hypothesized that burstiness should be higher in IDS than ADS (Daland, 2013), although we know of no systematic investigation of IDS corpora or the effects of burstiness on infant perception. Nonetheless, it is certain that burstiness should improve the word segmentation performance of our learner, since having a higher proportion of repetitions of the same word inside the short memory buffer would translate into a higher chance of detecting that word.

2 Methods

2.1 Corpus

2.1.1 Speakers

The twenty speakers in this study were ten mothers of 4-month-olds (M = 0;4.35, range: 0;3.95 -0;4.99) and ten mothers of 11-month-olds (M = 0;11.40, range: 0;11.120;12.01). The mothers were the child's primary caregiver, and native speakers of American English from a small Midwestern city. Infants were healthy full-terms with typical development and no known personal or familial history of hearing or language impairments, according to parental report.

2.1.2 Recording and human coding procedure

Full details on the corpus can be found on: `https://sites.google.com/site/acrsta/Home/nsf_allophones_corpora`. The key information for the present purposes is the following:

Speakers were provided with a set of objects and photos, each labeled with a target word. They were told that we were interested in how parents talk to their children about objects. The words containing the vowels did not constitute minimal pairs, so as not to make the parents overly conscious of the contrasts under study. The IDS portion was always carried out first, and during it, the caregiver and child were left alone. When the mother had finished going through all items, an experimenter returned accompanied by a confederate adult. The mother then repeated the task with the confederate.

The 20 speakers included in the present work are a subset of 36 mothers whose speech (excluding sections with overlapping noise or speech) had been analyzed in previous work (Cristia and Seidl, 2014). In that study, only one vowel per target word was coded and analyzed. A subset of caregivers was used for the present purposes because their speech had also been coded to investigate whether IDS and ADS differed to similar extents in the weak and strong vowels of bisyllabic and trochaic target word (Wang et al., 2015). This meant that we had access to the temporal location of both strong and weak vowels in some of the target words.

For the current study, since only the first two vowels of some words were coded in the corpus, we will use a proxy for words, which we call a target segment. It is defined as being the stretch of speech between the beginning of the first vowel and the end of the second vowel of a coded word. This definition is illustrated in Figure 1. We then kept the target segments appearing in both speech registers and collapsed all composed words classes into the class containing the first word only (e.g. picnic basket → picnic, peekaboo book → peekaboo), since the coded vowels actually belong to

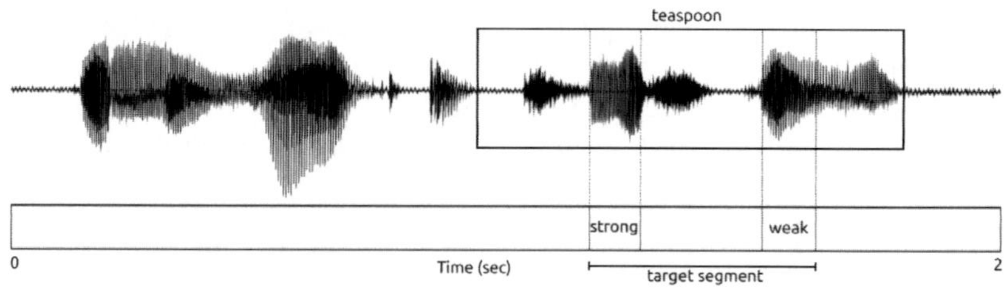

Figure 1: Example of target segment. The waveform and associated annotation of the utterance "Then we have a teaspoon" is illustrated. The annotation codes the position of the two vowels of the word "teaspoon". Below the vowel annotation we illustrate the target segment considered, defined as the stretch of speech between the beginning of the first vowel and the end of the second vowel of a given word. For comparison, the entire word is represented above the waveform.

the first word (e.g. picnic, peekaboo), not to the second one (e.g. basket, book). Composed words whose first word contained only one vowel were kept in their own separate class (e.g. tea-kettle, best-in-show). This gave us a total of 2298 target segments, 1300 in IDS and 998 in ADS. A complete list of the target segments is presented in Appendix A. Note that this coding was used only for evaluation purposes, as there is no training phase for the algorithm.

As can be seen in the example in Figure 1, the target segment only partially covers an actual word. We have estimated this coverage to be between 80-90%, in the case of words starting with a consonant-vowel (CV) sequence and ending in a vowel (e.g. bamboo, pesto) and around 50%, in the case of 4-syllable words (e.g. dictionary, tapioca). Since most of the target segments, both in terms of number of types and number of tokens, belong to the words starting with a CV sequence and ending with a vowel-consonant sequence (e.g. bacon, picnic), we could conclude that the majority of our target segments cover at least 2/3 of the actual word.

2.1.3 Corpus characteristics

In previous analyses comparing IDS and ADS on this subset of the corpus, pitch was found to be higher (particularly in stressed vowels) in IDS and there was also a trend for more peripherality in IDS, but no stable differences in vowel duration were seen (Wang et al., 2015). Also, an analysis of the whole corpus has shown greater variability in acoustic characteristics of stressed vowels in IDS than ADS (weak vowels had not been marked or analyzed) (Cristia and Seidl, 2014). Thus, the corpus represents well the prosodic and segmental characteristics of IDS alluded to in the introduction.

For the purposes of the present project, we further investigated potential differences in repetition. As expected, parents produced more repetitions of the target segments in IDS than ADS (significant according to a Wilcoxon's test, V (19) = 187, $p = 0.001$; mean for IDS = 3.358 repetitions per target segment, SD = 1.358; mean for ADS = 2.147, SD = 0.564).

Besides computing a measure of repetition, we have also attempted to measure differences in burstiness between IDS and ADS. Burstiness was defined as the reciprocal of the average distance (in seconds) between the end of the nth occurrence of a target segment and the beginning of the $n+1^{th}$ occurrence of the same word, provided that these two occurrences are not separated by another target segment. It was computed on a per-speaker basis and only for target segments appearing at least twice, in both the IDS and ADS recordings of the same speaker. About 4.618 seconds elapsed between two consecutive repetitions in ADS, compared to 7.371 in IDS. This meant that the average burst rate was 0.292 (SD = 0.186) in ADS, and 0.15 (SD = 0.065) in ADS. Thus, contrary to our expectations, a higher burstiness was obtained for ADS than for IDS.[1]

[1]We checked whether the difference in burstiness could be explained by the speech rate difference between the two registers. In order estimate speech rate, we calculated the average duration of the target words, all of which were bisyllables and occurred in both registers.The average duration was .311 s (SD = .042) in ADS and .362 (SD = .068) in IDS, in line with the view that IDS is slower than ADS.The speech rate difference (14%) does not seem to fully explain the difference seen in the burstiness between the two registers (48%). Nonetheless, this measure does not take into account pauses, which are likely to be considerably longer in IDS.

We have seen that the three IDS characteristics that might affect the performance of the model point in different directions. We lay out our predictions once our evaluation metrics have been introduced.

2.2 Algorithm

We used the open-source spoken term discovery system called MODIS (Catanese et al., 2013). Is it based on the seed discovery principle: it searches for matches of a short audio segment, referred to as the seed, in a larger segment, called a buffer. The search is performed by using a segmental variant of the dynamic time warping (DTW) algorithm. Once a match is found (decision taken based on a similarity threshold between the two speech segments), the seed will be extended and the match performed using the longer seed. This process will continue as long as the dis-similarity between the segments stays under the set threshold. When this threshold is reached, the term candidate is checked as to whether is complies with a minimum length requirement and stored in the motif library. An abstraction of the matched segments is stored in the library, represented by their median model. Next, this library of terms is compared against any new seed and only if no match is found in the library will the DTW search explained earlier take place. The match against the library terms employs also a self similarity matrix check. After the entire data set is searched, a post-processing of the obtained terms is performed in order to merge all overlapping segments into one single term.

The algorithm has several important parameters that must be set: the *seed size*, the minimum stretch of speech matched against the buffer, the *minimum term size* the algorithm will find, the *buffer size* in which the seed is searched and the *similarity threshold*, ϵ_{DTW}. Since the latter parameter influences the level of similarity between the members of the same term class, we have varied it in our experiment, while keeping the rest of the parameters constant. The seed length was set to 0.25 s, while the buffer length was set to 90 s, in order to model infants' short-term memory. The minimum term size considered was 0.5 s so as to be able to contain the majority of the target segments.

The variation of the similarity threshold can be seen as follows: When this parameter is low, even small deviances of similarity are rejected, representing a 'conservative' approach. When it is high, even large dissimilarities are accepted, representing a 'lax' approach. Based on previous infant word segmentation research, it appears that young children are conservative early on (Singh et al., 2012) – but how conservative? There is no principled way to set this parameter, as any decision we make would likely not have a clear basis in research. However, in order to restrain the search range of ϵ_{DTW} values on which we will perform our analysis, we ran MODIS on the combined ADS-IDS recordings of one speaker and we decided to take an interval of [2.0, 4.0]. The minimum value was the lowest threshold that returned any term classes, while the maximum value was the threshold value that gave a saturation point for the evaluation metrics measured.

We use as input features for the spoken term discovery system Mel frequency cepstral coefficients, a standard spectral representation used in speech applications. We compute the first 12 cepstral coefficients and the energy in a 20 ms window, every 10 ms, along with their delta (difference) and double delta (acceleration) coefficients.

2.3 Evaluation

As noted in the Introduction, our conceptual goal is to compare performance of this segmentation algorithm between IDS and ADS. We have also drawn several specific predictions. In this section, we explain how these predictions map onto the dependent variables used for the evaluation.

Since the corpus has not been exhaustively coded, we did not penalize the algorithm for clusters that do not include any target segments. Indeed, there may be other words that are repeated in the corpus (e.g., 'baby' or 'mommy') which have not been coded, so clusters could have been formed around these other words. Instead, we inspect only clusters that include at least one token of a target segment.

Given that word edges for target segments are not marked (only vowels), we consider a cluster to include a given token if one of the acoustic stretches included in that cluster covers the region between the beginning of the first vowel of the word and the end of the second vowel of that token. We derive a measure of *recall* as the number of tokens that appear in any given cluster divided by the total number of coded tokens. It is possible

We return to the potential limitations of our implementation of burstiness in the discussion.

that the higher repetition found in IDS will lead to higher coverage in this register as compared to ADS. At the same time, the opposite outcome could be expected if one would take into account the higher burstiness found in ADS. Thus, a clear prediction cannot be made.

As mentioned, there are target segments whose vowels were not coded because they overlap with speech or noise or were not produced with the intended vowel, nonetheless, it is possible for the algorithm to recognize matches for such uncoded words. Therefore, it would be unfair to penalize clusters that include target segments as well as stretches of speech other than the target segments that have not been coded by humans. However, when one cluster contains tokens from two or more different target segments, this will be penalized by our second dependent measure, namely cluster *purity*. It is defined as being the number of different target segments contained in a cluster, divided by the number of target segment classes. On the basis of our arguments above, we cannot make any clear prediction regarding how IDS and ADS will differ for this measure.

Third, we derive a measure that describes the amount of fragmentation of the found motif clusters. It is defined as being the percentage of clusters into which a particular target segment is found, out of the total number of clusters where target segments have been found. We will report the results in terms of *collocation*, defined as being equal to 1 - the amount of fragmentation. We expect IDS, with its greater variability, to yield a lower collocation.

3 Results

Analysis scripts and primary data and results files are available for download from `https://osf.io/y7kfw/`.

When no target segment is found by the algorithm for the speech of one caregiver, this results in missing data, as no recall, purity, or collocation can be calculated in these conditions. Therefore, we excluded from inspection all settings of the similarity threshold that resulted in missing data prior to carrying out statistical analyses. Data was included for settings 2.9-4 (at .1 intervals).

In general terms, we observed that performance is very good in terms of collocation and purity (above .6 for all individual speakers and for both registers), with performance for both of these decreasing and becoming more variable at the individual level as ϵ_{DTW} is set to laxer criteria. In contrast, recall performance is overall lower and more variable, with coverage increasing as laxer criteria are used.

Turning now to our key question, we calculated the difference in performance in IDS and ADS, for each measure and for each speaker. We tested for significant differences across the two registers in two ways: (1) keeping each ϵ_{DTW} value separate, and (2) collapsing across all ϵ_{DTW} values.

To evaluate for significance in the separate case, given that many such tests would have to be carried out (there are 12 levels for the similarity threshold in each evaluation measure), we wanted to control for repeated testing to avoid alpha risk inflation. Therefore, we used a step-down permutation resampling test (N = 10,000) and estimated the p-value for an observed t-statistic (from a one-sample t-test) through the rank of that p-value within the distribution of values for that statistic found under the null hypothesis.[2]

For the analyses collapsing across this threshold, we took the median across all threshold values within each caregiver, and used a Wilcoxon one-sample test to assess whether this average difference score was significantly different from zero for each evaluation dimension separately. We decided to employ the median followed by a Wilcoxon's non-parametric test based on the sum of the signed ranks because there was not clear evidence that such difference scores were normally distributed (the distributions were kurtotic with some outliers).

Both analyses revealed that there were some

[2]In the general permutation procedure, a distribution of a test statistic under the null hypothesis can be generated as follows: the sign of a random number and selection of individual difference scores is flipped (such that what used to indicate higher performance in IDS than ADS becomes the opposite) and the appropriate statistic (in this case, the t from a one-sample t-test, following usual practice van der Laan et al. (2004)) is calculated. The procedure is repeated many times, to generate a distribution of p-values under the null hypothesis. The adjusted p-value is then estimated as the rank of the absolute of the statistic in question against the distribution of absolute values found when the null hypothesis is true. The step-down version of the permutation procedure involves two changes. First, flipping the difference scores is done for all observations associated with the same individual together, which preserves the correlational structure of the data. Second, the distribution under the null is calculated once with all the data, and then repeated removing the strand of data (in our case, all the data associated with a given threshold parameter value) whose adjusted p-value is significant. The procedure stops when the adjusted value exceeds alpha.

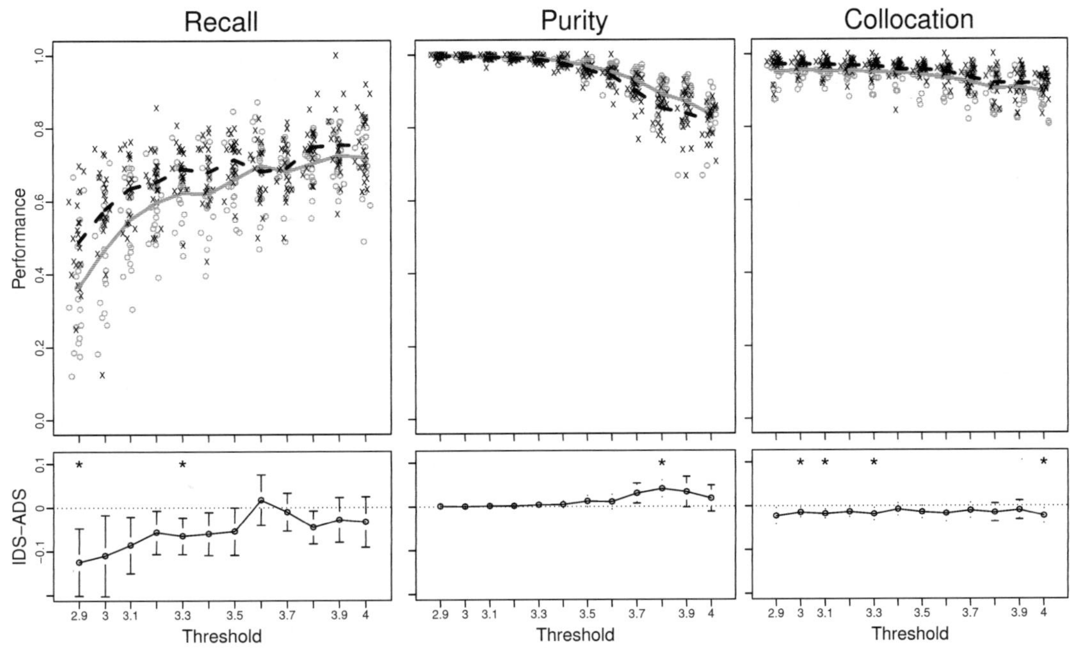

Figure 2: Performance (top panels; IDS in gray and ADS in black) and difference (IDS-ADS, bottom panels) for each of the three evaluation dimensions as a function of the ϵ_{DTW} threshold. Each point in the top panel represents a mother's score, separately for IDS (gray circles) and ADS (black crosses). The difference scores in the bottom represent the average difference and 95% confidence intervals across parents. Stars represent cases where the difference is significant at the $p < .05$ level, corrected for multiple comparison using a step-down permutation resampling test across parents.

significant differences across the registers for all the evaluation metrics computed. As shown in Figure 2, two of the ϵ_{DTW} values (both in the "conservative" region) lead to significantly higher performance in ADS than in IDS in terms of recall. This was replicated in our second analysis (based on the median across all ϵ_{DTW}): V(19) = 9, p=.016, 95% confidence interval (-0.087;-0.019), pseudo-median -0.050. As for purity, there was a trend for better performance in IDS than ADS that was significant for one ϵ_{DTW} value, closer to the liberal end of our threshold continuum. This advantage was replicated when looking at median values: V(19) = 55, $p = .006$, 95% confidence interval (.005;0.027), pseudo-median 0.016. As for collocation, performance was significantly better in ADS than IDS mostly in the same conservative region as with recall, a result replicated in the Wilcoxon's t-test on median difference scores: V(19) = 1, p=.003, 95% confidence interval (-.012;-0.006), pseudo-median -0.010.

Next, we had wondered whether greater repetition and burstiness would lead to better recall. The overall pattern of results appears to indicate this is not the case because although IDS has more repetitions, it has lower recall – although this could possibly relate to burstiness. As a first approach, we calculated Spearman correlations across speakers between recall performance (averaged across all parameters) and number of repetitions, on the one hand, or rate of burstiness, on the other, within each register separately.

As for repetitions, the estimate was moderate and positive in both registers, albeit significant for IDS r(18) = .549, $p = .014$, but only marginally in ADS r(18) = .430, $p = .060$. Thus, there appears to be some relationship between recall and repetition, but the greater number of repetitions in IDS over ADS is not sufficient for there to be a boost in recall in IDS over ADS overall.

Regarding burstiness, estimates were low, non-significant and surprisingly negative: IDS r(18) = -.159, p =.501; ADS r(18) = -.299, p =.199). The negative correlation would indicate that the higher burstiness is, the lower the recall – we return to this issue in the discussion.

4 Discussion

The first conclusion that must be drawn from the results of running our naïve learning algorithm on these data is that the difference in performance with IDS and ADS materials is subtle: Collapsing across threshold parameter values, it only amounts to absolute differences of between 1 and 5%. Nonetheless, these differences are there, since they surface in all three evaluation metrics, both when we use a multiple comparisons correction procedure, and when we average across all reasonable settings of the similarity threshold.

We had stated several predictions based on previous work. We had no clear expectation regarding *recall*, since the two factors that might affect it, repetition and burstiness, seemed to favour different registers. Overall, we observed an ADS advantage of about 5%, concentrated in the conservative regions of the similarity parameter. As for the relationship between repetition and recall, we found that while our IDS was more repetitious than the ADS, recall was lower for the former than the latter. However, the correlations in individual variation within each register were positive. This pattern of results partially supports our intuition: More repetition helps unsupervised motif discovery. However, the data go beyond our hunch in that differences in repetitiousness do not account for register differences. Regarding burstiness, we failed to confirm the prediction that IDS was more bursty, and we further found a negative non-significant correlation with recall. This may indicate that our corpus, elicited in a task where speakers did not have much lexical choice, was not ideal to measure burstiness differences. Additionally, the precise implementation we used may have confounded tempo differences, and an alternative burstiness definition, in terms of number of intervening words, could be more appropriate.

Turning to the second evaluation metric, *purity*, we also had no specific hypothesis, however, we found an overall advantage for IDS, with significant results for only one parameter value (located towards the liberal end of our continuum) as well as in analysis over median scores. Overall, performance with IDS was about 1.6% higher than that for ADS in this metric, this effect being mainly located in the more liberal region of the similarity threshold. This indicates that, at least for those parameter values, clusters tend to straddle over lexical categories slightly more in ADS than IDS, or, put differently, that it is more often the case that two targets are classified into a single motif in ADS than IDS. This is unexpected but interesting, because the target words studied in the present corpus were not necessarily very similar to one another (see Appendix A).

Finally, as we expected, target segments were more often split into multiple clusters (reflected in a lower *collocation* score) in IDS than ADS. This corroborates our suspicion that the acoustic implementation of words is more variable in IDS, which also explains why differences are particularly clear for conservative parameter values. Nonetheless, the difference across registers was small, only about 1%.

We provided results for all the values of the similarity threshold because we believe it can yield some insight into infants' performance at different points of development, since younger infants (7.5-month-olds) have been found to be more conservative than older ones (9-12 months of age, (Singh et al., 2012)). Our computational model suggests that, if they behave like our model learner, younger infants should both fail to recognize words across diverse instantiations (cf. our recall results) and postulate too many lexical entries (cf. our collocation results). In other words, our computational model predicts that signal-related effects of register on word segmentation performance will be greatest, with an IDS disadvantage, for younger rather than older infants. It is possible that our purity results suggest that the IDS disadvantage be reversed in these older ages, who are supposedly more liberal in their acoustic matching. Extant infant work showing IDS advantages has looked at 7- and 8-month-olds (Singh et al., 2009; Thiessen et al., 2005), so future work should test these specific predictions in even younger infants.

Together with (Kirchhoff and Schimmel, 2005), which relied on hand-segmented words, the present results are relevant to the interpretation of infant performance in word segmentation tasks which compare IDS and ADS. Specifically, since neither classification of segmented words, nor motif discovery, are overall more successful in IDS than ADS, then it follows that infants' improved segmentation performance for IDS is not due to words being physically (or segmentally) easier to find or classify in IDS than ADS. Instead, there must be something else in the spoken signal that boosts infant performance in IDS. This other factor may be attention/arousal: Perhaps infants attend more to IDS stimuli (which is clear in preferential studies (Dunst et al., 2012)). Alternatively, infant performance may reflect a more complex cognitive bias, for instance if they apply different learning strategies when prompted by IDS (as proposed in the Natural Pedagogy framework (Csibra and Gergely, 2009)). Similar explanations have been put forward to explain improved performance for boosts in word-meaning mapping tasks in IDS over ADS (Graf Estes and Hurley, 2013).

There are many open questions that need to be revisited in other research, such as to what extent motif discovery reflects meaningful features of the algorithm that real infant utilize during word segmentation in the lab and in the world, the integration of multimodal information, or the extent to which specific predictions made from MODIS versus competing models are born out by infant data.

5 Conclusions

In this paper, we focused mainly on one documented difference between IDS and ADS, namely phonetic variability, and considered two lexical parameters, repetition and burstiness. We found that performance was affected by register, with an overall trend for lower performance in IDS than ADS when three metrics was considered. The impact of register was greatest when our model learner, which relies on acoustic matching, was conservative. We believe this result suggests that register differences relate to the differences in phonetic variability that have been separately documented, although additional analyses (for instance using regressions to explore individual variation) are needed to confirm this hypothesis. Furthermore, it would be important to repeat these analyses with other corpora, particularly those gathered at home, which may vary more naturally along other dimensions we also intended to explore, such as repetition and burstiness.

Additionally, other models are needed to gain a more holistic understanding of how register features affect learners' performance, since we only explored effects of a few IDS characteristics, and others remain unexplored (see Table 1). For example, IDS contains shorter utterances (Albin and Echols, 1996; Aslin et al., 1996) and is produced with more exaggerated prosodic edge marking than ADS (Fernald and Mazzie, 1991; Kondaurova and Bergeson, 2011). If there are shorter utterances in IDS it means that more words will occur at utterance edges which are, as mentioned above, also marked with increased acoustic salience in IDS. These utterance edges have been shown to be hot-spots for word segmentation (Seidl and Johnson, 2006), so much so that even infants as young as 4 months are able to find words at utterance edges using this strategy (Johnson et al., 2014). Recent work on speech-based spoken-term discovery has shown that the integration of prosodic boundary information in such a system improves segmentation performance (Ludusan et al., 2014). Since this was found in corpora containing ADS, we would like to explore whether the prosodic structure would give a boost in performance when IDS is given as input to MODIS, compared to when ADS is employed.

Acknowledgments

This work was supported by the European Research Council (grant ERC-2011-AdG-295810 BOOTPHON), the Agence Nationale pour la Recherche (grants ANR-14-CE30-0003 MechELex, ANR-2010-BLAN-1901-1 BOOT-LANG, ANR-10-IDEX-0001-02 PSL*, and ANR-10-LABX-0087 IEC), the Fondation de France, and NSF grant number 0843959. Statement of contributions: AS collected the corpus and oversaw coding; BL carried out the MODIS experiments; AC and BL carried out the statistical analyses, with input from all authors; AC and BL wrote a first draft; all authors contributed to the design and writing.

Appendix A. List of target words: *baboon, bacon, bamboo, basil, bassinet, beetle, Benji, best-in-show, dancer, dancing, daycare, decker, dictionary, disney, pansy, paper, pedal, peekaboo, pegboard, pencil, pendant, pepsi, pesto, picnic, piglet, shopping, tambourine, tapioca, tassel, tea-kettle, teaspoon, teddy* and *tender*.

References

Drema Albin and Catharine Echols. 1996. Stressed and word-final syllables in infant-directed speech. *Infant Behavior and Development*, 19:401418.

Richard Aslin, Julide Woodward, Nicholas LaMendola, and Thomas Bever. 1996. Models of word segmentation in fluent maternal speech to infants. In J. Morgan and K. Demuth, editors, *Signal to Syntax: Bootstrapping from Speech to Grammar in Early Acquisition*. Lawrence Earlbaum Associates, Mahwah, NJ.

Heather Bortfeld, James Morgan, Roberta Golinkoff, and Karen Rathbun. 2005. Mommy and me: Familiar names help launch babies into speech stream segmentation. *Psychological Science*, 16:298–304.

Laurence Catanese, Nathan Souviraà-Labastie, Bingqing Qu, Sebastien Campion, Guillaume Gravier, Emmanuel Vincent, and Frédéric Bimbot. 2013. MODIS: an audio motif discovery software. In *Proceedings of Interspeech*.

Alejandrina Cristia and Amanda Seidl. 2014. The hyperarticulation hypothesis of infant-directed speech. *Journal of Child Language*, 41:913–934.

Alejandrina Cristia. 2013. Input to language: The phonetics and perception of infant-directed speech. *Language and Linguistics Compass*, 7:157–170.

Gergely Csibra and György Gergely. 2009. Natural pedagogy. *Trends in cognitive sciences*, 13(4):148–153.

Robert Daland. 2013. Variation in the input: a case study of manner class frequencies. *Journal of child language*, 40(5):1091–1122.

Carl Dunst, Ellen Gorman, and Deborah Hamby. 2012. Preference for infant-directed speech in preverbal young children. *Center for Early Literacy Learning*, 5(1).

Anne Fernald and Claudia Mazzie. 1991. Prosody and focus in speech to infants and adults. *Developmental Psychology*, 27:209–221.

Anne Fernald and Hiromi Morikawa. 1993. Common themes and cultural variations in Japanese and American mothers' speech to infants. *Child development*, 64(3):637–656.

Katharine Graf Estes and Karinna Hurley. 2013. Infant-directed prosody helps infants map sounds to meanings. *Infancy*, 18(5):797–824.

Derek Houston and Peter Jusczyk. 2003. Infants' long-term memory for the sound patterns of words and voices. *Journal of Experimental Psychology: Human Perception and Performance*, 29(6):1143.

Elizabeth Johnson, Amanda Seidl, and Michael Tyler. 2014. The edge factor in early word segmentation: utterance-level prosody enables word form extraction by 6-month-olds. *PLoS ONE*, 9(1):e83546.

Katrin Kirchhoff and Steven Schimmel. 2005. Statistical properties of infant-directed versus adult-directed speech: insights from speech recognition. *The Journal of the Acoustical Society of America*, 117(4):2238–2246.

Maria Kondaurova and Tonya Bergeson. 2011. The effects of age and infant hearing status on maternal use of prosodic cues for clause boundaries in speech. *Journal of Speech Language and Hearing Research*, 54:740–754.

Patricia Kuhl, Jean Andruski, Inna Chistovich, Ludmilla Chistovich, Elena Kozhevnikova, Viktoria Ryskina, Elvira Stolyarova, Ulla Sundberg, and Francisco Lacerda. 1997. Cross-language analysis of phonetic units in language addressed to infants. *Science*, 277:684–686.

Bogdan Ludusan, Guillaume Gravier, and Emmanuel Dupoux. 2014. Incorporating prosodic boundaries in unsupervised term discovery. In *Proceedings of Speech Prosody*, pages 939–943.

Andrew Martin, Thomas Schatz, Maarten Versteegh, Kouki Miyazawa, Reiko Mazuka, Emmanuel Dupoux, and Alejandrina Cristia. 2015. Mothers speak less clearly to infants than to adults a comprehensive test of the hyperarticulation hypothesis. *Psychological science*, 26(3):341–347.

Bob McMurray, Kristine Kovack-Lesh, Dresden Goodwin, and William McEchron. 2013. Infant directed speech and the development of speech perception: Enhancing development or an unintended consequence? *Cognition*, 129:362–378.

Gerald McRoberts, Colleen McDonough, and Laura Lakusta. 2009. The role of verbal repetition in the development of infant speech preferences from 4 to 14 months of age. *Infancy*, 14(2):162–194.

Amanda Seidl and Elizabeth Johnson. 2006. Infant word segmentation revisited: Edge alignment facilitates target extraction. *Developmental Science*, 9 (6):565–573.

Leher Singh, Sarah Nestor, Chandni Parikh, and Ashley Yull. 2009. Influences of infant-directed speech on early word recognition. *Infancy*, 14(6):654–666.

Leher Singh, Steven Reznick, and Liang Xuehua. 2012. Infant word segmentation and childhood vocabulary development: A longitudinal analysis. *Developmental Science*, 15:482–495.

Erik Thiessen, Emily Hill, and Jenny Saffran. 2005. Infant-directed speech facilitates word segmentation. *Infancy*, 7:53–71.

Sho Tsuji and Alejandrina Cristia. 2014. Perceptual attunement in vowels: A meta-analysis. *Developmental psychobiology*, 56(2):179–191.

Mark J van der Laan, Sandrine Dudoit, and Katherine S Pollard. 2004. Multiple testing. Part II. Step-down procedures for control of the family-wise error rate. *Statistical Applications in Genetics and Molecular Biology*, 3(1):1–35.

Yuanyuan Wang, Amanda Seidl, and Alejandrina Cristia. 2015. Acoustic-phonetic differences between infant-and adult-directed speech: the role of stress and utterance position. *Journal of child language*, 42(4):821–842.

Modeling dative alternations of individual children

Antal van den Bosch
Centre for Language Studies
Radboud University
PO Box 9103, NL-5000 HD Nijmegen
the Netherlands
a.vandenbosch@let.ru.nl

Joan Bresnan
Center for the Study of Language and Information
Stanford University
Stanford, CA 94305-4115
United States of America
bresnan@stanford.edu

Abstract

We address the question whether children can acquire mature use of higher-level grammatical choices from the linguistic input, given only general prior knowledge and learning biases. We do so on the basis of a case study with the dative alternation in English, building on a study by de Marneffe et al. (2012) who model the production of the dative alternation by seven young children, using data from the Child Language Data Exchange System corpus. Using mixed-effects logistic modelling on the aggregated data of these children, De Marneffe *et al.* report that the children's choices can be predicted both by their own utterances and by child-directed speech. Here we bring the computational modeling down to the individual child, using memory-based learning and incremental learning curve studies. We observe that for all children, their dative choices are best predicted by a model trained on child-directed speech. Yet, models trained on two individual children for which sufficient data is available are about as accurate. Furthermore, models trained on the dative alternations of these children provide approximations of dative alternations in caregiver speech that are about as accurate as training and testing on caregiver data only.

1 Introduction

The production of language is the result of a great number of choices made by the individual speaker, where each choice may be affected by various factors that, according to a large body of work, range from simple word frequencies to subtle semantic factors. For instance, which variant of the dative alternation speakers produce has been shown in a corpus study to be partially affected by the animacy and givenness of the recipient and theme (Bresnan et al., 2007). An inanimate recipient tends to co-occur with a prepositional dative construction ("bring more jobs and more federal spending to their little area").

Somehow and at some point in language acquisition, children learn these preferences, but it takes several years before children approximate adult language use. Monitoring and modeling this process of development may shed light on the inner workings of language learning in general, but to keep experiments under control, most studies, including the one presented here, zoom in on a representative but specific phenomenon. The dative alternation has been the topic of several studies in which computational models are trained on naturalistic data (Perfors et al., 2010; Parisien and Stevenson, 2010; Villavicencio et al., 2013; Conwell et al., 2011), such as offered by the Child Language Data Exchange System (CHILDES) (MacWhinney, 2000), a publicly available database of children's speech produced in a natural environment. These approaches address what is conventionally known as "Baker's paradox" (Baker, 1979; Pinker, 1989), which can be phrased as the question how children learn not to generalize a syntactic alternation to cases that block alternation, such as the verb 'donate', which only allows the prepositional dative construction.

In contrast, the present contribution continues a line of research introduced by de Marneffe et al. (2012), who formulate three research questions: (1) do children show sensitivity to linguistic probability in their own syntactic choices, and if so, (2) are those probabilities driven by the same factors that affect adult production? And finally, (3) do children assign the same weight to various factors as their caretakers? If so, then this may support the hypothesis that from early on children are sen-

Proceedings of the Sixth Workshop on Cognitive Aspects of Computational Language Learning, pages 103–112,
Lisbon, Portugal, 18 September 2015. ©2015 Association for Computational Linguistics.

sitive to (complex) variable distributional patterns.

At the highest theoretical level, the present study addresses the question whether children can acquire mature use of higher-level grammatical choices from the linguistic input, given only general prior knowledge and learning biases—or is a rich system of domain-specific abstract linguistic knowledge required from the outset? See, for example, Ambridge and Lieven (2015; Pine et al. (2013; Yang (2013; Conwell et al. (2011; Perfors et al. (2010), for a recent sample of the debate.

The present study addresses this question by applying a well-developed exemplar-based machine learning model incrementally to children's linguistic experiences, represented by samples of child and caregiver productions from the CHILDES corpora (MacWhinney, 2000), gathered for the prior study of de Marneffe et al. (2012). In terms of computational theory, the model used in the present study is one of the class of mathematical kernel methods from Machine Learning theory, which encompass classical learning models such as exemplar theory (Jäkel et al., 2009; Nosofsky, 1986).

More generally, we compare the predictions of an exemplar-based machine learning method to choices made by individual human subjects as a direct test of the model's cognitive plausibility for learning. Following Jäkel et al. (2009) we use the tools-to-theories heuristic of Gigerenzer (1991) in that we see our model as a mathematically and computationally simple and transparent emulation of the complex individual subject. What we emulate is the subject trying to model the data he or she observes as examples stored in memory (Jäkel et al., 2009).

2 The dative construction in English

Syntactic alternations such as the genitive, dative, or locative alternation in English are choices that speakers have in generating different syntactic forms that carry approximately the same meaning. Monitoring speakers and observing which particular choices they make in which context allows us to explore the predictive components in this context from which we can guess which choice is going to be made.

The English dative alternation, the focus of this contribution, refers to the choice between a prepositional dative construction (NP PP) as in "I gave the duck to my Mommy", where the NP is the theme and the PP contains the recipient, and a double object construction (NP NP) as in "I gave my Mommy the duck", where the first NP is the recipient and the second NP is the theme. A robust finding accross studies is that inanimate, indefinite, nominal, or longer arguments tend to be placed in the final complement position of the dative construction, while animate, definite, pronominal, or shorter arguments are placed next to the verb, preceding the other complement (de Marneffe et al., 2012). This means, for instance, that if a recipient of the dative construction is pronominal, such as *me*, it will tend to occur immediately after the verb, triggering a double object dative.

The dative construction is frequently used by children as well as their caregivers in child-directed speech (Campbell and Tomasello, 2001); this makes it a suitable focus for the computational modeling of syntactic alternations in child production.

While de Marneffe et al. (2012) use mixed-effects logistic regression to model dative alternation in children's speech, Theijssen (2012) compares regression-based and memory-based learning accounts of the dative alternation choice in adults. Theijssen's dataset consisted of 11,784 adult constructions of both types extracted from the British National Corpus (Burnard, 2000), 7,757 of which occur in transcribed spoken utterances, and 4,027 in written sentences. Her mixed-effects logistic regression approach uses automatically extracted higher-level determinants: animacy, definiteness, givenness, pronominality, and person of the recipient, and definiteness, givenness, and pronominality of the theme. Alternatively, Theijssen applied a memory-based learning classifier (Daelemans and Van den Bosch, 2005) which we also apply in this study. The memory-based approach she used included lexical information only: the identity (stem) of the verb, the recipient, and the theme.

Theijssen reports that MBL classifies unseen cases about as accurately (93.1% correct) into the two dative choices as regression analysis does, which attains a fit of 93.5%, while MBL does so without the higher-level features. According to Theijssen, the main factors for the success of the simple MBL approach are the strong licensing of one or the other dative construction by particular verbs, and the significant effect of length difference between recipient and theme. Both aspects of the input can be learned directly from from lexical input, while they remain hidden in the higher-level features. In this study we keep the available features identical to the earlier approach introduced by de Marneffe et al. (2012) in order to stay close to this particular study, which focused on datives with two verbs only (*give* and *show*).

3 Modeling learning curves of individual children

3.1 Memory-based learning

Memory-based learning is a computational approach to solving natural language processing problems. The approach is based on the combination of a memory component and a processing component. Learning happens by storing attested examples of the problem in memory. New unseen examples of the same problem are solved through similarity-based reasoning on the basis of the stored examples (Daelemans and Van den Bosch, 2005). In other words, memory-based learning offers a computational implementation of example-based or exemplar-based language processing.

Van den Bosch and Daelemans (2013) argue that from a cognitive perspective the approach is attractive as a model for human language processing because it does not make any assumptions about the way abstractions are shaped, nor does it make any a priori distinction between regular and exceptional exemplars, allowing it to explain fluidity of linguistic categories, and both regularization and irregularization in processing.

As a software tool for our experiments we use TiMBL[1] (Daelemans et al., 2010). In all our experiments we use the default setting of this implementation, which is based on the IB1 algorithm (Aha et al., 1991) and which adds an information-theoretic feature weighting metric. When the memory-based learning algorithm is asked to predict the class of an unseen test exemplar, it compares it to all training exemplars in memory, and constructs a ranking of the k nearest (or most similar) neighbors. The class that the algorithm predicts for the new exemplar is the majority class found among the k nearest neighbors.

To compute the similarity between an unseen test exemplar and a single training exemplar, the Overlap similarity function is used, weighted by gain ratio (Daelemans et al., 2010), expressed in Equation 1:

$$\Delta(X,Y) = \sum_{i=1}^{n} w_i \, \delta(x_i, y_i) \qquad (1)$$

where:

$$\delta(x_i, y_i) = \begin{cases} 0 & \text{if } x_i = y_i \\ 1 & \text{if } x_i \neq y_i \end{cases} \qquad (2)$$

and w_i represents the gain-ratio weight of feature i:

$$w_i = \frac{H(C) - \sum_{v \in V_i} P(v) \times H(C|v)}{si(i)} \qquad (3)$$

Where C is the set of class labels, $H(C) = -\sum_{c \in C} P(c) \log_2 P(c)$ is the entropy of the class labels, V_i is the set of values for feature i, and $H(C|v)$ is the conditional entropy of the subset of the training examples that have value v on feature i. The probabilities are estimated from relative frequencies in the training set. Finally, $si(i)$ is the so-called split info, or the entropy of the values, of feature i (Quinlan, 1993):

$$si(i) = -\sum_{v \in V_i} P(v) \log_2 P(v) \qquad (4)$$

The gain ratio weighting assigns higher weights to features that are more predictive with respect to the class. It is more robust than the simpler information gain metric, which overestimates the importance of features with many values (such as lexical features); the split info, the entropy of the values, acts as a penalty for a feature with many values. One effect of this weighting in the similarity function is that mismatches on features with a large gain ratio cause memory exemplars to be more distant than when the mismatch is on features with a small gain ratio. On the other hand, the gain ratio weight of a feature may be so prominent that it promotes a memory exemplar with a matching value on that feature to the top-ranking k nearest neighbors, despite the fact that other less important features carry non-matching values.

Memory-based learning can be likened to local regression or locally-weighted learning (Atkeson et al., 1997). It has similar issues with feature collinearity (gain ratio weights are computed separately for each feature; redundancy is not taken

[1]TiMBL, Tilburg Memory-Based Learner, is an open-source toolkit available from `http://ilk.uvt.nl/timbl`. We used version 6.4.5.

into account), but by limiting its decision to local evidence found close to the test exemplar, the algorithm is sensitive to subtle co-occurences of matching features in the k nearest neighbors.

The default version of TiMBL, used in this study, sets the number of neighbors to $k = 1$, which implies that an unseen test vector is compared to all training exemplars, and the dative choice label of the single most similar training exemplar is taken as the prediction of the test exemplar.

4 Experimental setup

4.1 Data collection

We used the same data as de Marneffe et al. (2012), which were extracted from the CHILDES database (MacWhinney, 2000). De Marneffe *et al.* focused on seven children: Abe, Adam, Naomi, Nina, Sarah, Shem, and Trevor, based on the amount of data available for them compared to other children, in terms of both their total number of utterances and the number of utterances containing one of the variants of the dative alternation. The utterances were taken from the children's production between the ages of 2–5 years. The data yielded a sufficient number of utterances to investigate two verbs in depth, *give* and *show*, which are the only ones considered in this study. On top of this filtering, De Marneffe *et al.* selected only dative constructions following the "verb NP NP" (double object) construction or "verb NP PP" (prepositional dative) construction.

For all seven children, conversations with caregivers were included as well. Table 1 lists the basic statistics of available child and child-directed utterances with dative alternations, and the age range of the individual children (in days). For two children, Adam and Nina, we have more than one hundred dative attestations in their own speech. For both children we also have more than one hundred datives in the speech directed to them by their caregivers; for a third child, Shem, we also have over a hundred caregiver utterances containing datives.

Following the encoding of the data by De Marneffe *et al.* in their computational modeling experiment with mixed-effects logistic regression, all attestations of both dative constructions in their utterance context are converted to feature vectors. Each vector (examplar) is metadated with the exact day of attestation, and labeled with the dative choice made by the child (i.e. a binary choice between the double object construction and the prepositional dative). Each vector is composed of fourteen feature values; the fourteen underlying features are listed in Table 2.

	# Datives in		Age (days)	
Child	child data	cds	First	Last
Abe	74	0	924	1,803
Adam	221	207	824	1,897
Naomi	21	0	767	1,733
Nina	146	443	747	1,193
Sarah	19	0	1,178	1,841
Shem	15	138	875	1,130
Trevor	33	0	757	1,452

Table 1: Basic statistics for the seven children used in the study: numbers of utterances and age range in days (cds = child-directed speech).

The Theme and Recipient length features are manually corrected due to the fact that in the original data used by De Marneffe *et al.* some recipients and themes mistakenly included other material such as adverbials.

The third column of Table 3 lists the gain ratio weights for each feature (cf. Equation 3). These weights seem to suggest four groups of features:

1. *Theme pronoun status* and *Recipient pronoun status* are by far the most predictive features. *Theme pronoun status* has a weight about 2.5 times higher than that of *Recipient pronoun status*, and over three times higher than the third highest weight;

2. There is a second-tier group of informative features with a gain ratio of about $0.07 - 0.08$: *Prime*, *Theme*, *Recipient*, *Recipient givenness levels*, *Theme corrected lenght*, and *Recipient corrected length*;

3. A third-tier group of features has weights in the range of $0.02 - 0.05$: *Theme givenness levels*, *Theme animacy*, and *Recipient toy animacy*;

4. A fourth-tier group has near-zero weights, carrying hardly any predictive information: *Verb*, *Recipient animacy*, and *Theme toy animacy*.

Perhaps somewhat surprisingly, the identity of the verb (*give* or *show*) is virtually unrelated to the

Name	Description	Gain ratio
Prime	The type of nearest previous occurrence of a dative construction, if any, within the 10 preceding lines. Three values are distinguished: 0 = none, NP = double NP-dative ("give me a hug"); PP = to-dative ("give it to me")	0.076
Verb	"give" or "show"; the two most frequent dative verbs collected in the childrens's speech	0.006
Theme	that which shown or given ("a hug" in "give me a hug"; "it" in "give it to me")	0.079
Recipient	to whom or which the theme is shown or given ("me" in "give me a hug" and "give it to me")	0.079
Theme givenness levels	either 'given': the referent of the theme was mentioned in the preceding ten lines or was denoted by a first or second person pronoun, "me", "us", or "you"; or 'new': not given	0.038
Recipient givenness levels	coded in the the same way as *Theme givenness levels*	0.086
Theme animacy	1 = the theme refers to a human or animal; 0 = other	0.022
Recipient animacy	coded in the same way as *Theme animacy*	0.005
Theme toy animacy	explicitly encodes toy themes as animate: 1 = the theme refers to a human or animal or toy; 0 = not animate	0.000
Recipient toy animacy	coded in the same way as *Theme toy animacy*	0.051
Theme pronoun status	'pronoun' = the theme is a definite pronoun ("it", "them") or a demonstrative pronoun ("this", "dis", "those", etc); 'lexical' = not pronoun	0.276
Recipient pronoun status	coded in the same way as *Theme pronoun status*	0.113
Theme corrected lenght	length of the theme in orthographic words	0.071
Recipient corrected length	length of the recipient in orthographic words	0.086

Table 2: The fourteen features used in the study, along with their gain ratio based on a concatenation of all children's data.

dative choice. In other words, the identity of the verb does not license one of the dative constructions.[2] The high weights for the pronoun status features imply that the likelihood of being a nearest neighbor is large when it has the same values on either of these features as the test exemplar. Yet, the weights of the other features, especially those in the second-tier group, are large enough to outweigh a mismatch on the pronoun features.

4.2 Learning curve evaluation

Our experiments are run per individual child, in an iterative experiment that tracks the child on a day-by-day basis and computes a learning curve. Figure 1 illustrates how the iterative learning curve experiment takes its first steps. At each point of the curve, all dative choices attested so far constitute the training set, while all new dative choices attested in the single next day on which datives are observed constitute the test set. Hence, the first training set is the first day on which the child generated one or more dative constructions; the first test set is derived from the next day the child produced datives. In the second step, the test set of the first step is added to the training data, and the next test set consists of all datives produced by the child on a next day.

At each step the incrementally learning memory-based classifier adds the new examples to memory, after which it classifies the new test set, which may only contain one or a handful of attestations. All single predictions per day are recorded as a sequence of predictions and whether these predictions were correct or incorrect. At each point of the curve a correctness score can be produced that aggregates over all predictions so far. At the end of the curve we achieve an aggregate score over all predictions.

The desired outcome of a learning curve experiment is obviously a metric expressing the success of predicting the right choices. In order for indi-

[2]This may be different for other verbs than *give* or *show*.

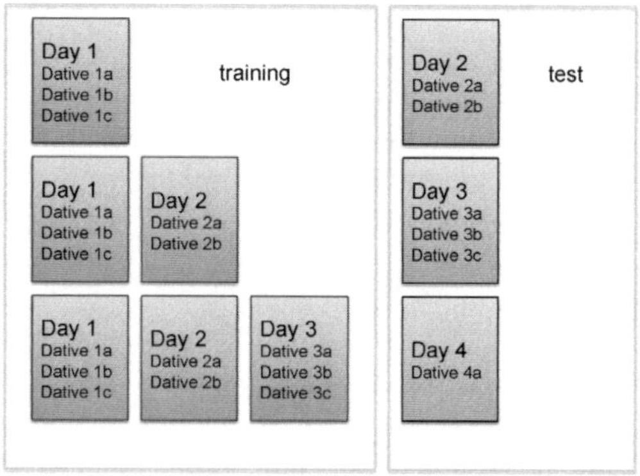

Figure 1: Visualisation of the first steps of a learning curve experiment. In the first step, the training material contains all dative attestations observed in the first day of attestations, and the test material contains all dative attestations found in the next day with datives. In the second, step, the latter material is added to the training set, and the third day of attestations is now the test set.

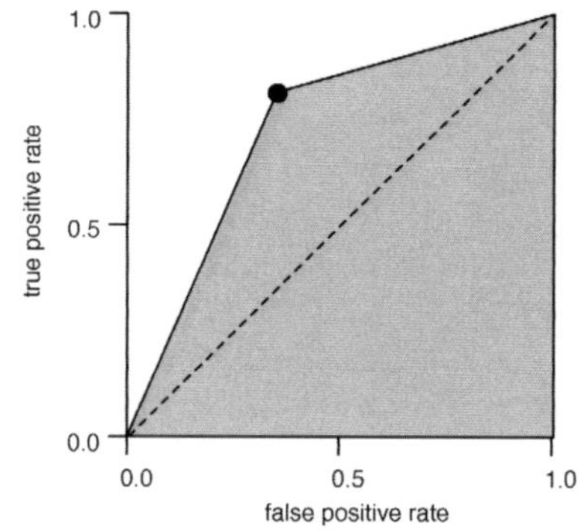

Figure 2: Illustration of the area under the curve (AUC) in the true positive rate–false positive rate space of the outcome of a point classifier (large dot).

vidual experimental outcomes to be comparable, they should not be based on different skews in the distribution between the two dative choices. Accuracy (the percentage of correct predictions) will not do, as it is biased to the majority class. When a child would choose one dative construction in 90% of the cases, a classifier trained on that child would easily score 90% accurate predictions by only guessing the majority outcome, while a classifier that is able to attain 80% correct predictions for a child that chooses between the two alternations in a 50%–50% distribution is intrinsically more successful and interesting.

To eliminate the effect that class skew may have on our evaluation metric we evaluate our classifier predictions in the learning curve experiments with the area under the curve (AUC) metric (Fawcett, 2004). The AUC metric computes, per class, the surface under a curve or a point classifier in the two-dimensional receiver operation characteristic (ROC) space, where the one dimension is the true positive rate (or recall) of predicting the class, and the other dimension is the false positive rate of mispredicting the class. Figure 2 displays the AUC score of the outcome of a classifier (a point classifier as it produces a single score rather than a curve) on a class, depicted by the large dot; the AUC score is the area of the gray surface.

We compute the AUC score of both dative choices, and take the micro-average of the two AUC scores; i.e. each score is weighted by the relative proportion of occurrence of its choice. The resulting number is a score between 0.5 and 1.0 that is insensitive to the skew between the two dative choices in a particular child's data, where 0.5 means baseline performance (random or majority guessing), and 1.0 means perfect prediction.

5 Results

As an illustration of the measurements taken during learning curve experiments, Figure 3 displays the curves for Adam and Nina, the children with most observations. Starting at 100% AUC score, the curves of both children initially drop considerably, and then rise to a score that appears to stabilize, at least for Adam for whom data is available into his fifth year. Later points in the curve are based on more training data.

At the end of each curve, the aggregated score can be measured, which in the best case would be a good approximation of the stabilized score we saw with Adam. Table 3 lists the aggregated score at the end of the curve for all seven children. Adam's dative choices can be predicted at an AUC score of 0.80, while Nina's choices are predicted with an AUC score of 0.71. For all other children the available data is insufficient to arrive at any above-chance performance.

To arrive at a sufficient amount of data per child we can add the data from all other children to all points of the learning curve, mixing the child's own data with substantially more data from other children. The fourth column of Table 3 shows that

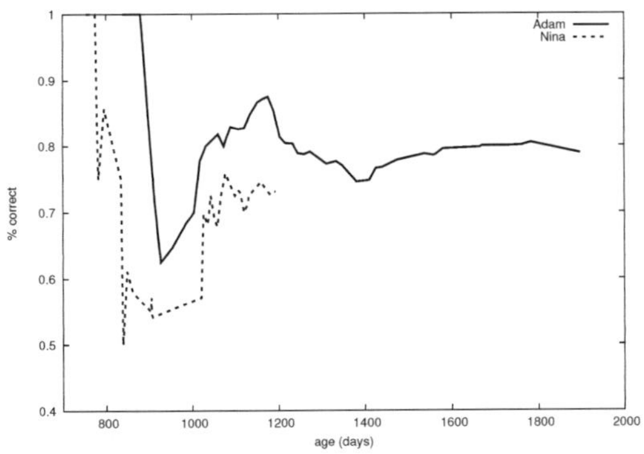

Figure 3: Individual learning curves for Adam and Nina, in terms of AUC scores on predicted dative alternation choices, trained on their own earlier data.

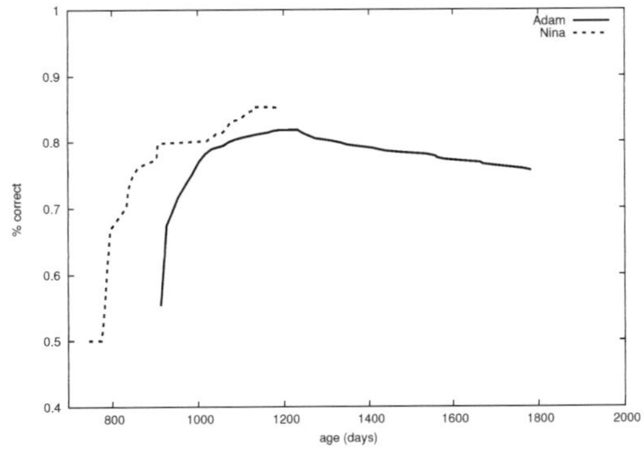

Figure 4: AUC scores on predicting dative alternation choices in child-directed speech from other children, based on increasing amounts of data from Adam and Nina.

this leads to above-chance performance of 0.7 or higher for all children except for Naomi (0.52). However, Adam's score is slightly lower after this mix (0.77 versus 0.80 on Adam's own data).

As De Marneffe *et al.*'s study suggests, it makes sense to predict the children's dative choices from child-directed speech, which represents one of the major sources of language input a child receives. To avoid any effects of alignment (such as the child repeating the caregiver), we constructed training sets for all children that exclude the utterances of their own caregivers. The fifth column of Table 3 lists the AUC scores obtained with this experiment. This leads to improved scores for all children, except for Adam; the score of 0.80 based on his own data is not surpassed.

Finally, the sixth column of Table 3 displays the scores at the end of the learning curve when all available data is used as additional data during all points of the curve, including all child-directed speech from other children and all other children's data. Surprisingly the advantage of having the maximal amount of training data is not visible in the scores, which are mostly lower, except for Adam (stable at 0.80) and Nina, the other child for which sufficient data was available (0.79).

Overall, the individual scores for all children range between 0.79 and 0.88, which could be considered accurate. For comparison, De Marneffe *et al* report a C score of 0.89 by their aggregate model. The C score (Harrell, 2001) is typically used for measuring the fit of regression models, and is to regression what AUC is to classification. It should be noted, though, that their C score is a fit, i.e. a test on the training data, whereas we test un unseen data only.[3] If memory-based learning is applied to classify its training data, its score is trivally 100%, as it memorizes all training exemplars.[4]

It is also possible to reverse the roles in the training and testing regimen, and test the predictive value of children's datives on caregiver datives. This experiment would show how well an child's speech approximates that of adults. Figure 4 displays learning curves (AUC scores) when training on increasing amounts of datives produced by Adam and Nina, tested on the caregiver speech of other children. The score starts out low, then increases, peaks (with both children) and then slowly decreases in the case of Adam.

To put the outcomes of these two learning curves in perspective, Table 4 compares their aggregrate score against a control experiment. The second column of Table 4 lists the end points of the aggregrate learning curves displayed in Figure 4. In the control experiment, the child-directed speech of Adam and Nina was used, respectively, as training data; the two trained models were again

[3]After reporting on the C score, de Marneffe et al. (2012) note that they do not know whether their model overfits. They then introduce a new experiment on two new children and datives with three verbs: *give*, *show*, and a new verb *bring*, and split the data into a 90% training set and 10% test set. On all three verbs they report a classification accuracy (not AUC, unfortunately) on the test set of 91.2% against a majority baseline of 68.4%. On the new verb *bring* the accuracy is 72.9%.

[4]Classification accuracy when testing on the training set may be lower than 100% when identical training exemplars exist with different dative choice labels.

Table 3: Aggregated AUC scores of MBL at the end of the learning curves of the seven children, training on four different selections of material. Best performances are printed in bold.

		Training on			
Child	# Datives (CDS)	Child only	+ Other children	CDS other children	All
Abe	74	*0.50*	0.84	**0.87**	0.86
Adam	221 (207)	**0.80**	0.77	**0.80**	**0.80**
Naomi	21	*0.50*	0.52	**0.81**	0.58
Nina	146 (443)	0.71	0.74	0.76	**0.79**
Sarah	19	*0.50*	0.83	**0.88**	0.83
Shem	15 (138)	*0.50*	0.74	**0.88**	0.74
Trevor	33	*0.50*	0.72	**0.86**	0.73

tested on the collective set of datives in other children's child-directed speech.

Child	# Datives (CDS)	Train child, test CDS	Train and test CDS
Adam	221 (207)	0.76	0.84
Nina	146 (443)	0.85	0.86

Table 4: Comparison of AUC scores when testing on CDS data from other children, trained either on the child's datives or on the child's caregiver's datives.

Training on Adam's datives, of which we have a higher number (221) than of Nina (146), we see at the end of the learning curve that datives in the child-directed speech of other children are predicted less accurately (0.76) than when training on Nina's datives (0.85). As the third column shows, the different caregiver input directed at the two children, when used as training data, does not differ notably in the approximation of child-directed speech directed at other children; more interestingly, we see that the AUC yielded by training on Nina's data (0.85) is about as high as training and testing on child-directed speech data (0.84 and 0.86). In other words, Nina's output is slightly harder to predict than Adam's (cf. Table 3), but it approximates adult caregiver output better.

6 Discussion

In this contribution we explored the notion of building a predictive computational, exemplar-based model for individual children. Despite the fact that we were only able to work with a limited number of children for which sufficient data was available, we believe we have delivered a proof of concept: we can model individual learning curves, and when sufficient data is available, the results indicate that models trained on this data have competing generalization performance to aggregate models trained on data from multiple individuals.

What is more, our results indicate that training on other children does not produce the best predictive models. Training on child-directed speech, however, does lead to the overall best generalization performances. This partially confirms De Marneffe *et al.*'s conclusions. Although we used the same data, we cannot directly compare to this work because, as noted before, De Marneffe *et al.* fit their models on the training data, whereas we test on unseen data not included in training.

We estimated to what extent the data from the children for which we had sufficient data, Adam and Nina, could be used as training data to predict caregiver datives. The comparisons produce slightly different results. Comparing Tables 3 and 4, we observe that Nina's dative choices are harder to predict than Adam's, but they approximate adult caregiver dative choices better. A comparative study of Nina's and Adam's productions may explain this difference, but goes beyond the scope of this paper. We restrict ourselves to noting that we observe more varied predictors in Nina's output than in Adam's, that she uses significantly more pronouns, and that the variance in the length of the themes used by Nina is significantly greater than Adam's.

Overall, both Adam's and Nina's datives can be said to approximate and predict caregiver datives about as accurately as adult data does.

7 Conclusion

Our case study shows that the computational modelling of a language acquisition phenomenon at the level of the individual is possible. The results indicate that models trained on individual data have competing generalization performance to aggregate models trained on data from multiple individuals. For two children, sufficient data was available to show that training a memory-based model on their own data produced about as accurate predictions as training on child-directed speech, which de Marneffe et al. (2012) had shown before, but with data aggregated over children.

We argue that memory-based learning is a suitable method for this type of micro-modelling. It can work with very small amounts of training data, and it can learn incrementally. In contrast, most non-local regression methods and supervised machine learning methods require complete retraining when training data changes (e.g. when new examples come in). Furthermore, as an implementation of exemplar-based reasoning it offers a computational, objectively testable, reproducible, and arguably cognitively plausible (Van den Bosch and Daelemans, 2013) exemplar-based account of language acquisition and processing (Jäkel et al., 2009).

This proof-of-concept case study suggests several strands of future work. First, different syntactic alternations could be studied in the same way based on the same data, such as the genitive alternation in English. Second, our present study copied the features of de Marneffe et al. (2012), but there is some evidence from studies on adult data that the dative alternation can also be predicted with memory-based learning on lexical surface features (words) only (Theijssen, 2012). It would be interesting to repeat this study only with the *Theme* and *Recipient* surface lexical features.

As a more general goal, we hope to arrive at a new framework for modeling language production processes in which we can address existing research questions at the individual level, so that we can start to address the contrast between idiolectal data and aggregated data—an issue that has so far been largely theoretical and has been rarely addressed empirically (Louwerse, 2004; Mollin, 2009; Stoop and Van den Bosch, 2014).

Acknowledgements

The authors would like to thank the organizers and participants of Radboud University's "New Ways of Analyzing Syntactic Variance" Workshop in November 2012 and CSLI's "Gradience in Grammar" workshop in January 2014 for fruitful discussions and feedback. This material is based in part upon work supported by the National Science Foundation under Grant No. BCS-1025602.

References

David W Aha, Dennis Kibler, and Marc K Albert. 1991. Instance-based learning algorithms. *Machine Learning*, 6:37–66.

Ben Ambridge and Elena Lieven. 2015. A constructivist account of child language acquisition. *The Handbook of Language Emergence*, pages 478–510.

Christopher G Atkeson, Andrew W Moore, and Stefan Schaal. 1997. Locally weighted learning. *Artificial Intelligence Review*, 11(1–5):11–73.

Carl L Baker. 1979. Syntactic theory and the projection problem. *Linguistic Inquiry*, 10(4):533–581.

Joan Bresnan, Anna Cueni, Tatiana Nikitina, and R Harald Baayen. 2007. Predicting the dative alternation. In G. Bouma, I. Krämer, and J. Zwarts, editors, *Cognitive foundations of interpretation*, pages 69–94. Royal Netherlands Academy of Arts and Sciences, Amsterdam, The Netherlands.

Lou Burnard. 2000. Reference guide for the british national corpus (world edition). Technical report, Oxford University, Oxford, UK.

Aimee L Campbell and Michael Tomasello. 2001. The acquisition of english dative constructions. *Applied Psycholinguistics*, 22(2):253–267.

Erin Conwell, Timothy J ODonnell, and Jesse Snedeker. 2011. Frozen chunks and generalized representations: The case of the English dative alternation. In *Proceedings of the 35th Boston University conference on language development*, pages 132–144.

Walter Daelemans and Antal Van den Bosch. 2005. *Memory-based language processing*. Cambridge University Press, Cambridge, UK.

Walter Daelemans, Jakub Zavrel, Ko Van der Sloot, and Antal Van den Bosch. 2010. TiMBL: Tilburg memory based learner, version 6.3, reference guide. Technical Report ILK 10-01, ILK Research Group, Tilburg University.

Marie-Catherine de Marneffe, Scott Grimm, Inbal Arnon, Susannah Kirby, and Joan Bresnan. 2012. A statistical model of the grammatical choices in child production of dative sentences. *Language and Cognitive Processes*, 27(1):25–61.

Tom Fawcett. 2004. ROC graphs: Notes and practical considerations for researchers. Technical Report HPL-2003-4, Hewlett Packard Labs.

Gerd Gigerenzer. 1991. From tools to theories: A heuristic of discovery in cognitive psychology. *Psychological review*, 98(2):254.

Frank E Harrell. 2001. *Regression modeling strategies: with applications to linear models, logistic regression, and survival analysis*. Springer.

Frank Jäkel, Bernhard Schölkopf, and Felix A Wichmann. 2009. Does cognitive science need kernels? *Trends in cognitive sciences*, 13(9):381–388.

Max M Louwerse. 2004. Semantic variation in idiolect and sociolect: Corpus linguistic evidence from literary texts. *Computers and the Humanities*, 38(2):207–221.

Brian MacWhinney. 2000. *The database*, volume 2 of *The CHILDES project: Tools for analyzing talk*. Lawrence Erlbaum, Mahwah, NJ.

Sandra Mollin. 2009. "i entirely understand" is a Blairism: The methodology of identifying idiolectal collocations. *Journal of Corpus Linguistics*, 14 (3):367–392.

Robert M Nosofsky. 1986. Attention, similarity, and the identification-categorization relationship. *Journal of Experimental Psychology: General*, 15:39–57.

Christopher Parisien and Suzanne Stevenson. 2010. Learning verb alternations in a usage-based Bayesian model. In *Proceedings of the 32nd Annual Meeting of the Cognitive Science Society*.

Amy Perfors, Joshua B Tenenbaum, and Elizabeth Wonnacott. 2010. Variability, negative evidence, and the acquisition of verb argument constructions. *Journal of Child Language*, 37(3):607–642.

Julian M Pine, Daniel Freudenthal, Grzegorz Krajewski, and Fernand Gobet. 2013. Do young children have adult-like syntactic categories? Zipf's law and the case of the determiner. *Cognition*, 127(3):345–360.

Steven Pinker. 1989. *Learnability and Cognition: The Acquisition of Argument Structure*. The MIT Press, Cambridge MA.

J Ross Quinlan. 1993. *C4.5: Programs for Machine Learning*. Morgan Kaufmann, San Mateo, CA.

Wessel Stoop and Antal Van den Bosch. 2014. Using idiolects and sociolects to improve word prediction. In *Proceedings of the 14th Conference of the European Chapter of the Association for Computational Linguistics*, pages 318–327, Gothenburg, Sweden, April. Association for Computational Linguistics.

Daphne Theijssen. 2012. *Making choices: Modelling the English dative alternation*. Ph.D. thesis, Radboud University Nijmegen, June.

Antal Van den Bosch and Walter Daelemans. 2013. Implicit schemata and categories in memory-based language processing. *Language and Speech*, 56(3):308–326.

Aline Villavicencio, Marco Idiart, Robert C Berwick, and Igor Malioutov. 2013. Language acquisition and probabilistic models: keeping it simple. In *Proceedings of the 51st Annual Meeting of the Association for Computational Linguistics (Volume 1: Long Papers)*, pages 1321–1330, Sofia, Bulgaria, August. Association for Computational Linguistics.

Charles Yang. 2013. Who's afraid of George Kingsley Zipf? or: Do children and chimps have language? *Significance*, 10(6):29–34.

Author Index

Barrett, Maria, 1, 6
Beekhuizen, Barend, 83
Berdicevskis, Aleksandrs, 65
Bloem, Jelke, 22
Bresnan, Joan, 103
Brochhagen, Thomas, 74

Cassani, Giovanni, 28, 33
Castilho, Sheila, 6
Çöltekin, Çağrı, 55
Cornudella, Miquel, 40
Cristia, Alex, 93

Daelemans, Walter, 28, 33
Dupoux, Emmanuel, 93

Faria, Pablo, 45

Gillis, Steven, 28, 33
Goodman, Noah, 14
Grimm, Robert, 28, 33

Klerke, Sigrid, 6

Ludusan, Bogdan, 93
Luong, Thang, 14

O'Donnell, Timothy, 14

Poibeau, Thierry, 40

Seidl, Amanda, 93
Søgaard, Anders, 1, 6
Stevenson, Suzanne, 83

van den Bosch, Antal, 103
Versloot, Arjen, 22

Weerman, Fred, 22

Association for Computational Linguistics
209 N. Eighth Street
Stroudsburg, Pennsylvania 18360

ISBN 978-1-5108-1193-5

CURRAN ASSOCIATES INC.
proceedings.com

Workshop on Vision and Language 2015 (VL'15)

Vision and Language Meet Cognitive Systems

Held at EMNLP 2015

Lisbon, Portugal
18 September 2015